D1639118

It's a French revelation from CGP!

OK, so GCSE French is tough... but this CGP Revision Guide will make your life a whole lot easier. It covers all the vocab and grammar you'll need for every topic!

But that's not all. We've also packed in plenty of exam-style reading, writing, translation, speaking and listening questions — with **free audio files** available from this page:

www.cgpbooks.co.uk/GCSEFrenchAudio

How to access your free Online Edition

You can read this entire book on your PC, Mac or tablet, with handy links to all the online audio files. Just go to **cgpbooks.co.uk/extras** and enter this code:

3741 1662 7757 1685

By the way, this code only works for one person. If somebody else has used this book before you, they might have already claimed the Online Edition.

CGP — still the best! ☺

Our sole aim here at CGP is to produce the highest quality books — carefully written, immaculately presented and dangerously close to being funny.

Then we work our socks off to get them out to you — at the cheapest possible prices.

CONTENTS

CONTENTS

Published by CGP

Editors:
Lucy Forsyth
Hannah Roscoe
Matt Topping

Contributors:
Marie-Laure Delvallée
Sophie Desgland
Jackie Shaw
Sarah Sweeney

With thanks to Christine Bodin, Sharon Knight, Louise Taylor and Karen Wells for the proofreading.
With thanks to Jan Greenway for the copyright research.

Acknowledgements:

Audio produced by Naomi Laredo of Small Print.

Recorded, edited and mastered by Graham Williams of The Speech Recording Studio,
with the assistance of Andy Le Vien at RMS Studios.

Voice Artists:

Danièle Bourdais
François Darriet
Perle Solvés

Edexcel material is reproduced by permission of Edexcel.

With thanks to iStock.com for permission to use the image on page 56.

Abridged and adapted extract from 'Madame Bovary', on page 19, by Gustave Flaubert.

Abridged and adapted extract from 'Les Misérables', on page 34, by Victor Hugo.

Abridged and adapted extract from 'Le tour du monde en quatre-vingts jours', on page 38, by Jules Verne.

ISBN: 978 1 78294 540 6
Printed by Elanders Ltd, Newcastle upon Tyne.
Clipart from Corel®

Based on the classic CGP style created by Richard Parsons.

Text, design, layout and original illustrations © Coordination Group Publications Ltd. (CGP) 2016
All rights reserved.

Photocopying more than one chapter of this book is not permitted. Extra copies are available from CGP.
0800 1712 712 • www.cgpbooks.co.uk

Numbers

First things first, you need to get to grips with numbers. You may feel like you're having to do an awful lot of maths just to say 'ninety', but don't worry, that's all part of the fun...

Un, deux, trois — *One, two, three*

Mary always kept track of her pocket money.

① 11 to 16 all end in 'ze'. But 17, 18 and 19 are 'ten-seven' etc.

0	zéro		
1	un		
2	deux	11	onze
3	trois	12	douze
4	quatre	13	treize
5	cinq	14	quatorze
6	six	15	quinze
7	sept	16	seize
8	huit	17	dix-sept
9	neuf	18	dix-huit
10	dix	19	dix-neuf

20	vingt
30	trente
40	quarante
50	cinquante
60	soixante
70	soixante-dix
80	quatre-vingts
90	quatre-vingt-dix

② Except 'vingt', most of the 'tens' end in 'nte'. Also, '70' is 'sixty-ten', '80' is 'four-20s', and '90' is 'four-20-ten'.

Grammar — un / une

For feminine nouns, use 'une' and 'et une' instead of 'un' and 'et un':
Il y a vingt et une filles et vingt et un garçons.
There are 21 girls and 21 boys.

③ In-between numbers are formed like English ones, but add 'et un' for numbers ending in '1'.

21	vingt et un
22	vingt-deux

④ For the 70s and 90s, add 11-19 to 'soixante' and 'quatre-vingt' (like 'quatre-vingts' (80) but without the 's'). '81' and '91' bend the rule explained in point 3 — they miss out the 'et', e.g. quatre-vingt-un (81).

71	soixante et onze	91	quatre-vingt-onze	100	cent	10.000	dix mille
72	soixante-douze	98	quatre-vingt-dix-huit	1000	mille	1.000.000	un million

⑤ For hundreds and thousands, put cent, deux cent, mille (etc.) before the number.

623	six cent vingt-trois	1947	mille neuf cent quarante-sept

In French, long numbers are broken up by full stops instead of commas. Also, French decimals use commas instead of decimal points.

Add '-ième' to the number to say second, third etc.

Here are a few more handy words to spice up your French. Watch out for 'first' — it doesn't follow the rule.

Use 'premier' for masculine nouns and 'première' for feminine ones.

A 'u' is added to 'cinq'.

1st	premier / première	5th	cinquième	10th	dixième
2nd	deuxième	6th	sixième	99th	quatre-vingt-dix-neuvième
3rd	troisième	7th	septième		
4th	quatrième	8th	huitième		
		9th	neuvième		

une douzaine	*a dozen*
une dizaine	*about ten*
une vingtaine	*about twenty*
un nombre de	*a number of*
des dizaines	*lots / dozens*

Numbers ending in 'e' lose the e.

The 'f' in 'neuf' changes to a 'v'.

(READING) *Your number's up — it's test time...*

*Read Mathieu's social media profile, and answer the questions **in French**. Write the numbers in full.*

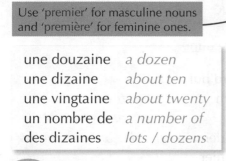

Salut ! Je m'appelle Mathieu, et j'ai dix-sept ans. Je suis le quatrième enfant de la famille — j'ai trois sœurs aînées. Nous habitons dans la première maison de la rue Phillipe — c'est la troisième rue après le parc. Il y a une vingtaine de maisons dans la rue.

e.g. Quel âge a Mathieu ? **Il a dix-sept ans.**
1. Il a combien de frères et de sœurs ? [1]
2. Quelle est sa maison ? [1]
3. Où se trouve la rue où Mathieu habite ? [1]
4. Combien de maisons y-a-t-il dans la rue ? [1]

2

Times and Dates

It's high time you learnt some more really useful stuff. This is essential for your exam — don't miss out.

Quelle heure est-il? — *What time is it?*

1) There are different ways to tell the time in French. Make sure you learn all of them. To say 'it's...o'clock' use 'il est...heure(s)'.

Il est une heure.   *It's 1 o'clock.*   Il est vingt heures.   *It's 8 pm.*

2) Use this vocab to say 'quarter past', 'half past' and 'quarter to'.

et quart	*quarter past*
et demie	*half past*
moins le quart	*quarter to*
du matin	*in the morning*
de l'après-midi	*in the afternoon*
du soir	*in the evening*

Il est deux heures et quart.   *It's quarter past two.*

Il est deux heures et demie.   *It's half past two.*

Il est trois heures moins le quart.   *It's quarter to three.*

Il est cinq heures du soir.   *It's five in the evening.*

To say 'in the evening' without referring to a specific hour of the day, just say 'le soir'. E.g. 'Le soir, j'ai dormi.' (*In the evening, I slept.*) The same rule applies for 'in the morning' and 'in the afternoon'.

Être à l'heure — *To be on time*

1) To say '...minutes past', you say the hour, then the number of minutes. You don't need any extra words.

Il est trois heures douze.   *It's 03:12.*

Il est vingt heures trente-trois.   *It's 20:33.*

The French use the 24-hour clock a lot — so make sure you can use it.

2) Use 'moins...' *(less)* to say '...to'.

Il est onze heures moins dix.   *It's ten to eleven.*

Grammar — 'à' with times
You use 'à' with times to say 'at'.
à dix heures   *at ten o'clock*

French grammar was all it took to turn study time into nap time.

Les jours de la semaine — *The days of the week*

In French, the days of the week are always lower case. They're also all masculine.

lundi	*Monday*		aujourd'hui	*today*
mardi	*Tuesday*		demain	*tomorrow*
mercredi	*Wednesday*		hier	*yesterday*
jeudi	*Thursday*		après-demain	*the day after tomorrow*
vendredi	*Friday*		avant-hier	*the day before yesterday*
samedi	*Saturday*		la semaine	*the week*
dimanche	*Sunday*		le week-end	*the weekend*

Grammar — le lundi (Mondays)
To say something happens regularly on a certain day, use the masculine definite article ('le') with the day — not a plural.
Le lundi, je fais du sport.
On Mondays, I do sport.

Je pars mardi.   *I'm leaving on Tuesday.*   the next day — le lendemain

Le week-end, j'aime faire la grasse matinée.   *At the weekend, I like to have a lie-in.*   During the week — Pendant la semaine

Elle voit son père le dimanche.   *She sees her father on Sundays.*   every day — tous les jours

Section 1 — General Stuff

Times and Dates

Learn these time and date phrases and you'll never miss a party in France...

Les mois de l'année — *The months of the year*

Months and seasons are <u>masculine</u> and <u>don't</u> begin with <u>capital letters</u>.

janvier	*January*	juillet	*July*	(en) hiver	*(in) winter*
février	*February*	août	*August*	**(au)** printemps	*(in) spring*
mars	*March*	septembre	*September*	(en) été	*(in) summer*
avril	*April*	octobre	*October*	(en) automne	*(in) autumn*
mai	*May*	novembre	*November*		
juin	*June*	décembre	*December*		

Watch out — 'in spring' is 'au printemps'.
All of the other seasons use 'en'.

Quelle est la date? — *What's the date?*

In French, you say '<u>the nine April</u>' or '<u>the seventeen November</u>'. The exception to this rule
is the <u>first day</u> of a month, where you use '<u>le premier</u>' (*the first*), like you would in English.

Aujourd'hui c'est le quinze mai.   *Today is the 15th of May.*

the first of August — le premier août

Mon frère est né le vingt-cinq
février mille neuf cent quatre-
vingt-dix-huit.   *My brother was born on
the 25th of February 1998.*

in the 90s — dans les années quatre-vingt-dix
in the year 2000 — en l'an deux mille

Ce matin / ce soir — *This morning / this evening*

These time phrases are really useful for <u>making arrangements</u>... and for your <u>exams</u>.

ce matin	*this morning*	la semaine prochaine	*next week*
cet après-midi	*this afternoon*	la semaine dernière	*last week*
ce soir	*this evening / tonight*	toujours	*always*
demain matin	*tomorrow morning*	quelquefois	*sometimes*
cette semaine	*this week*	(assez) souvent	*(quite) often*
ce week-end	*this weekend*	(assez) rarement	*(quite) rarely*

Qu'est-ce que tu fais ce soir?   *What are you doing this evening?*   this weekend — ce week-end

Le soir, je vais souvent au cinéma.   *In the evening, I often go to the cinema.*   rarely — rarement

La semaine prochaine, je vais danser.   *Next week, I'm going to dance.*   This afternoon — Cet après-midi

---

TRACK LISTENING 01

It's rarely the right time for a French exam...

*Listen to this French school-radio broadcast. Answer the questions **in English**.*

For the audio tracks go to www.cgpbooks.co.uk/ GCSEFrenchAudio.

e.g. For how long will the headmaster talk?   **five minutes**

1 a. When do most students get up?   *[1]*   **c.** On which days do dance classes take place?   *[1]*
   b. When do lessons start?   *[1]*   **d.** When was the school established?   *[1]*

Questions

You've probably got lots of burning questions, such as, "How long does it last?", "Please can you help me?" and "Have I finished yet?" Well, study these pages carefully and at least you'll be able to ask...

Les mots interrogatifs — *Question words*

quand?	*when?*
pourquoi?	*why?*
où?	*where?*
comment?	*how?*
combien?	*how much / many?*
qui?	*who?*
quoi?	*what?*
que?	*what?*
quel?	*which?*

These are known as interrogatives.

Grammar — quel, quelle, quels, quelles

'Quel' means 'which' or 'what'. It's an interrogative adjective, so it agrees with the noun it refers to. It has masculine, feminine, singular and plural forms:

quel (masc. singular)	quels (masc. plural)
quelle (fem. singular)	quelles (fem. plural)

→ **Quelles** filles aiment chanter?
Which *girls like singing?*
'Filles' (*girls*) is feminine and plural, so 'quelles' is used.

Clement was getting tired of being asked, "How's the weather up there?"

Pourquoi es-tu en retard?   *Why are you late?*

Qui vient avec moi?   *Who's coming with me?*

Où est la plage?   *Where is the beach?*

Ask questions by changing your tone of voice

1) The easiest way to ask a question in French is to say a normal sentence, but make your voice go up at the end. This works well for questions that are answered yes or no.

Tu as faim?   *Are you hungry?*

C'est loin?   *Is it far?*

Tu travailles le week-end?   *Do you work at the weekend?*

In writing, the only difference between this question and the statement 'C'est loin.' (*It's far.*) is the question mark.

"You don't need any more baguettes, do you?" — "Si!"

2) To answer 'yes' to a question containing a negative, use 'si'.

Est-ce que tu n'as pas faim? — Si, j'ai faim.   *Aren't you hungry? — Yes, I'm hungry.*

Use 'est-ce que' or 'qu'est-ce que' for questions

1) You can also turn a statement into a yes or no question by using 'est-ce que'.

Est-ce que tu as des frères ou des sœurs?   *Do you have any brothers or sisters?*

Est-ce que tu aimes jouer au tennis?   *Do you like playing tennis?*

2) You usually use 'qu'est-ce que' if your question starts with 'what'.

Qu'est-ce que tu fais dans ton temps libre?   *What do you do in your free time?*

You can use 'qu'est-ce qui' to ask 'what' when it's the subject of the sentence. See p.72 for more about using 'qui' and 'que' in questions.

Section 1 — General Stuff

Questions

Now you're ready to take your questions to the next level...

Put the verb first to form a question

You can ask questions in French by <u>swapping</u> the <u>verb</u> (see p.79) and the <u>subject</u> (the person or thing doing the action) around. Don't forget to add the <u>hyphen</u>, though.

Fais-tu **du sport**?	*Do you do any sport?*
Pouvez-vous **m'aider**?	*Can you help me?*
Aimes-tu **le hip-hop**?	*Do you like hip-hop?*

If the verb ends in a <u>vowel</u> and is followed by <u>il</u>, <u>elle</u> or <u>on</u>, you add a '<u>t</u>' to make it <u>easier to say</u>:

A-t-il **fini ses devoirs**?
Has he finished his homework?

Qu'est-ce que c'est? — *What is it?*

Here are some useful <u>questions</u> that you might want to ask:

À quelle heure?	*At what time?*	C'est de quelle couleur?	*What colour is it?*
Quelle heure est-il?	*What time is it?*	D'où?	*From where?*
C'est combien?	*How much is it?*	Pour combien de temps?	*For how long?*
C'est quelle date?	*What is the date?*	Que veut dire...?	*What does...mean?*
C'est quel jour?	*What day is it?*	Ça s'écrit comment?	*How is that written?*

Question	**Simple Answer**	**Extended Answer**
D'où viens-tu?	Je viens de Millom.	Je viens de Millom, dans le nord-ouest de l'Angleterre. C'est une petite ville rurale.
Where are you from?	*I'm from Millom.*	*I'm from Millom, in north-west England. It's a small, rural town.*

SPEAKING

I always thought 'Raquel' was a questionable name...

Here's a role play that Marie did with her teacher.

Grade **8-9**

Teacher: Est-ce que tu fais du sport ?

Marie: Oui, je fais du ski. Normalement je vais à **la piste de ski**[1] le lundi et le mercredi soir.

Teacher: Où est la piste de ski ?

Marie: La piste de ski **se trouve**[2] en centre-ville, près de la piscine.

Teacher: C'est loin de ta maison ?

Marie: Non, au contraire, c'est à quinze minutes à pied. C'est très pratique. Et vous, est-ce que vous aimez faire du ski?

Teacher: Oui, j'aime bien faire du ski en vacances.

Marie: Qu'est-ce que vous pensez du football?

Teacher: Le football ne me plaît pas. C'est ennuyeux.

[1]ski slope

[2]is (literally 'finds itself')

There's more info about role plays on p.93.

Tick list:
✓ correctly formed question
✓ time phrases
✓ present tense

To improve:
+ use an opinion phrase e.g. 'à mon avis...'

Use the instructions below to prepare your own role play. Address your friend as 'tu' and speak for about two minutes. [10 marks]

Tu parles du sport avec un(e) ami(e) français(e).

- *la natation — l'heure*
- *quand — jour(s)*
- *!*
- *? natation — opinion*
- *? sport préféré*

'!' means you'll need to answer a question you haven't prepared. When you see '?' you need to ask a question.

Being Polite

It would be a shame to waste all your hard work by being rude in the exam — so learn these expressions and wow everyone with your French charm. Bonne chance!

Bonjour...au revoir — *Hello...goodbye*

Learn these phrases — they're crucial.

bonjour	*hello*	au revoir	*goodbye*
salut	*hi*	à bientôt	*see you soon*
allô	*hello (on phone)*	à tout à l'heure	*see you soon / later*
bienvenue	*welcome*	à demain	*see you tomorrow*
bonsoir	*good evening*	Bon voyage!	*Have a good trip!*
bonne nuit	*good night*	Bonne chance!	*Good luck!*

Comment ça va?— *How are you?*

Make your conversation sparkle by using these little gems.

Comment ça va?	*How are you?*
Comment allez-vous?	*How are you? (formal)*
Et toi?	*And you? (informal)*
Et vous?	*And you? (formal)*
Ça va bien, merci.	*(I am) fine, thanks.*
Ça ne va pas bien.	*(I am) not well.*
Pas mal.	*Not bad.*
Je ne sais pas.	*I don't know.*
Super!	*Great!*
Je me sens...	*I feel...*
Comme ci, comme ça.	*OK.*

Grammar — using 'tu' and 'vous'

There are two ways of saying 'you' in French. 'Tu' is singular and informal. You should use it with a friend or family member. 'Vous' is for more than one person, or for one person in a formal situation, e.g. a stranger or someone older than you.

Comment ça va?	*How are you? (informal)*	How are you? (formal) — Comment allez-vous?
Je me sens fantastique.	*I feel fantastic.*	awful — affreux / affreuse
Pas mal.	*Not bad.*	well — bien

Puis-je vous présenter...? — *May I introduce...?*

Puis-je vous présenter Dave?	*May I introduce Dave?*
Voici Dave.	*This is Dave.*
enchanté(e)	*pleased to meet you*

'Enchanté' agrees with the gender of the speaker. It needs an extra 'e' ('enchantée') if the person saying it is female.

The conversation below shows how these phrases are used:

Madame Rollet :	Salut Delphine, comment ça va?	*Hi Delphine, how are you?*
Delphine :	Ça va bien. Comment allez-vous?	*I'm fine. How are you?*
Madame Rollet :	Comme ci, comme ça.	*O.K.*
Delphine :	Puis-je vous présenter Bruno?	*May I introduce Bruno?*
Madame Rollet :	Enchantée.	*Pleased to meet you.*

Delphine uses the polite 'vous' form — Madame Rollet is older than her.

If you're talking to someone you call 'tu', you say 'Puis-je te présenter...?' — it's informal.

Being Polite

This page is about asking politely. 'I want' never gets... Unless you want more exciting French vocab.

Je voudrais — *I would like*

'Je voudrais' and 'j'aimerais' are in the conditional tense. See p.87 for more.

1) '<u>Je voudrais</u>' and '<u>j'aimerais</u>' *(I would like)* are <u>more polite</u> than '<u>je veux</u>' *(I want)*.

Je voudrais **une tasse de thé**.	*I would like a cup of tea.*	We would like — Nous voudrions
J'aimerais **de l'eau**.	*I would like some water.*	He would like — Il aimerait

See p.4-5 for more about questions.

2) '<u>Puis-je...</u>' and '<u>Est-ce que je peux...</u>' both mean '*May I...*'.

Puis-je **avoir un café**?	*May I have a coffee?*	Est-ce que je peux **m'asseoir**?	*May I sit down?*

S'il vous plaît — *Please*

Don't forget these useful <u>polite words</u> — they could make all the difference...

s'il vous plaît	*please (formal)*	d'accord	*OK / fine*
s'il te plaît	*please (informal)*	pardon	*excuse me (informal)*
merci (beaucoup)	*thank you (very much)*	excusez-moi	*excuse me (polite)*
de rien	*you're welcome*	Je suis désolé(e).	*I'm sorry.*

'Désolé' has to agree with the subject, so you add an 'e' if you're female.

Je vous écoute — *I'm listening*

Here are some handy phrases to use for formal <u>phone calls</u> or <u>emails</u>.

à l'appareil	*on the line / speaking*	ne quittez pas	*stay on the line*
un instant	*one moment*	à l'attention de	*for the attention of*
je reviens tout de suite	*I'll be right back*	suite à	*further to / following*

WRITING

The joke has been deleted — apologies for any inconvenience...

Here's a script for you. Jean is introducing his friend, Michel, to his girlfriend, Aurélie.

Jean : Salut Michel ! Comment ça va ?

Grade 4-5

Michel : Oui, ça va bien merci — c'est le week-end ! Et toi ?

Jean : Pas trop mal. Puis-je te présenter Aurélie, ma **petite-amie**[1] ?

Michel : Enchanté.

Aurélie : Enchantée.

Michel : Comment allez-vous, Aurélie ?

Aurélie : Super, merci, mais **j'ai faim**[2].

Jean : Allons **chercher**[3] un sandwich. À tout à l'heure, Michel.

Michel : À bientôt !

[1]girlfriend
[2]I'm hungry
[3]to get

Tick list:
✓ variety of polite phrases
✓ gender agreement of enchanté(e)

To improve:
+ more detail to develop the ideas
+ different tenses (add a past or future)

Now it's your turn:

*Écris un script au sujet de deux personnes qui se présentent pour la première fois. Écris environ **40** mots **en français**.* [10 marks]

To get more tenses in your answer, you could make plans to meet in the future, or one person could say where they used to live. Try to include as many of the phrases you learnt on p.6 and 7 as you can.

Opinions

Having an opinion is a great way to pick up lots of marks in the exam, so don't hold back. Just make sure your rants are peppered with exciting phrases and vocab...

Qu'est-ce que tu penses de...? — *What do you think of...?*

There are <u>lots of ways</u> to ask someone their <u>opinion</u> in French... and to give your own.

Qu'est-ce que tu penses de...?	*What do you think of...?*	Je pense que...	*I think that...*
Quel est ton avis sur...?	*What's your opinion of...?*	À mon avis...	*In my opinion...*
Qu'est-ce que tu penses?	*What do you think?*	Je trouve que...	*I find that...*
Comment trouves-tu...?	*How do you find...?*	Je crois que...	*I believe that...*
Est-ce que tu le / la trouves sympa?	*Do you think he / she is nice?*	Personnellement...	*Personally...*

Qu'est-ce que tu penses de mon frère?
What do you think of my brother?

→ Je pense qu'il est très sympa.
I think that he's very nice.

He thought she was beautiful...
but how could he ever get to her?

Speak your mind — it'll sound impressive

Here's how to say what you <u>like</u> and <u>dislike</u>.

J'adore...	*I love...*	Je n'aime pas...	*I don't like...*
J'aime...	*I like / love...*	Ça ne me plaît pas.	*I don't like it.*
J'aime bien...	*I like...*	Ça ne m'intéresse pas.	*It doesn't interest me.*
Ça me plaît.	*I like it.*	Je trouve...affreux / affreuse	*I find...awful*
Je m'intéresse à...	*I'm interested in...*	Je déteste...	*I hate...*
Je trouve...chouette	*I find...great*	Ça ne me dit rien.	*It means nothing to me.*

Be careful — 'j'aime Pierre' can mean 'I like Pierre' OR 'I love Pierre'. If you only like him, it's safer to say 'je trouve Pierre sympathique' ('*I think Pierre is nice*') or 'j'aime bien Pierre' ('*I like Pierre*'). Otherwise you might be giving out the wrong message...

J'adore jouer au basket.   *I love playing basketball.*   I like — J'aime bien

Je m'intéresse à la musique.   *I'm interested in music.*   I'm not interested in — Je ne m'intéresse pas à

Je déteste les films d'horreur.   *I hate horror films.*   I find... awful. — Je trouve... affreux.

Es-tu d'accord? — *Do you agree?*

absolument	*absolutely*	bien sûr	*of course*	moi non plus	*me neither*
bien entendu	*of course*	ça dépend	*it depends*	ça m'est égal	*I don't care*

Es-tu d'accord avec moi?   *Do you agree with me?*   with that — avec ça

Bien sûr.   *Of course.*   *It depends.* — Ça dépend.

Opinions

You know what's even better than an exciting and varied rant? An exciting and varied rant stuffed full of justified opinions, of course.

Parce que — *Because*

The best way to justify your opinion is to give a reason. 'Parce que' and 'car' both mean <u>because</u>.

> J'aime ce film parce que les acteurs sont formidables.

> *I like this film because the actors are great.*

> Je trouve ce film affreux car l'histoire est ennuyeuse.

> *I think this film is awful because the story is boring.*

Alfred just couldn't stay awake during romcoms.

Use describing words to explain your opinions

Here are some <u>describing words</u> that you can use to <u>explain</u> your opinion.

affreux / affreuse	*awful*
amical(e)	*friendly*
amusant(e)	*funny*
barbant(e)	*boring*
beau / belle	*handsome / beautiful*
bon(ne)	*good*
chouette, super	*great*
doué(e)	*gifted / talented*
ennuyeux / ennuyeuse	*boring*
fantastique	*fantastic*
formidable	*great*
génial(e)	*brilliant*
mauvais(e)	*bad*
sympa, sympathique	*nice (person)*

> Ce film me plaît parce que les acteurs sont doués.

> *I like this film because the actors are talented.*

Remember, adjectives (describing words) need to agree with the noun they refer to — see p.61 for more.

These <u>phrases</u> might come in handy, too.

Ça m'énerve.	*It gets on my nerves.*
Ça me fait rire.	*It makes me laugh.*

> Je n'aime pas ce film car ça m'énerve.

> *I don't like this film because it gets on my nerves.*

You find French revision boring? Ça m'est égal...

*Sophie and Mayeul are talking about a French actor, Maurice le Pain. Have a look at the text, then answer the questions **in English**.*

Sophie : Quel est ton avis sur Maurice le Pain ?

Mayeul : Ça dépend. Je pense qu'il est assez bon dans les films d'action, mais je ne l'aime pas dans les comédies. Il n'est pas très amusant.

Sophie : Je ne suis pas d'accord ! C'est mon acteur préféré parce qu'il est vraiment doué. Ses films sont toujours formidables.

Mayeul : Il te plaît car il est beau. Moi, je préfère les acteurs qui ont du vrai talent.

Sophie : Tu es envieux ! Toutes mes amies adorent Maurice aussi. Nous le trouvons chouette.

e.g. What does Mayeul think about Maurice le Pain in action films?
He thinks he's quite good.

1. Why doesn't Mayeul like Maurice le Pain in comedies? [1]

2. Why is Maurice Sophie's favourite actor? [1]

3. What does Sophie say about Maurice le Pain's films? [1]

4. Why does Mayeul think that Sophie likes Maurice le Pain? [1]

5. What do Sophie's friends think of Maurice? [1]

Putting it All Together

You could get asked your opinion on any of the GCSE topics, so make sure you can bring all the stuff on these pages together. You'll feel like a right wally if you make a statement that you can't back up properly.

Talking about books, films, music...

'Ce' ('this' / 'that') becomes 'cette' in front of feminine nouns. For masculine nouns starting with a vowel, use 'cet'. See p.63 for more info.

In the exam, you might get asked if you <u>like</u> or <u>dislike</u> a band, film, book etc. If you don't have an opinion, just make one up. You won't get any marks for <u>shrugging</u>...

ce film	*this film*	ce groupe	*this band*
ce journal	*this newspaper*	cette équipe	*this team*
ce livre	*this book*	cet acteur	*this actor*
ce roman	*this novel*	cette actrice	*this actress*
ce magazine	*this magazine*	ce chanteur	*this singer (male)*
cette émission	*this programme*	cette chanteuse	*this singer (female)*
cette chanson	*this song*	cette vedette	*this star / celebrity*

Quel est ton avis sur cette équipe?   *What's your opinion of this team?*

J'aime bien cette équipe. À mon avis, les joueurs sont doués.   *I like this team. In my opinion, the players are gifted.*

With this routine, Brian couldn't fail to win the staff talent contest.

À mon avis — *In my opinion*

Question	**Simple Answer**	**Extended Answer**
Qu'est-ce que tu penses de la musique classique? *What do you think of classical music?*	C'est ennuyeux et agaçant. *It's boring and annoying.*	À mon avis, la musique classique est ennuyeuse. *In my opinion, classical music is boring.*

Qu'est-ce que tu penses de ce magazine?   *What do you think of this magazine?* — this actor — cet acteur

J'adore cette émission parce que ça me fait rire.   *I love this programme because it makes me laugh.* — it makes me cry — ça me fait pleurer

Je trouve ce chanteur affreux car sa musique est ennuyeuse.   *I find this singer awful because his music is boring.* — he is arrogant — il est arrogant

In my opinion, I deserve full marks. — Well, it's worth a try...

TRACK LISTENING 02

Deux amis parlent de leurs passe-temps. Complète les phrases en choisissant des mots dans la case.

1(i) a. Blandine aime bien jouer avec .... [1]
    b. Elle n'aime pas toujours faire du .... [1]
    c. Elle préfère .... [1]
(ii) a. En général, Marc pense que le sport est .... [1]
    b. Marc aime bien .... [1]
    c. À son avis, les comédies sont .... [1]

formidables	ennuyeux
son équipe	agaçantes
regarder des films	sport
natation	relaxant	lire
intéressant	le foot

About Yourself

Learning to tell the examiner about yourself is really important. Don't worry if you don't have much to say — just make stuff up. As long as you steer clear of big fat lies like being born in 3020, they'll never know...

Je m'appelle... — *My name is...*

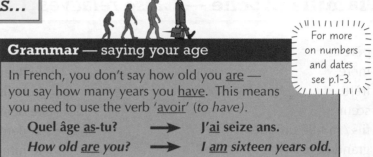

s'appeler	*to be called*
avoir... ans	*to be... years old*
le nom	*surname*
le prénom	*first name*
né(e) le...	*born on the...*
l'anniversaire (m)	*birthday*

Grammar — saying your age

In French, you don't say how old you <u>are</u> — you say how many years you <u>have</u>. This means you need to use the verb '<u>avoir</u>' (*to have*).

Quel âge <u>as-tu</u>? → **J'<u>ai</u> seize ans.**
How old <u>are</u> you? → ***I <u>am</u> sixteen years old.***

> For more on numbers and dates see p.1-3.

Je m'appelle Sara et j'habite à Natland.

I'm called Sara and I live in Natland.
> near to Kendal — près de Kendal

J'ai quinze ans, et je suis né(e) le neuf juin 2001.

I'm fifteen years old, and I was born on the ninth of June 2001.
> 'Né(e)' needs an extra 'e' on the end if you're female (see p.81).

Mon anniversaire, c'est le deux février.

My birthday is on the second of February.

English — anglais(e)		Welsh — gallois(e)
Scottish — écossais(e)		Irish — irlandais(e)

Je suis britannique mais je suis d'origine asiatique.

I'm British but I'm of Asian origin.

> Look at the vocab lists on p.105-106 for more nationalities.

Ça s'écrit... — *That's spelt...*

You might be asked to <u>spell out</u> your <u>name</u>, or another piece of information you've given. Generally, the French alphabet is <u>very similar</u> to English, but there are a few <u>tricky letters</u> to watch out for:

A — *'aah'*	H — *'ash'*	O — *'oh'*	V — *'vay'*
B — *'beh'*	I — *'ee'*	P — *'pay'*	W — *'doobluh vay'*
C — *'seh'*	J — *'djee'*	Q — *'koo'*	X — *'eex'*
D — *'deh'*	K — *'kah'*	R — *'air'*	Y — *'eegrek'*
E — *'euh'*	L — *'ell'*	S — *'ess'*	Z — *'zed'*
F — *'eff'*	M — *'em'*	T — *'tay'*	
G — *'djay'*	N — *'en'*	U — *'oo'*	

> In French, it's 'double V', not 'double U'.

Grammar — accents

For letters with accents, say the <u>letter</u> followed by the <u>accent</u>:

è — ***'euh accent <u>grave</u>'***
é — ***'euh accent <u>aigu</u>'***
ê — ***'euh accent <u>circonflexe</u>'***
ë — ***'euh <u>tréma</u>'***
ç — ***'seh <u>cédille</u>'***

SPEAKING *It's always about 'me', 'me', 'me' — typical...*

Read the question and Sophie's response below.
Parle-moi un peu de toi-même.

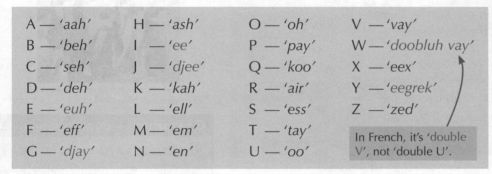

Je m'appelle Sophie. Ça s'écrit S-O-P-H-I-E. Je suis née le trois mars deux mille un et j'ai presque seize ans. Je suis anglaise et j'habite actuellement à Manchester, en Angleterre. Pourtant, je suis d'origine asiatique et mes parents sont nés à Hong Kong.

Grade 6-7

Tick list:
✓ tenses: present, perfect
✓ correct formation of dates
✓ conjunctions link phrases together
✓ correct adjective agreement

Now try to answer the same question.
Aim to talk for about two minutes. [10 marks]

You could say things like your name, age and where you're from.

To improve:
+ more varied conjunctions

Your Family

You need to be able to describe your family, too. It's a favourite with the examiners — no matter how many times they hear about students' lives, they never seem to get bored — so learn it well.

La famille proche — *Close relatives*

le père	*father*	la nièce	*niece*
la mère	*mother*	le beau-père	*step-father*
le frère	*brother*	la belle-mère	*step-mother*
la sœur	*sister*	le demi-frère	*half-brother*
le fils / la fille unique	*only child*	la demi-sœur	*half-sister*
le grand-père	*grandfather*	le jumeau	*twin brother*
la grand-mère	*grandmother*	la jumelle	*twin sister*
le / la petit(e) ami(e)	*boyfriend / girlfriend*	le / la partenaire	*partner*
le neveu	*nephew*	aîné(e)	*elder*

To say 'I'm an only child' in French, you don't need an article, e.g. 'je suis fils unique'.

When you're talking about something or someone that belongs to you, e.g. 'my sister', you need to use a possessive adjective (see p.63).

Parle-moi de ta famille — *Tell me about your family*

Question	Simple Answer	Extended Answer
As-tu une grande famille? *Have you got a big family?*	J'ai une petite famille — nous sommes quatre. *I've got a small family — there are four of us.*	J'ai une petite famille car ma mère est fille unique. J'ai un petit frère et une cousine. J'ai aussi une petite amie qui s'appelle Amy. *I've got a small family because my mum is an only child. I have a little brother and one cousin (female). I've also got a girlfriend called Amy.*

Dans ma famille, il y a neuf personnes.

In my family, there are nine people.

J'ai une grande famille car mes parents sont séparés et ils se sont tous les deux remariés.

I have a big family because my parents are separated and they have both remarried.

don't live together — ne vivent pas ensemble

are divorced — sont divorcés

J'ai deux frères qui sont plus âgés que moi.

I've got two brothers who are older than me.

younger — plus jeunes

Le partenaire de ma mère vient d'Italie, donc j'ai de la famille à l'étranger.

My mum's partner comes from Italy, so I have some family abroad.

isn't British — n'est pas britannique

Phillipe's family always looked out for each other.

Grammar — comparisons

To <u>compare</u> one person or thing to another, use '<u>plus</u> / <u>moins...que</u>' (<u>more</u> / <u>less...than</u>) with an <u>adjective</u> in the middle.

Elle est plus <u>âgée</u> / <u>jeune</u> que moi.
She is <u>older</u> / <u>younger</u> than me.

READING

Ma famille s'appelle 'The Addams Family'...

*A French friend has written a blog post and wants you to translate it **into English**. [7 marks]*

Dans ma famille, il y a trois personnes — ma mère, mon père et moi. Malheureusement, je n'ai ni frères ni sœurs donc je suis fils unique. Par contre, j'ai beaucoup de cousins et je les vois souvent. Le week-end dernier, par exemple, nous sommes allés au cinéma ensemble et nous nous sommes très bien amusés.

Look out for any changes in tense.

Describing People

Now you know how to name people in French, you can begin to describe them. This page is the perfect opportunity to learn how to insult an annoying brother or sister in flawless French, so don't let it slip by.

On décrit les autres — *Describing others*

It's really likely that you'll have to <u>describe</u> your family and friends, so learn these useful <u>adjectives</u>:

<u>les yeux (m):</u>	<u>eyes:</u>
marron / noisette	*brown / hazel*
<u>les cheveux (m):</u>	*hair:*
roux / bruns / blonds	*ginger / brown / blond*
longs / mi-longs / courts	*long / medium-length / short*
teints / bouclés / frisés / raides	*dyed / curly / curly / straight*
la barbe	*beard*
joli(e)	*pretty*
beau / belle	*handsome / beautiful*
laid(e)	*ugly*
grand(e)	*tall*
petit(e)	*short*
clair(e) / foncé(e)	*light / dark*
de taille (f) moyenne	*average height*

Grammar — agreements

Adjectives <u>agree</u> with the <u>person or thing</u> they're describing — if it's <u>feminine</u>, you need to add an '<u>e</u>' onto the <u>end of the adjective</u>. If it's <u>plural</u>, add an '<u>s</u>', and for something that's <u>feminine and plural</u>, add '<u>es</u>'.

Ma copine est très petite.
My girlfriend is very short.

Elle a les cheveux longs.
She has long hair.

'Marron' (*brown*) and 'noisette' (*hazel*) never agree with the noun they're describing.

Ils sont comment? — *What are they like?*

'Gros' (*fat*) becomes 'grosse' when it agrees with a feminine noun.

Ma sœur est assez grande et jolie. Elle a les yeux noisette et les cheveux longs et ondulés.

My sister is quite tall and pretty. She has hazel eyes and long, wavy hair.

fat — grosse
slim — mince

Ma meilleure copine a les yeux marron et les cheveux bruns. Elle porte des lunettes.

My best friend has brown eyes and brown hair. She wears glasses.

jewellery — des bijoux (m)

Mon frère aîné a beaucoup de boutons sur le visage et il a une moustache.

My older brother has lots of spots on his face and he has a moustache.

a scar — une cicatrice
a mole — un grain de beauté

Elles sont toutes les deux de taille moyenne.

They're both average height.

very beautiful — très belles

My brother's such a monkey — he's so hairy...

TRACK LISTENING 03

In this extract from a podcast, Fabien is being interviewed about his family. Find the true statement from the pair below.

e.g. A. Fabien lives with his parents.　　**B.** Fabien lives by himself.　　**A**

1. *There are two true statements in each list below. Choose the correct statements from each list.*

(i)　A. It's never quiet at Fabien's house.
　　B. Fabien is the youngest child at home.
　　C. His sisters have blue eyes.
　　D. Fabien's half-brother is older than him.
　　E. His half-brother lives at home. [2]

(ii)　A. Fabien's mother has long hair.
　　B. His mother has curly hair.
　　C. Fabien's father is tall.
　　D. His father has a beard.
　　E. Fabien looks like his father. [2]

Personalities

It's what's on the inside that counts, so it's probably a good idea to learn how to describe your personality. It isn't always easy to sum up your wonderful self in a few words, but use this page as a starting point.

Les personnalités (f) — *Personalities*

> Adjectives need to agree with the nouns they're describing. See p.61 for more.

gentil / gentille	*nice*	bavard(e)	*chatty / talkative*	égoïste	*selfish*
vif / vive	*lively*	aimable	*kind*	jaloux / jalouse	*jealous*
heureux / heureuse	*happy*	compréhensif / compréhensive	*understanding*	bête	*stupid / silly*
				fou / folle	*mad / crazy*

Question

Tu as quel genre de caractère?
What kind of personality do you have?

Simple Answer

Je suis gentil(le) et un peu bavard(e).
I'm nice and a bit chatty.

Extended Answer

Je suis assez vif / vive et bavard(e). Mes amis me disent que je suis vraiment généreux / généreuse, mais je sais que je suis parfois égoïste.
I'm quite lively and talkative. My friends tell me that I'm really generous, but I know that I'm sometimes selfish.

Olivier was always quite headstrong.

Grammar — imperfect tense

To describe someone in the <u>past</u>, use the <u>imperfect tense</u> (see p.82).

Elle <u>était</u> vive et bavarde.

She <u>was</u> lively and talkative.

Grammar — false friends

Some French words sound like English words, but have a <u>different</u> meaning.

sensible	*sensitive (not sensible)*
le caractère	*personality (not a fictional character)*
grand(e)	*big / tall (not grand)*

Parler des autres — *To talk about others*

It's useful to be able to say what <u>other people</u> are like too.

Mon frère est égoïste et il ne pense jamais aux autres. Pourtant, je suis très fier / fière de ma famille.	*My brother is selfish and he never thinks about others. However, I'm very proud of my family.*
Ma meilleure copine, Ann, est vraiment aimable et elle est toujours là pour moi quand j'ai un problème.	*My best friend, Ann, is really kind and she is always there for me when I have a problem.*

WRITING — *I hate mussels and prawns — they're so shellfish...*

Pierre has written a blog entry about his best friend.

Mon meilleur ami s'appelle Sunil. Il est sportif, intelligent et toujours heureux. Pourtant, au collège, il est un peu bavard et bête. Cependant il n'est jamais égoïste. Il veut toujours aider les autres et faire de bonnes actions. Le week-end, on va souvent au cinéma et on joue au foot ensemble dans le parc.

Grade 6-7

Tick list:
✓ good use of connectives
✓ wide range of adjectives

To improve:
+ use at least two tenses

Tu décris ton / ta meilleur(e) ami(e) pour ton blog.
*Tu **dois** faire référence aux points suivants :*
- *l'apparence et la personnalité de ton ami(e)*
- *pourquoi il / elle est ton / ta meilleur(e) ami(e)*
- *ce que vous faites ensemble le week-end*
- *ce que vous ferez ensemble dans l'avenir.*

*Écris **80-90** mots environ **en français**.* [20 marks]

Connectives can help you to express an opinion.
cependant / pourtant	*however*
de plus	*moreover*
donc	*so / therefore*

Pets

Love them or hate them, pets are often considered as part of the family and could appear in one of your exams (although hopefully not in physical form — I'm fairly certain animals aren't allowed in)...

Les animaux domestiques — *Pets*

la tortue	*tortoise*	l'oiseau (m)	*bird*	
le cochon d'Inde	*guinea pig*	le cheval	*horse*	
le lapin	*rabbit*	le poil	*animal hair*	
le poisson rouge	*goldfish*	sage	*well-behaved*	
le poisson tropical	*tropical fish*	méchant(e)	*naughty / nasty*	
le chat	*cat*	effronté(e)	*cheeky*	
le chien	*dog*	fidèle	*loyal / faithful*	
le hamster	*hamster*	paresseux /		
le serpent	*snake*	paresseuse	*lazy*	

Grammar — irregular adjectives

Some adjectives have <u>irregular feminine</u> forms (see p.61-62):

blanc (m) / blanche (f)	*white*
vieux (m) / vieille (f)	*old*
fou (m) / folle (f)	*mad*
beau (m) / belle (f)	*beautiful*

Question	Simple Answer	Extended Answer
As-tu un animal domestique? *Do you have a pet?*	Oui, j'ai deux chats. *Yes, I have two cats.*	Oui, j'ai deux chats chez moi. Ils sont blancs, à poils longs et assez vieux. J'avais un chien aussi, mais il est mort il y a cinq ans. *Yes, I've got two cats at home. They are white, long-haired and quite old. I used to have a dog too, but he died five years ago.*

Ils sont comment? — *What are they like?*

You should be able to describe your pet's <u>personality</u>, as well as their appearance.

J'ai un chien qui s'appelle César, et il a trois ans. Il est très vif. Je l'adore car il est mon meilleur ami.

I have a dog called César, and he's three years old. He's very lively. I love him because he's my best friend.

> I like to play with him — j'aime jouer avec lui

Malheureusement, je n'ai plus d'animaux, mais quand j'étais plus petit(e) j'avais un lapin. Il était très méchant!

Unfortunately, I don't have any pets anymore, but when I was younger I had a rabbit. He was very nasty!

> I can't have any pets anymore — je ne peux plus avoir d'animaux

Moi, je n'aime pas les animaux domestiques. Ils ont une mauvaise odeur, et ils ne sont pas hygiéniques.

I don't like pets. They smell bad, and they're unhygienic.

> I'm allergic to them — j'y suis allergique

J'adore les animaux domestiques, surtout les chiens. Ils sont toujours marrants et fidèles.

I love pets, especially dogs. They're always funny and loyal.

> affectionate — affectueux

Finish this page, then have a well-earned paws...

TRACK LISTENING 04

Listen to Romain talking about pets and answer the questions in English.

1 a. What does Romain do to help his neighbour? [1]

b. What reason does Romain give for Duc's misbehaviour? [1]

c. Why does Romain like guinea pigs? Give **one** reason. [1]

d. Which pets would Romain like to have when he's older? Give **two** details. [2]

Elodie's rabbit was pretty nosy.

Style and Fashion

Don't just describe your wardrobe in detail here — fashion is at the heart of tons of important debates (the importance of image, how celebrities influence others...), so make sure you've got some opinions ready.

Décris ton style — *Describe your style*

For more about clothes, see p.22 and p.102.

porter	*to wear*	la bague	*ring*	le costume	*suit*
se maquiller	*to put on make-up*	le maquillage	*make-up*	le parfum	*perfume*
le rouge à lèvres	*lipstick*	la jupe	*skirt*	le tatouage	*tattoo*
les bijoux (m)	*jewellery*	le short	*shorts*	la mode	*fashion*
les boucles (f) d'oreille	*earrings*	le collant	*tights*	teint	*dyed (hair)*

Grammar — 'en...' (made of...)

In French, use '<u>en</u>' to describe what something's made of.

en laine (f)	*made of wool*
en velours (m)	*made of velvet*
en cuir (m)	*made of leather*
en coton (m)	*made of cotton*

Je me fais couper les cheveux tous les mois. C'est cher, mais ça en vaut la peine.

I get my hair cut every month. It's expensive, but it's worth it.

Je voudrais un tatouage au poignet. Je vais le dessiner moi-même — ce sera une expression de ma personnalité.

I'd like a tattoo on my wrist. I'm going to design it myself — it'll be an expression of my personality.

La mode, est-elle importante? — *Is fashion important?*

The importance of <u>fashion</u> is a popular debate, so it's a good idea to <u>prepare</u> your opinion.

Pour moi, c'est très important d'être à la mode. Je fais toujours attention à ce que je porte, et j'aime être chic.

For me, it's very important to be fashionable. I am always careful with what I wear, and I like to be smart.

I'm passionate about fashion — Je suis passionné(e) par la mode

Moi, je ne m'intéresse pas à la mode. Je choisis toujours des vêtements confortables plutôt que les vêtements à la mode.

I'm not interested in fashion. I always choose comfortable clothes rather than fashionable ones.

practical — pratiques
second hand — d'occasion

Selon moi, ce n'est pas nécessaire de se maquiller pour être beau.

In my opinion, it isn't necessary to put on make-up to be beautiful.

make-up improves self-confidence — le maquillage améliore la confiance en soi

I've always been stylish — I was a model student at school...

Read the following online comments about fashion.

Pauline : Je suis passionnée par les vêtements et les bijoux ! J'aime porter des vêtements en velours parce que c'est à la mode. Par contre, je ne porte jamais de laine car personne de chic n'en porte aujourd'hui.

Jérôme : Moi, j'aime être individuel — je ne choisis pas des vêtements parce qu'ils sont à la mode, mais plutôt car je les aime. Cependant, j'aime me faire couper les cheveux et j'ai trois piercings et un tatouage.

Sylvie : Pour moi, l'apparence physique n'est pas très importante. Je préfère passer du temps en essayant d'être une personne gentille et sympathique plutôt qu'en choisissant des vêtements chics.

Who says each of these things about fashion? Choose either Pauline, Jérôme or Sylvie.

e.g. ....Pauline.... is passionate about fashion.

1. .... doesn't care about clothes. *[1]*   **3.** .... has a personal style. *[1]*

2. .... enjoys going to the hairdresser's. *[1]*   **4.** .... is influenced by others. *[1]*

Relationships

The examiners are also pretty interested in your relationships with other people — they're a nosy bunch. Luckily, it gives you a chance to practise some of those pesky reflexive verbs you know and love.

Les amis et les modèles — *Friends and role models*

se disputer	*to argue*
s'entendre (avec)	*to get on (with)*
connaître	*to know (a person)*
être fâché(e)	*to be angry*
se faire des amis	*to make friends*
casse-pieds	*a pain in the neck*
le sens de l'humour	*sense of humour*
jaloux / jalouse	*jealous*
équilibré(e)	*well-balanced*
soutenir	*to support*

Grammar — reflexive verbs

Reflexive verbs (see p.85) have an extra part — a reflexive pronoun.

Je m'entends bien avec...   *I get on well with...*
Nous nous disputons souvent.   *We often argue.*

In the perfect tense (see p.80-81), the pronoun goes before the present tense part of 'être' (to be).

Il s'est fait facilement des amis.   *He made friends easily.*

Mes modèles sont très influents. Ils m'inspirent à travailler dur car je veux être comme eux.

My role models are very influential. They inspire me to work hard because I want to be like them.

Je n'admire pas de célébrités. À mon avis, elles sont souvent gâtées et prétentieuses.

I don't admire celebrities. In my opinion, they are often spoilt and pretentious.

Tu t'entends bien avec...? — *Do you get on well with...?*

Tu t'entends bien avec ta famille?   *Do you get on well with your family?*   *I have a good relationship —* J'ai un bon rapport

Je m'entends bien avec mes parents.   *I get on well with my parents.*

Quelquefois je me dispute avec ma sœur aînée parce qu'elle est vraiment gâtée.   *Sometimes I argue with my older sister because she is really spoilt.*   *doesn't have a sense of humour —* n'a pas le sens de l'humour

SPEAKING My imaginary friend and I never fall out...

Read Ava's response to the picture task, then follow the instructions below.

Décris-moi la photo. La famille, semble-t-elle comme la tienne ?

Sur la photo, il y a une famille de cinq personnes — trois femmes et deux enfants. **Parmi**[1] les enfants, il y a un garçon et une fille. Le garçon **a l'air**[2] plus jeune que la fille. Ils ont l'air heureux et on dirait qu'ils s'entendent bien ensemble.

Moi, je m'entends très bien avec ma famille aussi. Mon père est plus strict que ma mère, mais il est raisonnable **quand même**[3]. Ma sœur est **mignonne**[4], mais elle m'énerve quelquefois.

(Grade 8-9)

[1]Amongst
[2]looks
[3]even so
[4]cute

Tick list:
✓ good use of comparatives like 'plus que'
✓ accurate use of reflexive verbs

To improve:
+ include a past tense

Regarde la photo et prépare des réponses sur les points suivants :

- *la description de la photo*
- *si la famille est comme la tienne*
- *si tu t'entendais bien avec ta famille quand tu étais plus jeune*
- *une activité que tu feras avec ta famille cette semaine*
- *!*

[24 marks]

You'll always be asked to describe the photo. Use 'Sur la photo, il y a...' to get started. Include as much detail as you can — look at the example for inspiration.

Socialising with Friends and Family

This may be a cruel topic to discuss while you're revising, but you can go back to having a social life soon...

Est-ce que tu es un(e) bon(ne) ami(e)? — *Are you a good friend?*

passer du temps avec	*to spend time with*	l'amitié (f)	*friendship*
traîner avec	*to hang out with*	indépendant(e)	*independent*
participer à	*to take part in*	joyeux / joyeuse	*happy*
la fête familiale	*family celebration*	le surnom	*nickname*

Question

Selon toi, quelles sont les qualités d'un(e) bon(ne) ami(e)?
In your opinion, what are the qualities of a good friend?

Simple Answer

Un(e) bon(ne) ami(e) te soutient toujours, et il / elle te fait rire.
A good friend always supports you, and they make you laugh.

Extended Answer

Un(e) bon(ne) ami(e) est quelqu'un qui te soutient et qui t'écoute. Il / elle est hônnete et il / elle te donne des conseils. Mais, à mon avis, la qualité la plus importante, c'est qu'il / elle a le même sens de l'humour que toi.

A good friend is someone who supports you and listens to you. They are honest and give you advice. But, in my opinion, the most important quality is that they have the same sense of humour as you.

Grammar — verb + infintive

When one verb <u>follows another</u>, the second verb is always in the <u>infinitive</u> (see p.79).

Il faut avoir les mêmes intérêts.
<u>You must have</u> the same interests.

Mon meilleur copain me <u>fait rire</u>.
My best friend <u>makes</u> me <u>laugh</u>.

Que fais-tu le week-end? — *What do you do at the weekend?*

Normalement, je passe le week-end en famille car je ne vois guère mes parents pendant la semaine. J'adore ça — je prends des nouvelles de tout le monde.

Normally, I spend the weekend with my family because I hardly see my parents in the week. I love it — I catch up with everyone.

Quand j'étais plus jeune, je passais beaucoup de temps en famille le week-end, mais maintenant, l'amitié est plus importante pour moi.

When I was younger, I used to spend a lot of time with my family at the weekend, but now, friendship is more important for me.

Le dimanche, je rends visite à mon grand-père. Je l'aide en faisant les tâches ménagères, et il cuisine pour moi.

On Sundays, I visit my grandad. I help him by doing the housework, and he cooks for me.

 ### *My friend Joe King always makes me laugh...*

Philippe a écrit un blog sur les activités qu'il fait avec sa famille.

Je suis très sociable, et pendant mon temps libre je sors beaucoup avec mes copains. Je vais chez eux le soir pendant la semaine. Le week-end, j'essaie de passer un peu de temps en famille, mais c'est difficile car j'ai deux petits frères et mes parents sont souvent **occupés**[1].

Quand j'étais plus petit, je passais plus de temps en famille — le samedi soir nous regardions un film ensemble. Maintenant, je préfère sortir avec mes copains.

 Grade 6-7

[1]busy

Tick list:
✓ tenses: present, imperfect
✓ time expressions ('pendant', 'le week-end')

To improve:
+ include conditional, future and perfect tenses
+ more advanced conjunctions
+ direct object pronouns

*Écris un blog sur les qualités d'un(e) bon(ne) ami(e). Tu **dois** faire référence aux points suivants :*

- *les qualités d'un(e) bon(ne) ami(e)*
- *si tu es un(e) bon(ne) ami(e)*
- *ce que tu fais avec tes ami(e)s*
- *tes projets pour l'été avec tes ami(e)s.*

*Écris **80-90** mots environ en **français**.* [20 marks]

Don't forget to justify your opinions using 'parce que' and 'car'.

Partnership

Seeing as Paris is the city of love, we couldn't let this topic slip by. Plus, you might have to talk about your views on love and marriage in the exam, so you need to know this stuff inside out and back to front.

Le mariage — *Marriage*

l'amour (m)	*love*	les fiançailles (f)	*engagement*	la femme	*wife*
célibataire	*single*	les noces (f)	*wedding*	épouser	*to marry*
la confiance	*trust*	le mari	*husband*	se marier	*to get married*

Le mariage montre au monde qu'on s'aime.

Marriage shows the world that you love each other.

À mon avis, le mariage commence à devenir démodé.

In my opinion, marriage is starting to become old-fashioned.

> These days / Today — De nos jours

Les noces sont trop chères. Avec l'argent, je préférerais acheter une maison.

Weddings are too expensive. With the money, I would prefer to buy a house.

> I think that — Je pense que
> In my opinion — Selon moi

Pour moi, le mariage est vraiment important. Je crois qu'il donne de la structure à la vie de famille.

For me, marriage is really important. I believe that it gives structure to family life.

Question

Tu voudrais te marier un jour?

Do you want to get married one day?

Simple Answer

Oui, à l'avenir je voudrais me marier et avoir des enfants.

Yes, in the future I'd like to get married and have children.

Extended Answers

Oui, pour moi le mariage est très important, et à l'avenir j'espère rencontrer l'homme / la femme de mes rêves et rester avec lui / elle pour toujours. Franchement, je ne comprends pas ceux qui ne veulent pas se marier.

Yes, marriage is very important for me, and in the future I hope to meet the man / woman of my dreams and stay with him / her forever. Frankly, I don't understand those people who don't want to get married.

Moi, je ne veux pas du tout me marier. Par contre, pour moi, ce qui est plus important c'est l'amour et la confiance. On peut être avec quelqu'un et avoir des enfants sans l'épouser.

I really don't want to get married. On the other hand, for me, what's more important is love and trust. You can be with someone and have children without marrying them.

Grammar — talking about the future

There are lots of different ways to talk about your <u>future plans</u>. You can use:

- The <u>future tense</u> (see p.84):
  je serai   *I will be*
- Or the <u>conditional tense</u> (see p.87):
  je voudrais   *I would like*
- Or use '<u>j'espère</u>' (*I hope*) + <u>infinitive</u>:
  J'espère me marier un jour.
  I hope to get married one day.

READING

Emotions run high at weddings — even the cakes are in tiers...

Read this extract from 'Madame Bovary' by Gustave Flaubert and choose the correct phrases.

Emma a, au contraire, désiré se marier à minuit, **aux flambeaux**[1]; mais le père Rouault n'a rien compris à cette idée. Il y avait donc des noces, où quarante-trois personnes sont venues, où l'on est resté seize heures à table, qui a recommencé le lendemain et quelque peu les jours suivants.

[1] in torchlight

1. Emma wanted to get married...
   A. the next day.
   B. in sixteen hours.
   C. at midnight.   *[1]*

2. Emma's wedding...
   A. was short and simple.
   B. suited her father's wishes.
   C. was exactly the way she wanted it.   *[1]*

Everyday Life

Tidying, cleaning, cooking... I'm sure you do all those things. Here's how to talk about them in French.

Une journée typique — *A typical day*

se lever	*to get up*	prendre le petit-déjeuner	*to eat breakfast*
se laver	*to wash (yourself)*	faire le lit	*to make the bed*
se doucher	*to shower*	se brosser les dents	*to brush your teeth*
s'habiller	*to get dressed*	se coucher	*to go to bed*

Véronique always found it
difficult to brush her teeth...

Question	**Simple Answer**	**Extended Answer**
Qu'est-ce que tu fais le matin?	Je quitte la maison à sept heures après avoir rangé la cuisine.	Je me lave, m'habille et prends mon petit-déjeuner en moins d'une heure. Mais l'année prochaine, j'aurai plus de temps car j'irai au lycée qui est plus proche.
What do you do in the morning?	*I leave home at seven after having tidied the kitchen.*	*I wash, get dressed and eat breakfast in less than an hour. But next year, I'll have more time because I will go to sixth form college which is closer.*

Grammar — reflexive

The 'se' part of reflexive verbs has to change:

Je	*me*
Tu	*te*
Il / elle / on	*se*
Nous	*nous*
Vous	*vous*
Ils / elles	*se*

See p.85 for more on this.

Gagner de l'argent de poche — *To earn pocket money*

les tâches (f) ménagères	*household tasks / chores*	faire du jardinage	*to do some gardening*
faire la lessive	*to do the laundry*	faire du bricolage	*to do some DIY*
faire la vaisselle	*to do the washing-up*	laver la voiture	*to wash the car*
mettre la table	*to lay the table*	garder des enfants	*to look after children / to babysit*

Je mets la table et je fais la vaisselle plusieurs fois par semaine. En plus, je range la cuisine le samedi.

I lay the table and I do the washing up several times a week. In addition, I tidy the kitchen on Saturdays.

I vacuum — je passe l'aspirateur

I clean — je nettoie (from nettoyer)

Mes parents font les courses et la lessive en rentrant du travail.

My parents do the shopping and the laundry once they get back from work.

Parfois, j'aide ma mère à faire du jardinage ou du bricolage le week-end.

Sometimes, I help my mum do some gardening or DIY at the weekend.

cook — cuisiner
bake (cakes etc.) — faire des pâtisseries

Je n'achète rien avec mon argent de poche car je veux l'économiser.

I don't buy anything with my pocket money because I want to save it.

READING

Tidying and cleaning — everyone's favourite activities...

Translate this blog entry about household chores **into English**. [7 marks]

Je reçois dix euros d'argent de poche par semaine. Mais je dois travailler pour gagner cet argent. Je participe tous les jours aux tâches ménagères pour aider mes parents. En plus, samedi dernier, j'ai gardé des enfants. J'achète beaucoup de musique en ligne, mais je vais essayer de faire des économies parce que j'aimerais partir en vacances avec mes copains.

Food

Food... my favourite topic. There's lots of vocab to learn — very useful for avoiding shocks in restaurants...

Qu'est-ce qu'on mange ce soir? — *What are we eating tonight?*

les légumes (m)	vegetables	les fruits (m)	fruit	le goût	taste
le chou-fleur	cauliflower	la pomme	apple	dégoûtant(e)	disgusting
le chou	cabbage	la poire	pear	épicé(e)	spicy
les haricots (m) verts	green beans	la framboise	raspberry	salé(e)	salty
le champignon	mushroom	la fraise	strawberry	sucré(e)	sweet
la pomme de terre	potato	les raisins (m)	grapes	amer / amère	bitter
les petits pois (m)	peas	l'ananas (m)	pineapple	bien cuit(e)	well cooked

le pain	bread	le lait	milk	la viande	meat	la saucisse	sausage
le riz	rice	le fromage	cheese	le poulet	chicken	le poisson	fish
les pâtes (f)	pasta	le beurre	butter	le bœuf	beef	le saumon	salmon
les frites (f)	chips	l'œuf (m)	egg	le jambon	ham	les fruits (m) de mer	seafood

Question	**Simple Answer**	**Extended Answer**
Quel est ton plat préféré?	Mon plat préféré c'est le steak frites, mais j'aime le potage aussi.	Je préfère manger du poisson plutôt que de la viande. Le poisson est meilleur pour la santé et plus nourrissant.
What's your favourite dish?	*My favourite dish is steak and chips, but I like soup too.*	*I prefer eating fish rather than meat. Fish is better for your health and more nourishing.*

Grammar — giving opinions

Use 'j'aime' (*I like*), '<u>je préfère</u>' (*I prefer*) and '<u>je déteste</u>' (*I hate*) to give a <u>range</u> of opinions.

    <u>**Je préfère**</u> **l'artichaut aux épinards.**   <u>***I prefer***</u> ***artichoke to spinach.***

    <u>**Je déteste**</u> **l'agneau mais** <u>**j'aime**</u> **la dinde.**   <u>***I hate***</u> ***lamb but*** <u>***I like***</u> ***turkey.***

For more food vocabulary, see the lists on p.101-102 and p.107.

Je mange... — *I eat...*

Get ready to talk about <u>what you eat</u>, <u>what you think</u> of it and <u>why</u>.

Je mange du saumon fumé — j'aime le goût.	*I eat smoked salmon — I like the taste.*
Je ne mange pas de plats cuisinés. Je préfère la cuisine faite maison car c'est plus sain.	*I don't eat ready meals. I prefer homemade food because it's healthier.*
Je devrais manger moins de nourriture sucrée parce que cela serait meilleur pour ma santé.	*I should eat less sugary food because that would be better for my health.*

tuna — du thon (m)
duck — du canard (m)

chocolate — chocolat (m)

cheese — fromage (m)

TRACK LISTENING 05

Hmm, I have 'un petit creux'* now...

Listen to Selina, Ahmed and Élodie. Choose the correct answer to complete each statement.

e.g. Selina never eats... **A.** lamb **B.** fish **C.** pork *C*

1 a. Ahmed particularly likes... **A.** raspberries **B.** mushrooms **C.** cauliflower *[1]*

  b. Élodie's sister eats... **A.** sweet food **B.** spicy food **C.** healthy food *[1]*

  c. Ahmed doesn't eat... **A.** ham **B.** peas **C.** vegetables *[1]*

  d. Selina hates... **A.** bananas **B.** pineapple **C.** strawberries *[1]*

Sid got caught doing a quick quality check of his dad's cooking.

*'avoir un petit creux' means 'to feel peckish'

Shopping

Whether you love fashion or you hate shopping, here's some stuff to help you talk about it in the exam.

Faire les magasins — *To go shopping*

'Faire les magasins' and 'faire des courses' refer to shopping in general. 'Faire les courses' refers to food shopping.

les vêtements (m)	*clothes*
la marque	*brand*
la mode	*fashion*
la carte bancaire	*bank card*
en espèces	*with cash*
la taille	*size*
le pantalon	*trousers*
la chemise	*shirt*
les chaussures (f)	*shoes*
en solde	*in the sale*
en vitrine	*in the window*
le ticket de caisse	*receipt*
l'étiquette (f)	*label*
rembourser	*to refund*
faire la queue	*to queue*

See p.102 for more clothes.

Question

Qu'est-ce que tu as acheté?
What did you buy?

Simple Answer

J'ai acheté un pull rouge et un T-shirt qui était en solde.
I bought a red jumper and a T-shirt that was in the sales.

Extended Answer

J'ai acheté une robe bleue. Elle était chère, donc j'ai dû payer par carte bancaire. J'ai voulu acheter un pantalon aussi, mais il ne m'allait pas.
I bought a blue dress. It was expensive, so I had to pay by card. I wanted to buy some trousers too, but they didn't suit me.

Grammar — aller à (to suit)

'Ça me va' means '*it suits me*'. The indirect object pronoun 'me' (see p.69) shows who it suits. The pronoun usually goes directly before the verb.

Je voudrais... — *I would like...*

Here are some useful phrases to use when you're shopping.

Autre chose?	*Anything else?*
Avec ça?	*Anything else?*
Ce sera tout?	*Is that everything?*
Ce sera tout.	*That's all.*
J'aimerais bien...	*I would like...*
Je regarde	*I'm browsing*

Grammar — rembourser (to refund)

'Rembourser' means 'to refund'.
Je vous rembourse. *I refund you.*
'Se faire rembourser' means 'to get a refund'.
Je me fais rembourser. *I get a refund.*
'Faire' doesn't agree in the perfect when followed by an infinitive: 'Elle s'est fait rembourser' *(She got a refund).*

Zoë was thrilled with the stylish new snowsuit her parents bought her...

J'adore l'écharpe en vitrine. Je peux l'essayer?	*I love the scarf in the window. Can I try it on?*
Je voudrais savoir si ce pull est en solde.	*I would like to know if this jumper is in the sale.*
Je voudrais acheter cette chemise, mais il n'y a aucune étiquette. C'est combien s'il vous plaît?	*I'd like to buy this shirt, but there's no label. How much is it please?*
Et l'avez-vous de taille moyenne?	*And do you have it in a medium size?*
Est-ce que vous avez cette robe en vert?	*Do you have this dress in green?*
Je cherche un jean blanc.	*I'm looking for white jeans.*
Je voudrais échanger ce pull contre un chapeau.	*I would like to exchange this jumper for a hat.*

the jeans — le jean
the raincoat — l'imperméable (m)

this hoodie — ce pull à capuche
this jacket — cette veste

in a large size — dans une grande taille
in a small size — dans une petite taille

pyjamas — un pyjama

some gloves — des gants (m)

Section 3 — Daily Life

Shopping

More shopping, you say? Well you're in luck — here's some stuff on quantities and online shopping...

Au magasin — *At the shop*

les courses (f)	*shopping*	la moitié	*half*	
une tranche	*a slice*	le quart	*quarter*	
tranché(e)	*sliced*	peser	*to weigh*	
un morceau	*a piece*	un gramme	*a gram*	
une portion	*a portion*	un kilogramme	*a kilogram*	
une boîte	*a box / tin*	un paquet	*a packet*	

Grammar — encore de (more)

'De' doesn't change with the <u>gender</u> or <u>number</u> of the noun after <u>quantifiers</u>. (See p.68.)

<u>'Encore de'</u> is an <u>exception</u> — it's followed by '<u>de</u>' and the <u>definite article</u> (du, de la, de l', des). **Je voudrais encore <u>du</u> pain. I'd like more bread.**

Je voudrais une tranche de pain.	*I would like a slice of bread.*
Nous voudrions une petite portion de flan.	*We would like a small portion of flan.*
Je pourrais avoir un demi-kilogramme de fromage, s'il vous plaît?	*Could I have half a kilogram of cheese, please?*
Voulez-vous un litre de lait?	*Do you want a litre of milk?*

half of this tart — la moitié de cette tarte

a piece of — un morceau de
more — encore du

half a litre — un demi-litre

Faire des courses en ligne — *To shop online*

Question	**Simple Answer**	**Extended Answer**
Est-ce que vous préférez faire des courses en ligne?	Oui, je trouve ça très pratique. On sait qu'on pourra trouver ce qu'on veut.	Je ne suis pas sûr. C'est vraiment pratique et les prix sont souvent moins chers en ligne. Mais j'aime pouvoir toucher et voir ce que j'achète. En plus, dans les magasins, on peut demander conseil aux vendeurs.
Do you prefer shopping online?	*Yes, I find it very convenient. You know you will be able to find what you want.*	*I'm not sure. It's really convenient and prices are often cheaper online. But I like being able to touch and see what I'm buying. In addition, in shops, you can ask for advice from the shop assistants.*

J'ai acheté des légumes en ligne mais ils étaient abîmés.	*I bought some vegetables online but they were damaged.*
Je préfère acheter les vêtements en ligne parce qu'ils sont livrés vite et les prix sont souvent réduits.	*I prefer to buy clothes online because they're delivered quickly and the prices are often reduced.*
Mais c'est difficile car on ne sait pas si on a choisi la bonne taille.	*But it's difficult because you don't know if you've chosen the right size.*

TRACK LISTENING 06

If only passing the exam was as easy as online shopping...

Listen to Sara and Pierre discussing the advantages and disadvantages of online shopping. Answer the following questions **in English**.

e.g. What does Sara think is the advantage of online shopping? **It's easier than going to the shops.**

1 a. Which disadvantage of online shopping does Sara mention? [1]
  b. What does Pierre find positive about online shopping? Give **two** details. [2]
  c. According to Pierre, what can't you be sure of when shopping online? [1]

Section 3 — Daily Life

Technology

Technology is a hot topic nowadays — it's difficult to imagine life without it. The examiners love asking questions that delve into its advantages and disadvantages, so it's worth going over these pages carefully.

Accro à mon ordinateur — *Addicted to my computer*

l'ordinateur (m) portable	*laptop*		le mail / le courrier électronique	*email*
la tablette	*tablet*		le mot de passse	*password*
le portable	*(mobile) phone*		l'écran (m) tactile	*touch screen*
le texto	*text message*			

envoyer	*to send*	télécharger	*to download*
recevoir	*to receive*	faire des achats (en ligne)	*to shop (online)*
tchatter	*to talk online*	être accro à	*to be addicted to*

Grammar — pouvoir / vouloir / devoir / il faut + infinitive

Some verbs can be followed directly by an infinitive (see p.79):

Je **peux acheter** de la musique en ligne.
I can buy music online.

Je **veux avoir** la dernière technologie.
I want to have the latest technology.

Les jeunes **doivent être** prudents en ligne.
Young people must be careful online.

Il **faut faire** attention sur les forums.
You must be careful on chat rooms.

Question	Simple Answer	Extended Answer
Utilises-tu souvent la technologie dans ta vie quotidienne? *Do you often use technology in your everyday life?*	Oui, j'utilise mon portable tous les jours et j'ai un ordinateur portable. *Yes, I use my mobile phone every day and I have a laptop.*	Oui, je suis accro à mon portable et j'envoie des messages à mes amis tout le temps. Par contre, je n'ai pas d'ordinateur portable. *Yes, I'm addicted to my mobile phone and I send messages to my friends all the time. On the other hand, I don't have a laptop.*

Jamais sans mon portable — *Never without my mobile phone*

J'ai eu mon premier portable à dix ans. — *I got my first mobile phone at age ten.*

J'envoie et je reçois des dizaines de textos par jour. — *I send and receive dozens of texts a day.*

Je ne pourrais pas vivre sans mon portable. — *I couldn't live without my mobile phone.*

Dans la vie quotidienne, les textos ont remplacé la conversation. — *In everyday life, text messages have replaced conversation.*
> we're constantly in contact with others — on est toujours en contact avec d'autres

On passe trop de temps sur nos portables. — *We spend too much time on our mobile phones.*
> lots of — beaucoup de
> little — peu de

Si je suis en retard, mes parents peuvent me téléphoner pour savoir où je suis. Je me sens en sécurité. — *If I'm late, my parents can phone me to find out where I am. I feel safe.*
> They find it very useful. — Ils le trouvent très utile.

Technology

Of course, technology isn't just about phones — the Internet practically runs the world, so it probably deserves a mention. It could come up in any one of your French exams, so learn it well.

Parlons d'Internet — *Let's talk about the Internet*

Views about the <u>Internet</u> vary massively, so it's worth considering its <u>advantages</u> and <u>disadvantages</u>.

Je peux faire des recherches pour mes projets scolaires en ligne. Les sites web factuels sont très utiles.	*I can do research for my school projects online. Factual websites are very useful.*
On peut trouver toutes les informations que l'on recherche rapidement.	*You can find all the pieces of information that you're looking for quickly.*
Je peux jouer à des jeux en ligne avec mes copains sans sortir de ma chambre.	*I can play online games with my friends without leaving my bedroom.*
Mon frère achète des billets de concert et de cinéma en ligne. C'est plus facile et pratique que de faire la queue au guichet.	*My brother buys concert and cinema tickets online. It's easier and more convenient than queuing at the box office.*

my family abroad — ma famille à l'étranger

Grammar — direct object pronouns (me, te, le, la, nous, vous, les)

A <u>direct object</u> is the <u>person or thing</u> (noun) that an action is <u>being done to</u>.

Elle joue <u>le jeu</u> en ligne.   *She plays <u>the game</u> online.*

<u>Direct object pronouns</u> (see p.69) <u>replace</u> that noun. In French, they come <u>before</u> the verb and are used to <u>avoid repetition</u>.

Elle <u>le</u> joue en ligne.   *She plays <u>it</u> online.*

> The direct object pronouns 'me', 'te', 'le' and 'la' drop their final letter and replace it with an apostrophe when they come directly before a word beginning with a vowel. E.g. 'Je peux t'aider.' (*I can help you.*)

Question	**Simple Answer**	**Extended Answer**
Selon vous, quels sont les dangers d'Internet? *In your opinion, what are the dangers associated with the Internet?*	Il faut faire attention à ce qu'on écrit sur Internet, surtout quand on met ses détails personnels en ligne. *You need to be careful with what you write on the Internet, especially when you put personal details online.*	Le problème principal, c'est de rester en sécurité. Il ne faut pas mettre de photos en ligne, ni afficher de détails personnels car tout le monde peut les voir. De plus, il faut faire attention en faisant des achats en ligne car il y a de la fraude. Il faut protéger tes détails personnels avec un mot de passe. *The main problem is staying safe. You mustn't put photos online, nor post personal details because everyone can see them. Furthermore, you need to be careful when shopping online because of fraud. You must protect your personal details with a password.*

WRITING — *I only use the Internet to watch cute cat videos...*

*Traduis le passage suivant **en français**. [12 marks]*

I got a new mobile phone for my birthday. My mum bought it for me. It's very useful because I can contact my parents and my friends when I want. I can also download music and games from the Internet. Tomorrow, I will use it to buy a book online.

Make sure you think about whether the nouns are masculine or feminine.

Camille knew that it'd be years before she got a new phone for her birthday.

Social Media

Social media is great for making friends — I've got nine hundred and they always remember my birthday...

Les réseaux sociaux — *Social networks*

le jeu	*game*
cliquer	*to click*
taper	*to type*
mettre en ligne	*to upload*
naviguer (sur)	*to browse*
l'écran (m)	*screen*
le forum	*chat room*

Grammar — irregular verb — envoyer (to send)

'Envoyer' is an irregular verb. Learn how to conjugate it properly — it's useful for talking about online communication.

j'envoie	*I send*	nous envoyons	*we send*
tu envoies	*you (inf. sing.) send*	vous envoyez	*you (form., pl.) send*
il / elle / on envoie	*he / she / one sends*	ils / elles envoient	*they send*

Question

Utilises-tu souvent les réseaux sociaux?

Do you often use social networks?

Simple Answer

Oui, j'utilise les réseaux sociaux chaque jour.

Yes, I use social networks every day.

deux fois par semaine	*twice a week*
de temps en temps	*from time to time*
tous les soirs	*every night*

Extended Answer

Oui, je suis un bloggeur. J'aime partager mes recettes et photos. Je passe en moyenne deux heures par jour sur les réseaux sociaux.

Yes, I am a blogger. I love to share my recipes and photos. On average, I spend two hours a day on social networks.

Je l'utilise parce que... — *I use it because...*

It's worth thinking about the different ways that people use social media and learning how to discuss them.

J'aime bien mettre mes vidéos en ligne pour les montrer à mes amis.

I like uploading my videos to show them to my friends.

my photos — mes photos
my blog posts — mes articles de blog

J'utilise les réseaux sociaux pour rencontrer ceux qui partagent les mêmes intérêts que moi.

I use social networks to meet those who share the same interests as me.

organise social events — organiser des événements sociaux

Les sites sociaux me permettent d'être à jour avec des nouvelles importantes.

Social media sites allow me to keep up to date with important news.

to stay in contact with my family — de rester en contact avec ma famille

 READING ## *Hang on a second — I just need to update my status...*

Lis les commentaires d'Anaïs, puis réponds aux questions en français.

En tout, je passe au moins trois heures par jour sur les réseaux sociaux. Je tchatte avec mes amis sur les sites sociaux **tout en faisant**[1] mes devoirs.

Je pense que, de nos jours, les réseaux sociaux sont indispensables. Par exemple, ils me permettent de savoir ce que fait mon cousin qui voyage en Amérique du Sud. Il met ses photos en ligne et je peux les regarder sur mon ordinateur. [1]*while doing*

e.g. Combien de temps par jour passe Anaïs sur les réseaux sociaux ?
au moins trois heures

1. Qu'est-ce qu'Anaïs fait pendant qu'elle complète ses devoirs ? [1]

2. Qu'est-ce qu'Anaïs pense des réseaux sociaux ? [1]

3. Comment est-ce que les sites sociaux l'aident à savoir ce que fait son cousin ? [1]

The Problems with Social Media

Of course, social media does have its drawbacks — even if you love it to bits, you still need to be able to talk about its disadvantages and give a balanced argument in the exam. Use this page to get some ideas.

Les inconvénients — *Disadvantages*

l'avantage (m)	*advantage*
l'inconvénient (m)	*disadvantage / drawback*
la cyber-intimidation	*cyber-bullying*
la vie privée	*private life*
à cause de	*as a result of*
au lieu de	*instead of*
grâce à	*thanks to*

Grammar — de (preposition)

à cause de and au lieu de both use the preposition 'de'. Remember, if 'de' is followed by 'le' or 'les', they combine:

de + le = du   de + les = des

À cause des réseaux sociaux...

As a result of social networks...

À mon avis — *In my opinion*

You might have to discuss the advantages and disadvantages of social media.

Moi, j'adore utiliser les réseaux sociaux — grâce à eux, je sais ce que font mes amis, même quand on ne s'est pas vu depuis longtemps.

I love using social networks — thanks to them, I know what my friends are doing, even when we haven't seen each other for a long time.

Cependant, je reconnais qu'il y a aussi des inconvénients. Par exemple, la vie privée n'est plus privée du tout — dès qu'on a mis une photo en ligne, tout le monde peut la voir.

However, I recognise that there are also drawbacks. For example, your private life is no longer private at all — as soon as you've put a photo online, everybody can see it.

De plus, la cyber-intimidation est un grand problème. Il y a des personnes qui écrivent des choses fausses et méchantes sur les sites sociaux.

Furthermore, cyber-bullying is a big problem. There are people who write fake and cruel things on social media sites.

SPEAKING

Want to know where I am? Just check my profile...

Have a look at Paul's answer to this question.

À ton avis, quels sont les avantages et inconvénients des réseaux sociaux ?

À mon avis, l'avantage le plus important des réseaux sociaux est que **n'importe qui**[1] peut être **écrivain**[2]. Moi, j'aimerais être journaliste un jour, et avec mon blog, j'ai l'opportunité d'écrire pour mes deux cents **abonnés**[3] — et c'est complètement gratuit !

Néanmoins[4], je les trouve parfois effrayants. De nos jours on est préoccupé des **centaines**[5] d'amis sur Internet, donc on abandonne souvent les rapports réels.

(Grade 6-7)

[1]anybody
[2]author
[3]subscribers
[4]nevertheless / however
[5]hundreds

Tick list:
✓ tenses: present, conditional
✓ superlative

To improve:
+ complex structures, e.g. pour + inf.
+ use quantifiers e.g. 'très' or 'vraiment'
+ more tenses: perfect, imperfect, future

Now answer the following questions.
Try to speak for about two minutes.   [12 marks]

- *Comment utilises-tu les réseaux sociaux ?*
- *À ton avis, quels sont les avantages des réseaux sociaux ?*
- *À ton avis, quels sont les inconvénients des réseaux sociaux ?*

Knowing a range of conjunctions will come in handy when giving both sides of an argument:

pourtant	*however*
néanmoins	*nevertheless*
par contre	*on the other hand*

Celebrations and Festivals

Time to celebrate — these pages are on festivals that are traditional in French-speaking countries.

Les fêtes françaises — *French festivals*

la fête	*festival / party*	la Saint-Sylvestre	*New Year's Eve*
fêter / célébrer	*to celebrate*	le Jour de l'An	*New Year's Day*
le jour férié	*bank holiday*	la fête des rois	*Epiphany / Twelfth Night*
le cadeau	*present*	la fête des mères / pères	*Mother's / Father's Day*
le défilé	*procession*	la Saint Valentin	*Valentine's Day*
la fête du travail	*May Day*	les feux (m) d'artifice	*fireworks*
la fête nationale	*Bastille Day*	Bon anniversaire!	*Happy birthday!*
le poisson d'avril	*April Fools' Day*	Bonne année!	*Happy New Year!*

Les écoles sont fermées les jours fériés.   *Schools are closed on bank holidays.*

On fête le Nouvel An à minuit et on prend des bonnes résolutions.   *People celebrate the New Year at midnight and make resolutions.*

La fête nationale — *Bastille Day*

Many events are held on <u>Bastille Day</u> to commemorate the <u>French Revolution</u>. It's the French <u>national day</u>.

Le quatorze juillet est le jour de la fête nationale. Il y a beaucoup d'événements pour la célébrer.   *14th July is Bastille Day. There are many events to celebrate it.*

Le quatorze juillet, beaucoup de gens s'habillent aux couleurs tricolores.   *On 14th July, lots of people dress in the colours of the French flag.*

J'aime regarder les feux d'artifice parce qu'ils sont toujours magnifiques.   *I like watching the fireworks because they're always amazing.*

J'aime la fête nationale parce qu'on peut la célébrer avec toute la famille.   *I like Bastille Day because you can celebrate it with the whole family.*

the processions — les défilés (m)
the dances — les danses (f)
impressive — impressionnant(e)s
it's an historical event — c'est un événement historique

Joyeux Noël! — *Merry Christmas!*

Nous mettons des cadeaux sous le sapin de Noël. Nous les ouvrons soit après la messe de minuit soit le jour de Noël.   *We put presents under the Christmas tree. We open them either after midnight mass or on Christmas Day.*

'Le réveillon' est le dîner qu'on mange après minuit la veille de Noël. Nous mangeons de l'oie pour le réveillon.   *'Le réveillon' is the dinner we eat after midnight on Christmas Eve. We eat goose for 'le réveillon'.*

Je pense que Noël est devenu trop commercial. Je préfère le fêter de façon traditionelle.   *I think that Christmas has become too commercial. I prefer to celebrate it in a traditional way.*

Le jour de Noël, j'aime regarder des films.   *On Christmas Day, I like to watch films.*

turkey — de la dinde
Christmas loaf — du pain calendal
yule log — de la bûche de Noël
to visit my family — rendre visite à ma famille
to eat a lot — beaucoup manger

Celebrations and Festivals

Even if you don't celebrate a particular festival, you can still talk about it, so here's some useful vocab.

La fête des rois — *Epiphany*

le roi	*king*
la reine	*queen*
la fève	*charm*
la couronne	*crown*
la galette des rois	*cake for Epiphany*
le gâteau des rois	*cake for Epiphany*

Dans une grande partie de la France on mange une 'galette des rois', qui est un type de gâteau rond.

In most of France people eat a 'galette des rois', which is a type of round cake.

On cache une fève dans la galette. La personne qui la trouve devient le roi / la reine.

A charm is hidden in the cake. The person who finds it becomes the king / the queen.

Question

Qu'est-ce que tu as fait pour la fête des rois?

What did you do for Epiphany?

Simple Answer

J'ai fait une galette des rois pour ma famille.

I made a 'galette des rois' for my family.

Extended Answer

Toute ma famille élargie était chez nous. Nous avons beaucoup mangé. J'ai trouvé la fève donc je suis devenu(e) le roi / la reine.

All my extended family were at our house. We ate a lot. I found the charm so I became king / queen.

D'autres fêtes religieuses — *Other religious festivals*

religieux / religieuse	*religious*	athée	*atheist*	le Pâques	*Easter*
juif / juive	*Jewish*	la Hanoukka	*Hanukkah*	la Carême	*Lent*
musulman(e)	*Muslim*	le ramadan	*Ramadan*	le vendredi Saint	*Good Friday*
chrétien(ne)	*Christian*	l'Aïd (f) al-Fitr	*Eid al-Fitr*	le Lundi de Pâques	*Easter Monday*

La Hanoukka est une fête juive. On allume des bougies et on prie ensemble.

Hanukkah is a Jewish festival. People light candles and pray together.

Au cours du Ramadan, les musulmans ne devraient ni manger ni boire de l'aube au coucher du soleil.

During Ramadan, Muslims should neither eat nor drink from dawn until sunset.

celebrate it for eight days — on la fête pendant huit jours
exchange gifts — on échange des cadeaux

Grammar — ne...ni...ni (neither...nor)

To say 'neither this nor that', use this structure: ne before the verb + ni ... ni ... .
Je ne fête ni Noël ni Pâques. *I celebrate neither Christmas nor Easter.*

TRACK LISTENING 07 *That's put you in a festive mood — ready for an exam question?*

Youssou is describing how he celebrated his birthday. Choose the correct option to finish each sentence.

e.g. Youssou is... *C*
- A. six years old.
- B. seventeen years old.
- C. sixteen years old.

1 a. He opened his gifts in the evening because...
- A. he didn't want to get up early to do it.
- B. he starts school early in the morning.
- C. he didn't want to do it at school. *[1]*

b. His sister made him...
- A. his favourite meal.
- B. a cake.
- C. some biscuits. *[1]*

c. There were fireworks...
- A. because it was Bastille Day.
- B. because it was May Day.
- C. to celebrate Youssou's birthday. *[1]*

'Low-key celebration' was not a concept that Marianne understood...

Books and Reading

Ahh, the noble book. You can use them for everything — decorating your coffee table, making paper aeroplanes, improving your posture... and revising for your French GCSE exams, of course.

Est-ce que tu aimes lire? — *Do you like reading?*

la lecture	*reading*
le livre	*book*
le roman	*novel*
la bande dessinée (BD)	*comic book*
le magazine / la revue	*magazine*
le journal	*newspaper*
la liseuse électronique	*e-reader*
le livre électronique	*e-book*

Grammar — 'donc' vs. 'comme'

'<u>Donc</u>' (*therefore / so*) expresses a <u>consequence</u>.

J'adore lire, <u>donc</u> j'ai acheté une liseuse électronique.
I love to read, <u>so</u> I bought an e-reader.

'<u>Comme</u>' (*as*) expresses a <u>reason</u> for something.

<u>Comme</u> elle est légère, je peux l'emmener partout.
<u>As</u> it's light, I can take it everywhere.

J'adore lire des romans policiers, car les intrigues sont toujours très passionnantes.

I love reading crime novels, because the plots are always very exciting.

On peut s'immerger dans un autre monde en lisant des romans fantastiques.

You can immerse yourself in another world by reading fantasy novels.

Les livres ne m'intéressent pas. Je préfère regarder les films, car on voit de l'action.

Books don't interest me. I prefer to watch films, because you see the action.

Would the zombie overlord be defeated? Vivienne couldn't wait to find out.

Question	**Simple Answer**	**Extended Answer**
Que penses-tu des livres électroniques?	À mon avis, ils sont très pratiques.	Ils sont géniaux. J'ai une liseuse électronique et je l'adore car il est très facile de télécharger des livres. En plus, il y a beaucoup de choix. Je crois qu'un jour, les livres électroniques remplaceront les livres en papier.
What do you think of e-books?	*In my opinion, they are very practical.*	*They are great. I have an e-reader and I love it because it is very easy to download books. In addition, there is a lot of choice. I believe that one day, e-books will replace paper books.*

SPEAKING — Think exams are a horror story? Not in my book...

Here's an example role play — Nasreen is talking to her teacher about reading.

Teacher: Est-ce que tu aimes lire?
Nasreen: Oui, je lis tout le temps, surtout les romans.
Teacher: Quel est ton opinion des livres électroniques?
Nasreen: Je ne les aime pas car je préfère tenir un vrai livre en main. Mais **j'avoue**[1] qu'ils sont plus pratiques.
Teacher: Qu'est-ce que tu as lu récemment?
Nasreen: Ce week-end, j'ai lu un roman historique, c'était super car je m'intéresse à l'histoire. Qu'est-ce que vous aimez lire?
Teacher: Moi, j'aime lire des biographies. [1] I admit
Nasreen: Avez-vous une liseuse électronique?
Teacher: Oui, j'en ai une. Je l'utilise souvent.

Grade 8-9

Tick list:
✓ tenses: present, imperfect, perfect
✓ correctly-formed questions

To improve:
+ use different conjunctions to link phrases

Prepare the role play card below. Use 'vous' and speak for about two minutes. [10 marks]

Tu parles de la lecture avec ton professeur.
- *si tu aimes lire*
- *livres électroniques — opinion*
- *!*
- *? genre de livres préféré*
- *? liseuse électronique*

Music

Music's a great topic to talk about in the exam, so whack on some 13th century monk chanting and start learning this vocabulary. You'll soon get into the swing of it...

La musique — *Music*

jouer	*to play*
(d'un instrument)	*(an instrument)*
la chanson	*song*
le musicien / la musicienne	*musician*
le chanteur / la chanteuse	*singer*
le genre	*genre*
le concert	*concert*
apprendre à	*to learn to*
faire partie de	*to be part of*
le groupe	*band*
la chorale	*choir*
l'orchestre (m)	*orchestra*
répéter	*to rehearse*

Grammar — jouer de

'jouer' is followed by 'de', 'du', 'de la' or 'des' when you're talking about playing a musical instrument. For more on how 'de' changes see p.60.

Je joue du violon et de la flûte.
I play the violin and the flute.

Grammar — imperfect tense

To talk about what you 'used to' do, use the imperfect tense. See p.83 for more.

Je chantais. *I used to sing*.

Question

Est-ce que tu joues d'un instrument de musique?

Do you play a musical instrument?

Simple Answer

Oui, je joue de la guitare et du piano.

Yes, I play the guitar and the piano.

Extended Answer

Oui, maintenant je joue de la batterie. Quand j'étais petit(e), je jouais de la trompette et je chantais dans une chorale.

Yes, now I play the drums. When I was younger, I used to play the trumpet and sing in a choir.

Écouter de la musique — *To listen to music*

It's worth thinking about how to express your opinions about music.

Je préfère le rap à la musique classique.	*I prefer rap to classical music.*
Mon grand-père détestait écouter de la musique classique quand il avait mon âge, mais maintenant c'est son genre de musique préféré.	*My grandad hated listening to classical music when he was my age, but now it is his favourite music genre.*
À mon avis, les chansons techno sont quelquefois trop bizarres.	*In my opinion, techno songs are sometimes too weird.*

dance music — la dance
rock music — la musique rock
pop music — la musique pop

See p.8-9 for more on opinions.

The French language is like musique to my ears...

Écoute cette interview avec le musicien Joël Lejoueur. Complète les phrases en choisissant un mot ou des mots dans la case. Il y a des mots que tu n'utiliseras pas.

1(i) a. L'instrument préféré de Joël est .... [1]
  b. Il n'aimait pas .... [1]

(ii) a. Joël préfère jouer .... [1]
  b. Selon Joël, pour devenir un bon musicien, il faut .... [1]

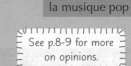

être doué
la guitare
collège
en groupe
répéter
son collège
seul
le violon
son professeur

Film and TV

Everyone loves a good film or TV show — and they're great to talk about in the exam. Make sure you know the names for different types of film and programme and that you can give and justify your opinions.

Allons au cinéma — *Let's go to the cinema*

See p.103-104 for more film vocab.

le film d'action / d'aventure	*action film*	les sous-titres (m)	*subtitles*
le film d'horreur / d'épouvante	*horror film*	les effets (m) spéciaux	*special effects*
le film d'amour / romantique	*romantic film*	la bande-annonce	*trailer*
le film d'animation	*animated film*	le billet de cinéma	*cinema ticket*

J'aime aller au cinéma pour voir des films sur grand écran, surtout les films comiques. Pourtant, les bandes-annonces m'énervent.

I like going to the cinema to see films on the big screen, especially comedies. However, the trailers annoy me.

> the tickets are expensive — les billets sont chers

Si le film est ennuyeux et les acteurs ne sont pas bons, je m'endors avant la fin.

If the film is boring and the actors aren't good, I fall asleep before the end.

> the special effects — les effets spéciaux

Je n'ai pas aimé le film. L'intrigue n'était pas croyable et les personnages étaient agaçants.

I didn't like the film. The plot wasn't believable and the characters were annoying.

Qu'est-ce qu'il y a à la télé? — *What's on TV?*

'On' is usually translated as 'sur' in French, but remember, you say 'à la télé'.

à la télé	*on TV*	l'émission (f)	*programme*	le documentaire	*documentary*
la publicité	*advert*	le feuilleton	*soap opera*	le jeu télévisé	*game show*
regarder	*to watch*	la télé réalité	*reality TV*	la chaîne de télé	*TV channel*
diffuser	*to broadcast*	les informations (f)	*the news*	célèbre	*famous*

Question

Qu'est-ce que tu as regardé à la télé hier soir?

What did you watch on TV last night?

Simple Answer

J'ai regardé un jeu télévisé et un feuilleton.

I watched a game show and a soap.

Extended Answer

J'ai regardé une émission de télé-réalité. Je trouve ce genre d'émission intéressant parce qu'on peut suivre la vie quotidienne des personnes célèbres. L'épisode que j'ai regardé hier était très divertissant.

I watched a reality TV show. I find this type of programme interesting because you can follow celebrities' daily lives. The episode that I watched yesterday was very entertaining.

Grammar — 'qui' and 'que'

'Qui' refers to the <u>subject</u> of the sentence. 'Que' refers to the <u>object</u>. See p.72 for more.

La personne <u>qui</u> regarde la télévision. *The person <u>who</u> watches television.*

La télévision <u>que</u> la personne regarde. *The television <u>that</u> the person watches.*

Ian wasn't in a horror film — he'd just had a bad day at the office.

I wouldn't mind a few ad breaks in the exam...

Traduis le passage suivant **en français**. [12 marks]

My friend and I went to the cinema last weekend. We watched a horror film. I wasn't scared, but my friend screamed during the film. I like going to the cinema. It is always entertaining. Next month, I will go to see the new action film.

Read each sentence fully before you decide which tense you need.

Sport

Whether you like sport or not, you need to be able to give your opinion on it. On your marks... get set... GO!

Faire du sport — *To do sport*

le foot / football	*football*	le hockey	*hockey*	l'aviron (m)	*rowing*
le rugby	*rugby*	le netball	*netball*	pratiquer un sport	*to do a sport*
le tennis	*tennis*	le basket	*basketball*	faire une randonnée	*to go on a walk*
l'équitation (f)	*horse riding*	la natation	*swimming*	faire du vélo	*to cycle*

Je joue au badminton deux fois par semaine, et parfois je fais de la voile aussi.

I play badminton twice a week, and sometimes I also go sailing.

on Mondays — le lundi

J'aime faire des randonnées avec mes parents et je voudrais essayer le tir à l'arc.

I like going on walks with my parents and I would like to try archery.

fencing — l'escrime (f)
scuba diving — la plongée sous-marine

Question

Est-ce que tu pratiques un sport régulièrement?

Do you do a sport on a regular basis?

Simple Answer

Oui, j'aime le sport et je joue au rugby le mercredi. Je regarde des matchs de tennis à la télé aussi.

Yes, I like sport and I play rugby on Wednesdays. I watch tennis matches on TV as well.

Extended Answer

Oui, je suis très sportif / sportive. Je fais partie d'une équipe de football et nous nous entraînons trois fois par semaine. La semaine dernière, nous avons perdu le match, mais j'ai marqué un but.

Yes, I'm very sporty. I'm part of a football team and we train three times a week. Last week, we lost the game, but I scored a goal.

Mon sport préféré c'est... — *My favourite sport is...*

le terrain de sport	*sports field*
s'entraîner	*to train*
le centre sportif	*sports centre*
le stade	*stadium*
la course	*race*
le tournoi	*tournament*
fana de	*a fan of*
à l'intérieur	*inside*
à l'extérieur	*outside*

Je préfère les sports individuels aux sports d'équipe. Ils sont plus compétitifs parce qu'on joue seulement pour soi-même.

I prefer individual sports to team sports. They're more competitive because you're playing just for yourself.

Moi, je joue au tennis. Cependant, je préfère m'entraîner avec d'autres personnes donc je fais de l'aviron aussi.

I play tennis. However, I prefer to train with other people so I do rowing as well.

READING — *Revising in your sweatpants is basically like doing sport...*

Read the advert. What does it tell us? Choose the three correct letters from the list below. [3 marks]

Le nouveau centre sportif est ouvert tous les jours, sauf le dimanche. On peut jouer au tennis et nager dehors dans la piscine chauffée. En plus, il y a des terrains de sport à l'extérieur, où on peut pratiquer des sports en équipe. Il y a aussi trois terrains de badminton. Le centre organise des tournois régulièrement — hier, il y a eu un tournoi de tennis de table. Si vous aimez courir, venez participer à la course qui aura lieu ici vendredi prochain.

A. The centre is open every day.
B. You can go swimming outdoors.
C. You can't play any raquet sports.
D. There are weekly table tennis tournaments.
E. You can take part in competitions.
F. There's going to be a race at the centre.
G. It's not possible to do team sports there.

Talking About Where You Live

Whether it's in the middle of nowhere or the inner city, you need to be able to describe where you live...

Où habites-tu? — *Where do you live?*

le centre-ville	*town centre*	les transports (m)		
le marché	*market*	en commun	*public transport*	
la poste	*post office*	la gare (routière)	*(bus) station*	
le tabac	*newsagent's*	la zone piétonne	*pedestrian zone*	
la boulangerie	*bakery*	la circulation	*traffic*	
la boucherie	*butcher's*	l'embouteillage (m)	*traffic jam*	
la bibliothèque	*library*	la piste cyclable	*cycle path*	
la campagne	*countryside*	l'usine (f)	*factory*	

Grammar — noun endings

Most nouns ending in '-ie' are feminine, e.g. la bijouterie (*the jeweller's*). Have a look at p.59 for a list of common masculine and feminine endings.

J'habite dans une ville à la campagne. | *I live in a town in the countryside.*

Je préfère habiter dans une ville. | *I prefer living in a town.*

by the sea — au bord de la mer
in the mountains — à la montagne
a city — une grande ville

Parle-moi de ta ville — *Tell me about your town*

Le système des transports en commun **marche** bien. Il aide à réduire la circulation en ville. | *The public transport system works well. It helps to reduce the traffic in the town.*

the noise — le bruit

Il n'y a pas beaucoup à faire dans ma ville. Il n'y a aucun cinéma, par exemple. | *There isn't a lot to do in my town. There's no cinema, for example.*

theatre — théâtre (m)
supermarket — supermarché (m)
shopping centre — centre commercial (m)

Dans ma ville, il y a un grand centre-ville et de nombreux magasins. | *In my town, there's a big town centre and numerous shops.*

Ma ville est pittoresque. Dans mon quartier, il y a une grande place avec des fountaines. | *My town is picturesque. In my area, there is a big square with fountains.*

READING — I don't know about you, but my town's really Misérable...

Read this extract from 'Les Misérables' by Victor Hugo, and answer the questions below in English. It describes how, after moving to Montreuil-sur-mer, père Madeleine profited from the black jet industry.

Montreuil-sur-mer était devenu **un centre d'affaires**[1] considérable. L'Espagne, qui consomme beaucoup de **jais noir**[2], y commandait chaque année des grands achats. [...] L'argent que père Madeleine a gagné était tel que, dès la deuxième année, il avait pu construire une grande usine dans laquelle il y avait deux vastes **ateliers**[3], l'un pour les hommes, l'autre pour les femmes. N'importe qui avait faim pouvait s'y présenter, et était sûr de trouver là de l'emploi et du pain. [...] Le chômage et la **misère**[4] étaient inconnus.

[1] a centre of trade
[2] black jet (a gemstone)
[3] workshops
[4] poverty

e.g. Which country bought a large amount of black jet?   Spain

1. When had père Madeleine earned enough money to build a factory?   [1]
2. Why did père Madeleine build two workshops?   [1]
3. How did père Madeleine help people who were hungry? Give **two** details.   [2]
4. Name **two** things which were unheard of in Montreuil-sur-mer.   [2]

The Home

Home sweet home... this page will help you describe where you live using some super French sentences.

La maison — *The home*

le quartier	*area*	l'immeuble (m)	*block of flats*	la salle de bains	*bathroom*
la maison...	*...house*	la pièce	*room*	les meubles (m)	*furniture*
individuelle	*detached*	le salon	*living room*	le lit	*bed*
jumelée	*semi-detached*	la cuisine	*kitchen*	le placard	*cupboard*
mitoyenne	*terraced*	la chambre	*bedroom*	l'armoire (f)	*wardrobe*

J'habite dans une maison mitoyenne. Nous avons six pièces. | *I live in a terraced house. We have six rooms.*

Dans ma chambre, il y a une chaise bleue, un lit et un bureau. | *In my bedroom, there's a blue chair, a bed and a desk.*

Grammar — adjectives

Most adjectives go <u>after</u> the noun, but some go <u>in front</u>:
un <u>beau</u> quartier   a <u>beautiful</u> area
See p.62 for more.

C'est comment chez toi? — *What's your home like?*

You need to vary which <u>adjectives</u> you use and learn some <u>descriptive phrases</u>.

J'habite dans un appartement. | *I live in a flat.*

J'aime habiter dans une maison jumelée. | *I like living in a semi-detached house.*

La cuisine est au rez-de-chaussée. | *The kitchen is on the ground floor.*

Nous avons un canapé confortable qui est dans le salon. | *We have a comfortable sofa which is in the living room.*

in a council house — dans une habitation à loyer modéré (une HLM)

on a farm — dans une ferme

on the first floor — au premier étage

I've got a fifty bedroom castle with a swimming pool...

Mahmoud has written a letter to his British exchange partner about his new flat.

Mon appartement a cinq pièces et se situe dans un immeuble **tout neuf**[1]. J'ai **emménagé**[2] il y a dix jours — j'habitais à la campagne avant cela. Ma chambre n'est pas très grande, donc la semaine prochaine j'achèterai des meubles plus petits. La cuisine est **carrément**[3] géniale. Il y a une grande **baie vitrée**[4] alors on y voit le soleil et la mer. J'aime beaucoup le bureau aussi. J'y fais mes devoirs car il y a une bibliothèque pour ranger mes livres. Et comme c'est à côté de la cuisine, c'est l'idéal pour **grignoter**[5]. Cependant, si la cuisine était plus loin, ce serait plus facile de manger moins de chocolat !

Grade 8-9

[1]brand new
[2]moved in
[3]absolutely
[4]bay window
[5]snacking

Tick list:
✓ tenses: present, perfect, imperfect, future, conditional
✓ correct pronoun position
✓ complex vocabulary
✓ use of 'si' clause

To improve:
+ use more exciting adjectives

Vous écrivez un blog sur votre maison / votre appartement pour un site Internet français.
*Vous **devez** faire référence aux points suivants:*

- *une description de votre maison / de votre appartement*
- *ce que vous pensez de votre quartier*
- *où vous habitiez dans le passé*
- *où vous aimeriez habiter à l'avenir.*

*Justifiez vos idées et vos opinions. Écrivez **130-150** mots environ **en français**.   [28 marks]*

Weather

British people are famous for moaning about the weather. Now you even get to do it in a different language...

Le temps — *The weather*

> 'Pleuvoir' and 'neiger' are impersonal verbs that can only be used with 'il' — see p.91.

le climat	*climate*			**Il fait...**	*It is...*		pleuvoir	*to rain*
Il y a...	*It is...*			beau	*fine*		neiger	*to snow*
du vent	*windy*			mauvais	*bad*		ensoleillé(e)	*sunny*
du soleil	*sunny*			chaud	*hot*		nuageux / nuageuse	*cloudy*
du brouillard	*foggy*			froid	*cold*		sec / sèche	*dry*

Tom was thrilled to be holidaying in Britain...

Il pleut.   *It's raining.* ← *It's snowing.* — Il neige.

It's hailing. — Il grêle.

Le climat là est doux.   *The climate there is mild.*

C'est nuageux et il pleut beaucoup.   *It's cloudy and it's raining a lot.*

stormy — orageux

misty — brumeux

Grammar — il y a (there is)

'Il y a' *(there is)* is often used to discuss the weather. 'Il y aura' is the future form and 'il y avait' is the imperfect — both are useful for talking about weather.

La météo — *The weather forecast*

Question	Simple Answer	Extended Answer
Quel temps fera-t-il demain? *What will the weather be like tomorrow?*	Il va faire beau et chaud, mais il va pleuvoir le soir. *It will be fine and hot, but it will rain in the evening.*	Il fera beau le matin, mais au cours de la journée le temps deviendra plus nuageux et orageux. Il pleuvra en fin d'après-midi. Il restera couvert le soir. La température moyenne sera de 16 degrés. *It will be fine in the morning, but during the day the weather will become more cloudy and stormy. It will rain late in the afternoon. It will remain overcast in the evening. The average temperature will be 16°C.*

Demain, le temps sera variable.   *Tomorrow, it's going to be changeable.*

Le week-end, il y aura des éclaircies.   *At the weekend, there will be bright spells.*

Ce sera orageux et il va neiger.   *It will be stormy and it will snow.*

Il fera mauvais et froid. Il y aura des orages dans le sud.   *The weather will be bad and cold. There will be storms in the south.*

lightning — des éclairs (m)

thunder — du tonnerre

freeze — geler

showers — des averses (f)

 READING ## *My brain's gone a bit foggy after all that...*

Read the weather forecast and decide whether each sentence is true or false.

- Voici les provisions météo. Ce matin, le temps **reste agité**[1] dans le sud-est, et il y aura des nuages orageux. Pourtant, cet après-midi, il fera plus beau et sec.

- Un peu de neige est attendue sur les Pyrénées au-dessus de 2000 m. Des averses orageuses et des coups de tonnerres se produiront dans le sud-ouest.

- En revanche, pour les régions au nord de Bordeaux, il y aura du brouillard le matin, et **un ciel**[2] ensoleillé l'après-midi.

[1]remains turbulent   [2]a sky

e.g.   In the south-east, it will be cloudy and stormy all day.   **false**

1.   It will snow in the Pyrenees above 2000 m.   [1]

2.   There will be showers and thunder in the south-west.   [1]

3.   It will be foggy all day in the regions north of Bordeaux.   [1]

Where to Go

We're all going on a summer holiday... This page is all about different countries and places you can go to.

Les pays (m) du monde — *The countries of the world*

l'Angleterre (f)	*England*	l'Inde (f)	*India*
la Grande-Bretagne	*Great Britain*	l'Amérique (f)	*America*
les États-Unis (m)	*United States*	l'Afrique (f)	*Africa*
l'Allemagne (f)	*Germany*	l'Asie (f)	*Asia*
la Chine	*China*	l'Europe (f)	*Europe*
l'Espagne (f)	*Spain*	à l'étranger	*abroad*
la Russie	*Russia*	la mer	*sea*
la Belgique	*Belgium*	la plage	*beach*
la Suisse	*Switzerland*	la Méditerranée	
le Pays de Galles	*Wales*		*the Mediterranean*

Grammar — to go to...

To say you're going to a country, you need the correct form of 'aller' *(to go)* and the correct preposition. Use:

- au for masc. sing. countries starting with a consonant.
- aux for plural countries.
- en for masc. sing. countries starting with a vowel and all fem. sing. countries.

If you're going to a town, you just need 'à'.

Les vacances (f) — *Holidays*

la Bourgogne	*Burgundy*	la Picardie	*Picardy*	la Guyane	*French Guiana*
la Normandie	*Normandy*	la Corse	*Corsica*	la Réunion	*Reunion*

These are all administrative regions of France.

Je vais aller en Bretagne, et après ça, j'irai en Écosse pour trois jours.

I'm going to go to Brittany, and after that, I will go to Scotland for three days.

J'ai passé les vacances au bord de la mer.

I spent the holidays at the seaside.

to Paris — à Paris
to India — en Inde
to the Netherlands — aux Pays-Bas (m)

Question

Quels sont vos projets pour les vacances?

What are your plans for the holidays?

Simple Answer

Je vais passer deux semaines en Algérie.

I'm going to spend two weeks in Algeria.

Extended Answer

À la fin d'août, j'irai dans le sud de l'Inde pour trois semaines avec deux amis. Nous visiterons des sites historiques.

At the end of August, I will go to the south of India for three weeks with two friends. We'll visit historical sites.

I wanted a trip to research this — my boss said, 'Get away!'...

*Lis l'email de Françoise qui parle de ses vacances. Réponds aux questions **en français**.*

Salut Marc,

Les grandes vacances sont arrivées enfin ! Mais je ne suis pas contente : ma famile n'a pas de projets pour les vacances. Nous ne pouvons pas arriver à une décision. Moi, je voudrais aller en Angleterre parce que j'ai envie de voir un match de football anglais. Ma sœur pense que nous devrions passer les vacances au bord de la mer. Elle veut aller chaque jour à la plage. Ma mère préférerait aller à Berlin car elle s'intéresse aux musées. Cependant, mon père dit que nous allons tous rester en France. Il croit que nous devrions faire du camping car il adore la vie en plein air. Et toi, où vas-tu passer les vacances ?

Françoise

1. Comment veut-elle passer les vacances ? Donne **deux** détails. [2]
2. Qu'est-ce qu'elle dit au sujet de sa sœur ? Donne **deux** détails. [2]
3. Que veut faire son père ? Donne **deux** détails. [2]

It was going to be a long night...

Accommodation

I know it's hard thinking about holidays while you're revising, but here's some stuff on accommodation.

Le logement — *Accommodation*

loger	*to stay*		faire du camping	*to go camping*
l'hôtel (m)	*hotel*		l'auberge (f) de jeunesse	*youth hostel*
le camping	*campsite*		la chambre d'hôte	*bed and breakfast*
la tente	*tent*		la colonie de vacances	*holiday camp*

Il cherche un hôtel au bord de la mer. — *He's looking for a hotel at the seaside.*

Est-ce qu'il y a une auberge de jeunesse ici? — *Is there a youth hostel here?*

in the town centre — au centre-ville

in Nice — à Nice

Où aimez-vous loger? — *Where do you like to stay?*

Question

Quel est votre type de logement préféré?

What's your favourite type of accommodation?

Simple Answer

J'aime loger dans les hôtels car c'est plus pratique.

I like staying in hotels because it's more practical.

Extended Answer

Je préfère faire du camping parce qu'il y a beaucoup de choses qu'on peut faire à la campagne. En plus, je trouve qu'on peut voir plus de choses de l'endroit qu'on visite.

I prefer to go camping because there are many things you can do in the countryside. Also, I find that you can see more of the place you're visiting.

Je préfère loger dans une auberge de jeunesse parce que c'est moins cher qu'un hôtel.

I prefer to stay in a youth hostel because it is less expensive than a hotel.

I like getting to know other people — j'aime faire la connaissance de nouvelles personnes

J'aime faire du camping parce que j'adore la vie en plein air.

I like camping because I love life in the open air.

nature — la nature

to explore the countryside — explorer la campagne

On peut se détendre plus si on loge dans un hôtel parce qu'on ne doit pas cuisiner.

You can relax more if you stay in a hotel because you don't have to cook.

because the rooms are already prepared — parce que les chambres sont déjà préparées

READING

'Une auberge de jeunesse' — *sounds like a vegetable to me...*

*Read this extract from 'Le tour du monde en quatre-vingts jours' by Jules Verne. Answer the questions **in English**.*

Lorsque Passepartout est arrivé à International-Hôtel, il ne lui semblait pas qu'il avait quitté l'Angleterre. Le rez-de-chaussée de l'hôtel était occupé par un immense «bar», sorte de buffet ouvert gratis à tout passant. Viande sèche, soupe aux huîtres, des biscuits et du fromage, y sont apparus sans que le consommateur ait dû payer. Cela paraissait «très-américain» à Passepartout. Le restaurant de l'hôtel était confortable. Mr. Fogg et Mrs. Aouda s'installaient devant une table et étaient abondamment servis.

1. What surprised Passepartout when he arrived at the International-Hôtel? *[1]*
2. Where was the hotel bar? *[1]*
3. What was provided in the buffet? Give **two** details. *[2]*
4. What was positive about the hotel? Give **two** details. *[2]*

Getting Ready to Go

And the boring but necessary admin bit... This page is about booking your holiday and getting ready to go.

Les préparatifs (m) — *Preparations*

réserver	*to book / to reserve*
la valise	*suitcase*
les bagages (m)	*luggage*
la pièce d'identité	*ID*
le passeport	*passport*
l'agence (f) de voyages	*travel agency*
la climatisation	*air conditioning*
le sac de couchage	*sleeping bag*
l'emplacement (m)	*pitch*
la chambre	*room*
le lit à deux places	*double bed*
les lits (m) jumeaux	*twin beds*
donner sur	*to overlook*

Grammar — from...to...

To say 'from...to...' when booking something, use 'du...au...'.

Je voudrais réserver une chambre du 25 août au 27 août.
I'd like to reserve a room from the 25th August to the 27th August.

Mmm...lovely décor. I've always wanted to sleep in a frilly pink bed...

J'ai mis mon passeport et mes lunettes de soleil dans ma valise.
I put my passport and my sunglasses in my suitcase.

J'ai réservé une chambre du 5 mai au 12 mai.
I booked a room from the 5th May to the 12th May.

Faire une réservation — *To make a reservation*

Je voudrais réserver une chambre avec un lit à deux places.
I would like to book a room with a double bed.

with twin beds — à lits jumeaux
with bunk beds — à lits superposés

Nous voudrions réserver un emplacement pour une tente du 13 juillet au 17 juillet. Nous sommes deux adultes et un enfant.
We would like to reserve a pitch for one tent from the 13th July to the 17th July. We are two adults and one child.

a campervan — un camping-car
a caravan — une caravane

Je préfère avoir une chambre simple avec climatisation qui donne sur la mer.
I prefer to have a single room with air conditioning which overlooks the sea.

SPEAKING — *Hope you've got all that vocab packed and ready for the exam...*

Jo is having a conversation with a French travel agent about booking a hotel.
Read her responses, then have a go at doing your own role play using the instructions below.

Tu parles avec un agent de voyage (AV). **Grade 8-9**

AV : Bonjour. Je peux vous aider ?

Jo : Bonjour ! Je voudrais réserver une chambre dans un hôtel à Toulouse, s'il vous plaît.

AV : Pour combien de personnes et pour combien de nuits ?

Jo : Pour deux adultes, du 3 juin au 5 juin, s'il vous plaît.

AV : D'accord. Vous avez des préférences particulières ?

Jo : Je préférerais une chambre **climatisée**[1] parce qu'il fera chaud. Est-ce qu'il y a un hôtel avec une piscine ?

AV : Oui, il y en a plusiers, par exemple l'Hôtel Ensoleillé.

Jo : Combien ça coûtera par nuit ?

AV : Ça coûte cent euros par nuit. [1]air-conditioned

Tick list:
✓ tenses: present, future, conditional
✓ complex and relevant vocab

To improve:
+ more varied conjunctions

Address the travel agent as 'vous' and speak for about two minutes. [10 marks]

Tu parles avec un agent de voyage.
• *réservation*
• *!*
• *dernières vacances — où*
• *? climatisation*
• *? activités pour enfants*

How to Get There

One vital thing about going on holiday is getting there. The transport vocab will be useful in other contexts too.

Comment y aller — *How to get there*

l'arrivée (f)	*arrival*	la voiture	*car*	conduire	*to drive*
le départ	*departure*	l'autobus (m)	*bus*	l'autoroute (f)	*motorway*
manquer	*to miss*	le train	*train*	la route	*way / road*
la carte	*map*	l'avion (m)	*plane*	le vol	*flight*
l'horaire (m)	*timetable*	le bateau	*boat*	louer	*to rent / to hire*

Voyager — *To travel*

Je suis allé(e) en train.	*I went by train.*
Je préfère les voitures aux bus car les bus sont peu fiables.	*I prefer cars to buses because buses are not very reliable.*
Nous avons manqué le bateau.	*We missed the boat.*

Grammar — monter, descendre

Use 'monter <u>dans</u>' to say 'to get <u>on</u>'.
Je monte <u>dans</u> le train. *I get <u>on</u> the train.*
Use 'descendre <u>de</u>' to say 'to get <u>off</u>'.
Il descend <u>du</u> bus. *He gets <u>off</u> the bus.*

Nous allons louer une voiture. Puis, selon la carte, nous devons prendre l'autoroute.	*We're going to hire a car. Then, according to the map, we need to take the motorway.*
J'ai regardé l'horaire — le TGV devrait arriver à six heures. Mais il est en retard.	*I looked at the timetable — the TGV should arrive at six o'clock. But it's late.*

'TGV' stands for 'train à grande vitesse' (high-speed train). The French national rail company is called SNCF.

En avion — *By plane*

Il faut arriver à l'aéroport deux heures avant l'heure de départ.	*You must arrive at the airport two hours before the departure time.*	check in — s'enregistrer
Le vol était retardé à cause d'un problème technique.	*The flight was delayed due to a technical problem.*	to bad weather — du mauvais temps

I liked flying until I had a go in this plane...

Question	**Simple Answer**	**Extended Answer**
Est-ce que tu aimes voler?	Oui, les avions sont le moyen de transport le plus sûr.	J'ai peur de voler parce que mon imagination me fait toujours envisager le pire. Mais les avions sont si pratiques et rapides!
Do you like flying?	*Yes, aeroplanes are the safest mode of transport.*	*I'm scared of flying because I always imagine the worst. But planes are so convenient and fast!*

Exams have been delayed due to fog — sorry, only kidding...

*Translate this social media post about holidays **into English**.* [7 marks]

La semaine prochaine, je vais aller en vacances aux États-Unis. En particulier, je voudrais voir New York. J'y ai réservé un hôtel de luxe avec une grande piscine. Cependant, le voyage m'inquiète beaucoup. J'ai peur de voler, et je serai dans l'avion pendant sept heures.

What to Do

So you've chosen a destination, booked your accommodation and got there... now what do you do?

Le tourisme — *Tourism*

l'office (m) de tourisme	*tourist office*	la cathédrale	*cathedral*	le tour	*tour*
les renseignements (m)	*information*	le château	*castle*	le plan de ville	*town plan*
le site touristique	*tourist attraction*	le musée	*museum*	la carte postale	*postcard*
le parc d'attractions	*theme park*	la visite guidée	*guided tour*	se faire bronzer	*to sunbathe*

En vacances, j'ai visité... — *On holiday, I visited...*

Question

Qu'est-ce que tu as fait en vacances?

What did you do on holiday?

Simple Answer

J'ai visité une cathédrale et je suis allé(e) à la plage.

I visited a cathedral and I went to the beach.

Extended Answer

J'ai décidé d'aller au musée pour apprendre autant que possible sur la région. Ça m'intéressait beaucoup.

I decided to go to the museum to learn as much as possible about the region. It was really interesting.

I wanted a nice day on the beach, but it was sealed off.

L'un de mes plus grands plaisirs, c'est acheter des souvenirs.

One of my greatest pleasures is buying souvenirs.

J'adore me faire bronzer à la plage. Malheureusement, j'ai oublié ma crème solaire.

I love sunbathing at the beach. Unfortunately, I forgot my suncream.

La cathédrale m'a beaucoup plu.

I liked the cathedral a lot.

going on a boat tour — faire un tour en bateau

my swimming costume — mon maillot de bain

my sunglasses — mes lunettes (f) de soleil

the zoo — le zoo

Grammar — plaire and pleuvoir

'Plaire' means *'to please'* and 'pleuvoir' means *'to rain'*. They both have the same past participle — 'plu'.

Il m'a beaucoup plu. *I liked it a lot. (It pleased me a lot.)* **Il a beaucoup plu.** *It rained a lot.*

How do beaches greet each other? They just wave...

Jack has written a blog about his plans for his holiday in France.

Cet été, je vais passer deux semaines à Cherbourg pour améliorer mon français. J'ai quelques projets pour réaliser ce **but**[1]. Je logerai avec une famille française, donc je parlerai français tous les jours. Je vais faire une visite guidée pour essayer de faire la connaissance de la ville et des gens français.

Je vais visiter les sites historiques car on peut y apprendre beaucoup. L'été dernier, je suis allé à Vienne et j'ai visité un château historique — les histoires des gens qui y ont vécu m'ont beaucoup intéressées.

J'irai sur la **côte**[2] aussi parce que je veux passer des jours relaxants à la plage.

Grade 8-9

[1]aim
[2]coast

Tick list:
- ✓ tenses: present, perfect, both futures
- ✓ correct use of 'y'

To improve:
- + use the conditional
- + give opinions using adjectives

Écrivez un article sur vos projets pour les vacances. Vous devez faire référence aux points suivants :

- *ce que vous aimez faire en vacances*
- *les vacances dernières*
- *vos projets pour cet été*
- *vos vacances de rêve.*

Justifiez vos idées et vos opinions. Écrivez **130-150** *mots environ* **en français**. *[28 marks]*

Eating Out

It would be a real waste to go to France and miss out on the delicious cuisine, so here's some useful vocab.

Qu'est-ce que vous voudriez? — *What would you like?*

There's more vocab. on p.107.

la boisson	*drink*	le hors d'œuvre	*starter*
la carte	*menu*	le plat principal	*main meal*
l'eau (f) plate / gazeuse	*still / fizzy water*	le dessert	*dessert*
le thé	*tea*	commander	*to order*
le café	*coffee*	végétarien(ne)	*vegetarian*
le vin	*wine*	fermé (le lundi)	*closed (on Mondays)*
la bière	*beer*	le serveur / la serveuse	*waiter / waitress*
la pression	*beer (from the pump)*	l'addition (f)	*the bill*

Je voudrais un verre de jus d'orange et une portion de frites, s'il vous plaît.

I would like a glass of orange juice and a portion of chips, please.

Marcel had everything he kneaded in life.

Allons au restaurant — *Let's go to the restaurant*

J'aime manger au restaurant parce qu'on peut goûter des plats qu'on ne cuisinerait jamais chez soi. J'ai essayé la cuisine chinoise, par exemple.

I like eating in restaurants because you can try food that you would never cook at home. I tried Chinese food, for example.

Indian — indienne
Mexican — mexicaine

Je suis végétarien(ne) donc c'est difficile de trouver des restaurants où je peux manger.

I'm vegetarian so it's hard to find restaurants where I can eat.

vegan — végétalien(ne)
allergic to... — allergique à...

J'ai commandé des escargots au restaurant français. Comme dessert, j'ai mangé une glace à la fraise.

I ordered snails in the French restaurant. For dessert, I ate a strawberry ice cream.

frogs' legs — des cuisses de grenouille
the fixed price menu — le menu à prix fixe

 SPEAKING

Waiter! This exam is overcooked — it's too tough...

Here's an example role play — Yann is talking to Fatima about a visit to a restaurant.

Fatima :	Qu'est-ce que tu as commandé au restaurant ?
Yann :	J'ai commandé du potage comme hors d'œuvre et du poulet avec des haricots verts comme plat principal.
Fatima :	Tout s'est bien passé ?
Yann :	**Je me suis plaint**[1] du poulet parce qu'il était froid.
Fatima :	Qu'est-ce que tu as aimé le plus ?
Yann :	J'ai aimé les haricots verts car ils étaient bien cuisinés.
Fatima :	Quel est ton repas préféré ?
Yann :	Le poulet avec les petits pois et les pommes de terre. Et toi, quel est ton repas préféré ?
Fatima :	Mon repas préféré est les fruits de mer.
Yann :	Qu'est-ce que tu mangeras ce soir ?
Fatima :	Je mangerai des pâtes avec des petits pois et des champignons. J'aime manger ça avec du fromage.

Grade 8-9

Tick list:
✓ tenses: perfect, imperfect, present, future
✓ opinion phrases
✓ correctly formed question

To improve:
+ use adjectives, e.g. 'délicieux', to avoid repeating 'aimer'

Prepare the role play card below. Use 'tu' and speak for about two minutes. [10 marks]

[1] I complained

Tu parles avec ton ami(e) d'une visite au restaurant.
* *les plats commandés*
* *problème*
* *!*
* *? repas préféré*
* *? ce soir — restaurant*

Practical Stuff

It's always good to know how to get out of a spot of bother on holiday. Even more importantly, you'll want to be able to tell your hilarious and embarrassing stories to your French friends. Learn this page well.

J'ai perdu mon billet — *I've lost my ticket*

> On public transport in France, you normally have to validate your ticket in a machine before you travel.

le bureau des objets trouvés	*lost property office*	le retard	*delay*
le commissariat	*police station*	le quai	*platform*
l'accueil (m)	*reception*	composter	*to validate (ticket)*
le portefeuille	*wallet*	laisser	*to leave (behind)*
le pneu	*tyre*	voler	*to steal*
les freins (m)	*brakes*	tomber en panne	*to break down*

Qu'est-ce qui t'est arrivé? — *What happened to you?*

Holiday <u>mishaps</u> are just waiting to happen — especially when another <u>language</u> is involved.

Grammar — 'se faire' + infinitive

The <u>perfect tense</u> (see p.80-81) of '<u>se faire</u>' followed by an <u>infinitive</u> is a way of saying that <u>something happened to you</u>. It's often used when we would say '<u>got</u>' in English, e.g. 'they got stranded.' Remember — all reflexive verbs use '<u>être</u>' in the perfect tense.

Il s'est fait piquer par un moustique.   *He got bitten by a mosquito.*
Hier, je me suis fait voler mon portefeuille.   *Yesterday, my wallet was stolen.*

En faisant du ski aux Alpes, j'ai glissé et je suis tombé(e) sur mon bras. J'ai dû aller aux urgences.

Je suis allé(e) au Maroc en famille. Nous sommes tombés en panne dans les montagnes — c'était un cauchemar.

L'année dérnière, j'ai rendu visite à un ami en France. J'ai oublié de composter mon billet de train, alors j'ai reçu une amende.

Whilst skiing in the Alps, I slipped and I fell on my arm. I had to go to A&E.

I went to Morocco with my family. We broke down in the mountains — it was a nightmare.

Last year, I visited a friend in France. I forgot to validate my train ticket, so I received a fine.

I broke my leg — je me suis cassé la jambe
We got a flat tyre — Nous avons eu un pneu crevé
I had to go to customer services — j'ai dû aller au service client
the ticket inspector was angry — le contrôleur / la contrôleuse était en colère

This page could be your ticket out of a tricky situation...

Marc has written a report describing an incident that happened during a recent trip.

La semaine dernière, je suis allé à Paris. Après avoir pris le métro, je me suis rendu compte que je n'avais plus mon portefeuille ! Je suis allé au bureau des objets trouvés, mais c'était évident que quelqu'un l'avait volé. J'étais en colère, et je n'avais plus d'argent ; j'ai dû aller au commissariat pour déclarer le vol. Les policiers étaient compréhensifs et ils m'ont aidé à **remplir les formulaires**[1].

Grade 8-9

Tick list:
✓ tenses: perfect, imperfect, pluperfect
✓ perfect infinitive
✓ negative construction

[1]to fill out the forms

To improve:
+ use the present, conditional and future
+ more varied conjunctions

Un site Internet touristique cherche des articles sur les problèmes et les solutions en vacances. Écrivez **130-150** mots environ **en français**. Vous **devez** faire référence aux points suivants :

• où vous êtes allé(e) et ce que vous avez fait
• un problème qui vous est arrivé
• ce que vous avez fait pour résoudre le problème
• si vous reviendriez au même endroit.   *[28 marks]*

Giving and Asking for Directions

Feeling lost? Then this is the page for you. It's got all you need to know about getting to where you want to go.

Où est...? — *Where is...?*

situé(e)	*situated*	en face de	*opposite*	environ	*about*
se trouver	*to be situated*	juste à côté de	*right next to*	jusqu'à	*until*
traverser	*to cross*	ici	*here*	le nord	*north*
à gauche	*on / to the left*	là-bas	*over there*	le sud	*south*
à droite	*on / to the right*	loin de	*far from*	l'est (m)	*east*
tout droit	*straight ahead*	près de	*near*	l'ouest (m)	*west*

Giving directions is easy... isn't it?

La poste est située en face de l'église.
Allez tout droit pour environ deux minutes, puis prenez la première rue à droite.

The post office is situated opposite the church. Go straight ahead for about two minutes, then take the first street on the right.

Traversez la rue, puis tournez à gauche.
La boulangerie est juste à côté de l'école.

Cross the street, then turn left. The bakery is right next to the school.

Le village est au sud-ouest de la ville.
La ville est dans le sud du pays.

The village is south-west of the town. The town is in the south of the country.

> Remember, if you're talking to someone you don't know, use the 'vous' form of the verb.

C'est loin d'ici? — *Is it far from here?*

It's useful to use <u>landmarks</u> when describing how to get somewhere.

la rue	*street*	les feux (m) (de signalisation)	*(traffic) lights*
la place	*square*	le rond-point	*roundabout*
le pont	*bridge*	le carrefour	*crossroads*
le trottoir	*pavement*	le panneau	*sign*

Grammar — imperative

The <u>imperative</u> form is used to give <u>instructions</u>:
Traversez! *Cross!*
See p.88 for more.

Pour aller à la gare, continuez tout droit, et tournez à gauche au carrefour.

To go to the train station, keep going straight ahead, and turn left at the crossroads.

to the bank —	à la banque
to the theatre —	au théâtre
to the café —	au café

Suivez le panneau 'toutes directions', et allez jusqu'aux feux, mais ne traversez pas le pont.

Follow the sign for 'all directions', and go up to the lights, but don't cross the bridge.

the toll —	le péage
the hospital —	l'hôpital (m)
the town hall —	l'hôtel (m) de ville

La banque est située en face de l'épicerie, juste à côté de la mosquée.

The bank is opposite the grocer's, right next to the mosque.

on the other side of — de l'autre côté de

Left! No, the other left! Directions are hard enough in English!

TRACK LISTENING 09

Your friend left a message on your voicemail. Choose the correct answers to complete the statements.

1 a. You should change bus at the... **A.** park **B.** cinema **C.** bus station [1]

b. The Grand-Place is... **A.** by the market **B.** near the supermarket **C.** on the coast [1]

c. After turning left you should... **A.** go as far as the library **B.** pass the library **C.** walk 100 m [1]

d. Then, you should... **A.** turn right **B.** cross at the traffic lights **C.** keep going for 200 m [1]

School Subjects

Talking about subjects is pretty straightforward — plus, you're probably bursting to say that you adore all things French-related. Explaining your opinion will get you more marks, so use this page to prepare properly.

Les matières (f) — *Subjects*

For more school subjects, see p.107-108.

For how to pronounce the letters of the French alphabet, look at p.11.

l'allemand (m)	*German*	la matière obligatoire	*compulsory subject*
l'espagnol (m)	*Spanish*	la littérature anglaise	*English literature*
le français	*French*	le dessin	*art*
la biologie	*biology*	l'EPS (éducation physique et sportive) (f)	*PE (physical education)*
la chimie	*chemistry*		
la physique	*physics*	l'informatique (f)	*IT (information technology)*

Ma matière préférée c'est... — *My favourite subject is...*

Moi, j'adore l'EPS. C'est chouette parce que je ne dois pas me concentrer et les cours sont détendus.

I love PE. It's great because I don't have to concentrate and the lessons are relaxed.

À mon avis, la physique est affreuse. C'est trop compliqué et je n'aime pas faire les expériences.

In my opinion, physics is awful. It's too complicated and I don't like doing the experiments.

my teacher is funny — mon / ma professeur est amusant(e)

I love doing exercise — j'adore faire de l'exercice

is boring — est ennuyeuse

is useless — ne sert à rien

Question	**Simple Answer**	**Extended Answer**
Quelle est ta matière préférée? *What's your favourite subject?*	J'aime assez les maths. *I quite like maths.* j'aime bien *I really like* j'adore *I love*	J'aime assez les maths car c'est logique, cependant, je préfère la littérature anglaise. C'est fascinant et je m'intéresse aux histoires des autres. *I quite like maths because it's logical, however, I prefer English literature. It's fascinating and I'm interested in other people's stories.*

I think all of these opinions are pretty subjective...

Cho a envoyé un email à sa copine pour lui parler de ses matières préférées.

Au lycée, ma matière préférée c'est le français parce que c'est tellement intéressant. J'aime assez le dessin et la technologie, mais je les trouve difficiles car je n'ai pas de **côté artistique**[1]. L'année dernière, j'ai étudié l'espagnol, et je m'intéressais beaucoup à cette matière. Malheureusement, le professeur d'espagnol a quitté le lycée, et j'ai dû **laisser tomber**[2] cette matière.

Je déteste l'allemand — pour moi c'est vraiment une langue affreuse. C'est dommage car j'aime apprendre les langues. Je voudrais étudier d'autres langues dans l'avenir et, si j'ai de la chance, peut être je pourrais devenir **traductrice**[3].

Grade 8-9

Tick list:
- ✓ tenses: present, perfect, imperfect, conditional, future
- ✓ si clause
- ✓ good use of conjunctions

[1] artistic side
[2] to drop
[3] translator

To improve:
+ include more varied sentence structures, e.g. 'pour' + infinitive

Écris un email à un(e) copain / copine pour donner ton avis sur les matières scolaires.
*Tu **dois** faire référence aux points suivants :*

- *les matières que tu aimes / n'aimes pas au collège et pourquoi*
- *les matières que tu as trouvées difficiles cette année*
- *pourquoi tu penses que les matières que tu étudies sont utiles (ou pas)*
- *les matières que tu voudrais faire dans l'avenir.*

*Écris **80-90** mots environ **en français**.*   [20 marks]

School Routine

You could probably sleepwalk through your school routine by now — the only thing left is to 'Frenchify' it...

Aller à l'école — *To go to school*

For more modes of transport, see p.40.

la salle de classe	*classroom*
le cours	*lesson*
l'emploi (m) du temps	*timetable*
la récré(ation)	*break*
les vacances (f)	*holidays*
le trimestre	*term*
la semaine	*week*
la rentrée	*return to school (after the summer)*
en retard	*late*
de bonne heure	*early*
tous les jours	*every day*
aller à pied	*to go on foot*

Question

Comment vas-tu à l'école?
How do you get to school?

Simple Answer

J'y vais à pied.
I walk there.

Extended Answer

Normalement, j'y vais à pied parce que j'habite près du lycée. Par contre, quand il pleut, ma mère m'emmène en voiture.
Normally, I walk there because I live close to college. However, when it's raining, my mum takes me in the car.

Grammar — 'y' (there)

'Y' is a pronoun that means 'there'. It can replace nouns that are <u>locations</u>, to avoid repetition. It normally goes <u>before the verb</u> — see p.70-71.

J'y vais ce week-end.
I'm going there this weekend.

Une journée typique — *A typical day*

See p.2 for more about stating the time.

La journée scolaire commence à neuf heures, et elle finit à quinze heures trente. Il y a deux récrés de vingt minutes, et on prend le déjeuner à midi.

The school day starts at nine o'clock, and it finishes at three thirty pm. There are two twenty-minute breaks, and we have lunch at midday.

J'ai un cours de maths chaque jour. Par contre, je ne fais qu'une heure d'EPS par semaine.

I have a maths lesson every day. On the other hand, I only do one hour of PE a week.

C'est une journée fatigante. Si j'avais le choix, je commencerais les cours plus tard.

It's a tiring day. If I had the choice, I would start lessons later.

Pendant la récré — *During break*

Je fais partie de l'équipe scolaire de natation, donc je m'entraîne souvent pendant la récré.

I'm part of the school swimming team, so I often train during break.

Normalement, je reste dehors avec mes amis et nous jouons au football. Mais parfois nous allons à la cantine.

Normally, I stay outside with my friends and we play football. But sometimes we go to the canteen.

the holidays — les vacances

the term — le trimestre

Make sure you go over this again and again and again...

TRACK LISTENING 10

Nicolas parle de son emploi du temps. Complète les phrases en choisissant des mots dans la case.

son frère	libres	le mardi	~~la chimie~~	stressés	d'EPS	la voiture	le soir	fatigués

e.g. Nicolas adore .... *la chimie* ....

1 a. Nicolas dit qu'il arrive à l'école en retard à cause de .... [1]

b. Nicolas se sent très fatigué après les cours .... [1]

c. Le mercredi, les élèves sont .... [1]

Nicolas was always ec-static in science lessons.

School Life

The French system is a little different to ours, and you need to understand it in case it pops up in your exams.

La vie scolaire — *School life*

bien équipé(e)	*well equipped*	l'élève (m / f)	*pupil*
mal équipé(e)	*badly equipped*	l'internat (m)	*boarding school*

apprendre — *to learn*
être en seconde — *to be in year 11*

Où vas-tu à l'école? — *Where do you go to school?*

Grammar — present tense + 'depuis'

To say you've been doing something since a certain age, use the present tense with 'depuis' (*since*).

J'étudie le français depuis l'âge de six ans.
I've been studying French since the age of six.

See p.79 for more about depuis in the present tense.

(2 - 6 years)	la maternelle	*nursery school*
(6 - 11 years)	l'école (f) primaire	*primary school*
(11 - 15 years)	le collège	*secondary school*
(15 - 18 years)	le lycée	*sixth form college*
(15 - 18 years)	le lycée professionnel	*technical college*

Je vais au collège près de chez moi. Je l'aime bien, et mes professeurs ont un bon sens de l'humour.

I go to the secondary school close to my home. I really like it, and my teachers have a good sense of humour.

are very engaging — sont très passionnants

Mon école est un internat. J'y vais depuis l'âge de onze ans.

My school is a boarding school. I've been going there since the age of eleven.

a state / private / religious school — une école publique / privée / confessionnelle

Décris ton école — *Describe your school*

Mon collège est très vieux, mais c'est génial à l'intérieur. Les couloirs sont vifs et pleins de couleur.

My school is very old, but it's great inside. The corridors are lively and full of colour.

it's modern — c'est moderne
the atmosphere is very different — l'ambiance (f) est très différente

Au total, il y a environ trois cents élèves. Il y a deux terrains de sport.

In total, there are around three hundred pupils. There are two sports pitches.

swimming pools — piscines (f)
sports halls — gymnases (m)

Revision means I don't have any kind of life...

Read these forum comments about school life, then answer the questions below.

Karine : Je vais au lycée à Paris et je suis en seconde. Les cours de sciences me fascinent car nos laboratoires sont très bien équipés : on peut faire plein d'expériences.

Alain : Je vais au lycée professionnel, et je prends des cours pour devenir mécanicien. Malheureusement, il faut que tout le monde étudie les maths. Je les déteste : le prof est vraiment ennuyeux, donc je n'arrive pas à m'intéresser aux cours.

Vusi : Je vais au collège. Il y a une piscine, donc je peux faire de l'exercice après les cours, ce qui m'aide à me relaxer.

Who says what about school life? Choose either Karine, Alain or Vusi.

1. .... says that sport is relaxing. [1]
2. .... says that having good resources encourages learning. [1]
3. .... says that the teacher's personality makes a big difference. [1]

The new science teacher was a real dinosaur.

School Pressures

School can be pretty stressful — and I'm not just talking about outfits on non-uniform day. Trying to study and get the grades you need whilst maintaining a social life is no mean feat. Here's your chance to let it all out...

Le règlement — *School rules*

> Watch out — 'passer un examen' doesn't mean 'to pass an exam', it means 'to take an exam'.

la pression	*pressure*	le bulletin scolaire	*school report*
les devoirs (m)	*homework*	la retenue	*detention*
la note	*mark*	permettre	*to allow*
les résultats (m)	*results*	passer un examen	*to sit an exam*
l'examen (m)	*examination*	échouer	*to fail*
l'erreur (f)	*error / mistake*	réussir un examen	*to pass an exam*
les incivilités (f)	*rudeness*	redoubler	*to resit the year*

It was important not to break formation in Mathieu's school.

L'uniforme scolaire aide à rendre tous les élèves égaux.
School uniform helps to make all pupils equal. ← *prevents students from being individual* — empêche les élèves d'être individuels

Il est interdit de courir dans les couloirs.
It is forbidden to run in the corridors. ← *to wear make-up at school* — de se maquiller à l'école
to be rude to the teachers — d'être impoli(e) envers les professeurs

Si on enfreint le règlement, on sera en retenue.
If you break the school rules, you'll be in detention. ← *If you forget your homework* — Si on oublie ses devoirs
If you're late — Si on est en retard

Être sous pression — *To be under pressure*

If you're asked for your <u>views on school</u>, this is a great chance to <u>add detail</u> to your answer.

Il y a beaucoup de pression à l'école à obtenir de bonnes notes.
There's a lot of pressure at school to get good marks. ← *to be fashionable* — d'être à la mode

J'ai étudié dur cette année donc j'espère réussir mes examens.
I studied hard this year so I hope to pass my exams. ← *to get a good school report* — obtenir un bon bulletin scolaire

Je me sens sous forte pression car j'ai peur de devoir redoubler.
I feel under lots of pressure because I'm scared of having to repeat the year. ← *my older brother is very gifted* — mon frère aîné est très doué

SPEAKING *Assez 'stressed', you say 'out' — stressed, out, stressed, out...*

Read the example then have a go at the photo question below. Aim to talk for about three minutes.

Es-tu sous pression dans ta vie scolaire ?

Moi, je me sens sous assez de pression. Il y a des devoirs chaque semaine pour l'anglais, les mathématiques et les sciences ; d'ailleurs, si nous n'obtenons pas de bonnes notes, les profs nous en donnent plus. Je voudrais aller à l'université, donc je dois réussir tous mes examens. Pourtant, il est difficile de trouver assez de temps pour étudier et aussi de passer du temps avec ses amis.

Grade 8-9

Tick list:
- ✓ tenses: present, conditional
- ✓ pronouns ('nous', 'en')
- ✓ reflexive verb

To improve:
- + talk about the past
- + include intensifiers, e.g. 'très'

Regarde la photo et prépare des réponses sur les points suivants :

- *la description de la photo*
- *ton opinion sur le règlement scolaire*
- *comment était ton école primaire*
- *comment tu changerais la vie scolaire si tu avais le choix*
- *!*

[24 marks]

School Events

Being able to talk about school events is pretty handy — we all love a good moan about parents' evening...

Faire un échange — *To do an exchange*

participer à	to take part
l'échange (m) (scolaire)	(school) exchange
l'excursion (f) scolaire	school trip
à l'étranger	abroad
le car de ramassage	school bus
un(e) correspondant(e)	penfriend
la remise des prix	prize giving
la réunion	meeting
la rencontre parents-professeurs	parents' evening

Grammar — perfect infinitive

The <u>perfect infinitive</u> (see p.89) is formed by '<u>après avoir</u>' + <u>past participle</u>. It means '<u>after having done</u>' something.

> **Après avoir écrit à mon / ma correspondant(e)...**
> ***After having written to my penfriend...***

If the verb takes '<u>être</u>' instead of 'avoir' in the perfect tense, use '<u>après être</u>' + <u>past participle</u>.

> **Après être rentré(e)(s) chez moi...**
> ***After having returned home...***

Question

As-tu participé à un échange scolaire?

Have you taken part in a school exchange?

Simple Answer

Oui, j'ai fait un échange scolaire cette année.

Yes, I did a school exchange this year.

Grammar — 'Il y a' + period of time

'<u>Il y a</u>' followed by a <u>period of time</u> means '<u>ago</u>'.

> **Il y a deux ans.**   ***Two years <u>ago</u>.***

Extended Answer

Oui, j'ai participé à un échange il y a six mois. J'ai une correspondante française qui s'appelle Anna, et je suis resté(e) chez elle pendant une semaine. Après avoir fait cet échange, j'ai vraiment envie de passer plus de temps à l'étranger.

Yes, I took part in a school exchange 6 months ago. I have a French pen pal who's called Anna, and I stayed at her house for one week. After having done that exchange, I really want to spend more time abroad.

Des événements scolaires — *School events*

L'année dernière, je suis allé(e) au musée avec ma classe d'histoire. Pendant la visite guidée, nous avons pris des notes pour faire une rédaction.

Last year, I went to the museum with my history class. During the guided tour, we took some notes to write an essay.

À la fin de l'année scolaire, j'assisterai à une remise des prix. J'ai eu les meilleures notes de la classe pendant toute l'année, et ma prof m'a attribué(e) le prix d'excellence.

At the end of the school year, I will attend a prize giving. I have had the best marks in the class all year, and my teacher has awarded me the top prize.

> I went on a school trip — je suis parti(e) en excursion scolaire

My penfriend 'Philippe Phlop' wouldn't shut up about shoes...

Listen to Marie talk about her French exchange, and then answer the questions below.

e.g. Marie's exchange...
  A. happened last year.   **B.** happened this year.   **C.** will happen next year.   **A**

1. (i) Before the exchange, Marie...
  A. wrote to Marc once.
  B. wrote to Marc every two weeks.
  C. had never written to Marc.
  D. wrote to Marc often.   *[1]*

(ii) During the exchange, Marie...
  A. improved her French.
  B. offended Marc's family.
  C. never watched the TV.
  D. went to the zoo.   *[1]*

The French students thought a week in England wasn't really a fair exchange.

Education Post-16

It's more than likely you've given this a lot of thought already, so you've already done the hardest part. All that's left is to work out how to say it in French — here's a little something to help you on your way...

L'enseignement postscolaire — *Further education*

You might have to discuss your plans for <u>future studies</u>, so it's important to know some <u>key vocabulary</u>.

laisser tomber	*to drop*
former	*to train*
en première	*in year 12*
en terminale	*in year 13*
le conseiller d'orientation / la conseillère d'orientation	*careers adviser*
le bac(calauréat)	*A-levels*
l'apprentissage (m)	*apprenticeship*
l'apprenti(e) (m / f)	*apprentice*
la licence	*degree*
l'université (f), la faculté	*university*
l'année (f) sabbatique	*gap year*

'Collège' means 'secondary school' in French. The French equivalent of technical college is a 'lycée professionnel'. For more about the school system, see p.47.

Grammar — 'avoir' constructions + infinitive

'Avoir envie de' means '<u>to want</u>' to do something. '<u>Avoir l'intention de</u>' means '<u>to intend</u>' to do something.

Both of these constructions are followed by an infinitive (see p.79).

J'ai envie d'<u>aller</u> à l'université.
I want <u>to go</u> to university.

Elle a l'intention de <u>faire</u> un apprentissage.
She intends <u>to do</u> an apprenticeship.

Mes études à l'avenir — *My future studies*

Question	Simple Answer	Extended Answer
Pourquoi as-tu choisi de passer / ne pas passer le bac? *Why have you chosen to do / not to do A-levels?* 	J'ai besoin du bac pour faire mon métier préféré. *I need A-levels to do my preferred job.* Je préférerais faire une formation. *I'd prefer to do some training.*	Pour moi, ce n'est pas un choix. Il faut avoir une licence pour faire mon métier préféré, et pour faire ça, j'ai besoin du bac. *For me, it isn't a choice. You have to have a degree to do my preferred job, and to do that, I need A-levels.* Pour moi, il s'agit de l'argent. Je voudrais trouver un emploi et gagner de l'argent dès que possible. De plus, j'ai parlé au conseiller d'orientation et il m'a conseillé de faire un apprentissage. *For me, it's about money. I would like to find a job and earn money as soon as possible. Moreover, I've spoken to the careers adviser and he advised me to do an apprenticeship.*

J'ai l'intention d'aller au lycée l'année prochaine pour passer le bac.

I plan to go to sixth form next year to do A-levels.

to study history, maths and French — pour étudier l'histoire, les maths et le français

Avant d'aller à l'université, j'aimerais prendre une année sabbatique pour découvrir le monde.

Before going to university, I would like to take a gap year to discover the world.

do some voluntary work — faire du travail bénévole

 ## *If this page isn't educational, I don't know what is...*

Traduis le passage suivant **en français**. [12 marks]

To celebrate the end of the exams, I watched films with my friends. We are very happy because it is the holidays. Next September, I will go to the sixth form college to do A-levels and I would like to get good results. However, my best friend wants to do an apprenticeship.

Amil couldn't get many on board his apprenticeship.

Career Choices and Ambitions

Deciding what to do with your life isn't exactly plain sailing, but don't worry about having to reveal your grand plans to the world in French. If you're uncertain, don't let it stop you — just make something up.

Le monde du travail — *The world of work*

le petit job	*part-time job*
le boulot	*job (informal)*
l'emploi (m)	*job (formal)*
l'employé(e) (m / f)	*employee*
l'employeur (m) /	
l'employeuse (f)	*employer*
le débouché	*job opportunity / prospect*
le / la patron(ne)	*boss*
le salaire	*salary*
l'ingénieur (m / f)	*engineer*
l'avocat(e) (m / f)	*lawyer*
l'infirmier (m) /	
l'infirmière (f)	*nurse*

See the vocab list on p.109 for more jobs.

Grammar — articles with jobs / professions

In French, you <u>don't need</u> an indefinite article ('<u>un</u>' / '<u>une</u>') when you describe someone's job.

Ma mère <u>est avocate</u>. *My mother's <u>a lawyer</u>.*

Je veux <u>être infirmier</u>. *I want <u>to be a nurse</u>.*

Grammar — venir + de + infinitive

'<u>Venir + de + infinitive</u>' means '<u>to have just done something</u>'.

Don't forget that 'venir' (to come) is an <u>irregular</u> verb.

Je <u>viens d'aller</u> à un entretien.
I <u>have just been</u> to an interview.

Mon père <u>vient de prendre</u> sa retraite.
My dad <u>has just taken</u> his retirement.

Ton métier idéal — *Your ideal job*

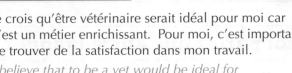

Question	**Simple Answer**	**Extended Answer**
Quel est ton métier idéal? Pourquoi?	Je rêve d'être médecin afin de soigner les malades.	Je crois qu'être vétérinaire serait idéal pour moi car c'est un métier enrichissant. Pour moi, c'est important de trouver de la satisfaction dans mon travail.
What is your ideal job? Why?	*I dream of being a doctor so that I can care for sick people.*	*I believe that to be a vet would be ideal for me because it's an enriching job. For me, it's important to find job satisfaction.*

As-tu un petit-job? — *Do you have a part-time job?*

Je suis vendeur / vendeuse. Je travaille le week-end pour gagner de l'argent.

I'm a shop assistant. I work at the weekend to earn money.

I babysit — Je fais du babysitting

I work at a hairdresser's — Je travaille dans un salon de coiffure

Je travaille dans un café. Mon salaire n'est pas très bon, mais je travaille dur.

I work in a café. My salary isn't very good, but I work hard.

I like working there — j'aime y travailler

Je fais du travail bénévole. C'est gratifiant d'aider les autres.

I do voluntary work. It's rewarding to help others.

an interesting challenge — un défi intéressant

Phew — it's all work, work, work in this section...

Your French pen pal sends you this message. Translate it **into English**. *[7 marks]*

Quand j'étais plus jeune, j'avais envie d'être boulanger parce que j'adorais faire des gâteaux. Aujourd'hui, je m'intéresse toujours à la cuisine, et j'aimerais être chef quand je quitterai l'école. J'ai un petit job dans la cuisine d'un restaurant. Je ne gagne pas beaucoup d'argent, mais j'espère que l'expérience sera utile dans l'avenir.

Languages for the Future

Learning a language isn't just about getting a qualification — it's meant to create opportunities. Knowing the local lingo could get you an amazing holiday deal, or even land you with the love of your life.

Apprendre une langue étrangère — *To learn a foreign language*

It's worth thinking about <u>the importance</u> of foreign languages — try to give a <u>balanced view</u>.

rencontrer quelqu'un	*to meet someone*
discuter	*to talk*
s'exprimer	*to express oneself*
obtenir un métier	*to get a job*
parcourir le monde	*to travel the world*
communiquer	*to communicate*
parler couramment	*to speak fluently*
les vacances (f) scolaires	*school holidays*
l'assistant(e) (m / f) de langue	*language assistant*
les langues (f) étrangères	*foreign languages*
les possibilités (f) d'avancement	*promotion prospects*

Question

Devrait-on apprendre une langue étrangère?

Should you learn a foreign language?

Simple Answer

Oui, car tout le monde ne parle pas couramment l'anglais.

Yes, because not everyone speaks English fluently.

Extended Answer

Oui, absolument. Le monde se compose de langues différentes, et elles sont toutes importantes.

Yes, absolutely. The world is made up of different languages, and they are all important.

Non, je pense qu'apprendre une autre langue est une perte de temps. Tout le monde parle anglais donc c'est déjà facile de communiquer.

No, I think that learning another language is a waste of time. Everyone speaks English so it's already easy to communicate.

Grammar — 'si' + imperfect + conditional

If you use '<u>si</u>' (*if*) with the <u>imperfect tense</u> (see p.82-83), the next verb should be in the <u>conditional tense</u> (see p.87).

<u>Si j'apprenais</u> **une autre langue, <u>j'aurais</u>** plus de débouchés.

<u>**If I learnt**</u> **another language, <u>I'd have</u> more job prospects.**

Pourquoi parler une autre langue? — *Why speak another language?*

Si on parle une deuxième langue, c'est plus facile de trouver un emploi: les entreprises s'intéressent au marché mondial.

If you speak a second language, it's easier to get a job: businesses are interested in the global market.

Quand je vais en vacances, j'aime pouvoir comprendre ce que disent les gens du pays.

When I go on holiday, I like to be able to understand what the locals are saying.

Je veux apprendre des langues étrangères pour me faire des amis quand je ferai mon année sabbatique.

I want to learn foreign languages to make friends when I take my gap year.

we live in a multicultural society — on vit dans une société multiculturelle

the signs — les panneaux (m)
the menus — les menus (m)

 Languages are a langue but rewarding process...

*Read Hélène's blog post, then answer the questions below **in English**.*

En ce moment, j'étudie deux langues au collège : l'anglais et l'allemand. Je pense que ce sera utile plus tard car je veux être **hôtesse de l'air**[1] et parcourir le monde. D'ailleurs, si je me marie avec un étranger, je voudrais que nous puissions nous parler dans leur **langue maternelle**[2]. À mon avis, pour comprendre la culture d'un pays il faut parler sa langue.

e.g. *Which languages is Hélène learning?* **English and German** [1] air hostess [2] native language

1. *Why would these languages be useful in her preferred job?* [1]
2. *Why does Hélène think that learning another language could be useful in her future personal life?* [1]
3. *According to Hélène, what does speaking a language help you to understand?* [1]

Applying for Jobs

Applying for jobs isn't always fun, but at least when you're pretending there's a little less pressure...

Poser sa candidature — *To apply for a job*

postuler	*to apply*
faire un stage	*to do work experience*
remplir un formulaire	*to fill in a form*
le poste	*position*
l'offre (f) d'emploi	*job offer*
l'annonce (f) de recrutement	*job advertisement*
la lettre de motivation	*application letter*
le salaire	*salary*
l'entretien (m)	*(job) interview*
les conditions (f) d'emploi	*terms of employment*
à temps plein	*full-time*
à temps partiel	*part-time*
au chômage	*unemployed*

Question

Quelles qualités faut-il pour trouver un emploi?
What qualities do you need to find a job?

Simple Answer

Il faut être motivé(e) et bien organisé(e).
You must be motivated and well organised.

Extended Answer

Il faut être ambitieux / ambitieuse et bien préparé(e) pour l'entretien. Il faut aussi avoir des diplômes.
You must be ambitious and well-prepared for the interview. You must also have qualifications.

Vous devez me recruter car... — *You should hire me because...*

Je suis la meilleure personne pour ce poste parce que je suis patient(e) et travailleur / travailleuse.

I'm the best person for this job because I'm patient and hardworking.

J'ai beaucoup d'expérience et de compétences.

I have lots of experience and skills.

> the required qualifications — les diplômes requis

J'ai fait un stage dans un hôpital l'été dernier, et on m'a donné beaucoup de responsabilités.

I did work experience in a hospital last summer, and I was given lots of responsibilities.

 SPEAKING

The zoo said I lacked the necessary koala-fications...

Read the sample role play. Mehul is talking to an employee at the job centre.

Employé : Où est-ce que vous aimeriez travailler ?

Mehul : Je voudrais devenir éditeur, donc j'aimerais travailler pour une **maison d'édition**[1].

Employé : Pourquoi vous y intéressez-vous ?

Mehul : Je pense que ce serait un métier varié et enrichissant. En plus, j'adore écrire.

Employé : Avez-vous de l'expérience dans ce domaine ?

Mehul : Oui, en effet. L'été dernier, j'ai fait un stage au journal local. J'y ai beaucoup appris, c'était très intéressant. Est-ce qu'il y a des postes à Paris ?

Employé : Oui, il y a un poste chez «Curiosité», une maison d'édition.

Mehul : Quelles sont les conditions d'emploi ?

Employé : Le salaire est de €2100 par mois. Vous aurez vingt-cinq **jours de congés**[2] par an.

Grade 8-9

Tick list:
✓ tenses: present, imperfect, perfect, conditional
✓ correctly-formed questions
✓ opinion phrases

To improve:
+ use different conjunctions to link phrases

Prepare the role-play card below. Use 'vous' and speak for about two minutes. [10 marks]

Tu passes un entretien pour un emploi d'été dans une colonie de vacances.

- *travailler pendant les vacances — raison*
- *travail — ton expérience*
- *!*
- *? heures de travail*
- *? commencer — quand*

[1]publishing house　　[2]days' leave

Environmental Problems

That's right — it's time to start thinking about all things green, natural and... erm... polluted.

L'environnement (m) — *The environment*

l'effet (m) de serre	*the greenhouse effect*	le pétrole	*oil*
le réchauffement de la Terre	*global warming*	jeter	*to throw away*
la couche d'ozone	*ozone layer*	gaspiller	*to waste*
augmenter	*to increase*	les déchets (m) / les ordures (f)	*rubbish*
mondial(e)	*worldwide*	pollué(e)	*polluted*
le charbon	*coal*	le déboisement	*deforestation*
le gaz carbonique	*carbon dioxide*	détruire	*to destroy*
le gaz d'échappement	*exhaust fumes*	l'eau (f) douce	*fresh water*

Ce n'est pas écologique — *It's not environmentally friendly*

Les gens jettent souvent des choses recyclables dans la poubelle.

People often throw recyclable things in the bin.

> paper — du papier
> glass — du verre

Un sac en plastique peut prendre des années à se décomposer.

A plastic bag may take years to decompose.

> an aluminium can — une boîte en aluminium

L'emballage est un gaspillage des ressources naturelles de la Terre.

Packaging is a waste of the Earth's natural resources.

> of raw materials — des matières (f) premières

Nous gaspillons de l'eau dans la vie quotidienne.

We waste water in everyday life.

> electricity — de l'électricité (f)

La pollution est un risque sanitaire — *Pollution is a health hazard*

La pollution est causée par les activités humaines.

Pollution is caused by human activity.

Parfois, les usines contaminent les lacs et les rivières avec des produits chimiques nocifs.

Sometimes, factories contaminate lakes and rivers with harmful chemicals.

Dans les grandes villes, la pollution de l'air peut provoquer des problèmes de santé.

In cities, air pollution may cause health problems.

La destruction des habitats — *The destruction of habitats*

Le déboisement contribue à l'effet de serre et mène à la perte des écosystèmes.

Deforestation contributes to the greenhouse effectand leads to the loss of ecosystems.

Certaines espèces sont menacées d'extinction. Elles ne survivraient pas les effets du réchauffement de la Terre.

Certain species are threatened by extinction. They would not survive the effects of global warming.

Environmental Problems

You might prefer hiding away in a darkened room to roaming the hills and basking in the glories of nature, but you still need to have an opinion about environmental problems, so listen up...

Les catastrophes naturelles — *Natural disasters*

l'incendie (m)	*fire*	l'ouragan (m)	*hurricane*
l'inondation (f)	*flood*	la sécheresse	*drought*
le tremblement de terre	*earthquake*	le désastre	*disaster*

Des milliers de personnes ont dû quitter leurs maisons après les inondations l'année dernière.

Thousands of people had to leave their homes after the floods last year.

Un incendie a ravagé le village.

A fire devastated the village.

Le gouvernement prend des mesures pour aider les victimes du tremblement de terre.

The government is taking measures to help the victims of the earthquake.

Il y a des problèmes graves — *There are some serious problems*

Question

À ton avis, quelles sont les plus grandes menaces pour l'environnement?

In your opinion, what are the biggest threats to the environment?

Simple Answer

Je crois que les plus grandes menaces sont le déboisement, le réchauffement de la Terre et la pollution de l'air.

I believe that the biggest threats are deforestation, global warming and air pollution.

Extended Answer

D'abord, il y a l'utilisation mondiale des énergies fossiles, comme le charbon, qui mène à une augmentation du gaz carbonique. Cela est responsable du réchauffement de la Terre.

En plus, je trouve qu'on a trop de déchets — une famille moyenne jette plus d'une tonne de déchets chaque année!

Enfin, il y a le gaspillage de l'eau. Malgré les 780 millions personnes dans le monde qui n'ont pas d'eau potable, ici on gaspille de l'eau chaque jour.

Firstly, there is the global use of fossil fuels, like coal, which leads to an increase in carbon dioxide. This is responsible for global warming.

Furthermore, I find that we have too much rubbish — an average family throws away more than a tonne of rubbish each year!

Lastly, there's water wastage. Despite the 780 million people in the world who don't have drinking water, we waste water each day here.

> ### Grammar — adjective position
>
> In French, adjectives usually come after the noun. However, this isn't always the case, e.g.
>
> **Il y a un <u>grand problème</u>.** *There is a <u>big problem</u>.*
>
> Adjectives such as <u>beau</u> — *beautiful*, <u>joli</u> — *pretty*, <u>jeune</u> — *young*, <u>gentil</u> — *kind*, <u>grand</u> — *big*, <u>petit</u> — *small* usually come before the noun. See p.62 for more.
>
> **Le déboisement abîme le <u>beau paysage</u>.**
> *Deforestation ruins the <u>beautiful landscape</u>.*
>
> **Les <u>petites actions</u> peuvent avoir un <u>grand effet</u>.**
> *<u>Small actions</u> can have a <u>big impact</u>.*

I think we should use more wind turbines — I'm a big fan...

*Traduis le passage suivant **en français**.* [12 marks]

Samit thinks that we must protect the planet. He believes that global warming has caused some serious problems, like droughts and hurricanes. In his opinion, people waste too many natural resources. He thinks that, in the future, we will have to use renewable energy instead of coal and oil.

Caring for the Environment

You might be feeling a bit down about the state of the world, but fear not — there's plenty you can do to make things better. Just don't go recycling this revision guide before you've learnt it all...

Comment pouvons-nous aider? — *How can we help?*

éteindre	*to switch off*	l'énergie (f) renouvelable	*renewable energy*
le manque (de)	*lack (of)*	les produits (m) bio	*green products*
protéger	*to protect*	le centre de recyclage	*recycling centre*
faire du compost	*to make compost*	faire du recyclage / recycler	*to recycle*
l'énergie solaire (f)	*solar power*	être vert(e)	*to be green*
l'énergie éolienne (f)	*wind power*	l'organisation charitable (f)	*charity*
sauvegarder	*to keep safe*	le commerce équitable	*fair trade*

Pour conserver l'énergie, il faut se souvenir d'éteindre les lumières quand on quitte la maison.

To save energy, you must remember to switch off the lights when you leave the house.

Il faut privilégier les énergies renouvelables.

We must give priority to renewable energy.

Grammar — se souvenir de

'Se souvenir de' means 'to remember'. It's a reflexive verb so it needs a reflexive pronoun (p.85 has more about this).

Je me souviens toujours de trier mes déchets quand je fais du recyclage.
I always remember to sort my rubbish when I recycle.

Question

Que fais-tu pour protéger la planète?
What do you do to protect the planet?

Simple Answer

Je trie mes ordures et je fais du compost. En plus, je fais du recyclage.
I sort my rubbish and I make compost. Also, I recycle.

Extended Answer

Je fais autant que possible dans la vie quotidienne. Par exemple, je prends des mesures pour économiser l'eau, comme prendre une douche au lieu d'un bain. Cette année, je vais organiser un événement dans ma ville pour promouvoir les produits bio qui endommagent moins l'environnement.

I do as much as possible in my daily life. For example, I take action to save water, such as having a shower instead of a bath. This year, I am going to organise an event in my town to promote green products, which harm the environment less.

SPEAKING — *I've given up washing in order to save the environment...*

Have a look at the sample response, then answer the questions below. Talk for about three minutes.

Est-ce que tu fais du recyclage ? Pourquoi / pourquoi pas ?

À mon avis, protéger l'environnement, c'est très important. Je recycle autant que possible — le verre, le plastique et même mes vieux vêtements. En plus, j'ai mené une campagne à l'école pour encourager les élèves à faire du recyclage. Je pense que si chaque personne prenait une ou deux mesures pour combattre le gaspillage des ressources, nous pourrions sauver la planète.

(Grade 6-7)

Tick list:
- ✓ detailed answer
- ✓ tenses: perfect, imperfect, present, conditional

To improve:
- + more adjectives and adverbs
- + use 'il faut...' or 'on doit...'
- + add a future tense

Regarde la photo et prépare des réponses sur les points suivants :

- *la description de la photo*
- *si l'environnement est important pour toi*
- *une mesure que tu as prise récemment pour protéger la Terre*
- *ce que tu pourrais faire pour être plus vert(e)*
- *!*   *[24 marks]*

Problems in Society

Unfortunately, there's more to social problems than preferring your pyjamas to parties, so learn this stuff well.

Les problèmes sociaux — *Social problems*

'SDF' stands for 'sans domicile fixe' *(without a permanent home).*

l'égalité (f)	*equality*	les SDF, les sans-abri (m / f)	*homeless people*
effrayant(e)	*frightening*	le chômage	*unemployment*
voler	*to steal*	la pauvreté	*poverty*
la guerre	*war*	mal nourri(e)	*malnourished*
mourir	*to die*	affamé(e)	*starving*

L'inégalité sociale — *Social inequality*

Le chômage est un problème grave dans les pays européens.
Unemployment is a serious problem in European countries.

Racism — Le racisme
Discrimination — La discrimination

Il faut lutter contre les mentalités racistes et sexistes.
We need to fight against racist and sexist mentalities.

combat — combattre
eradicate — éradiquer

Le problème principal est... — *The main problem is...*

Question

À ton avis, quels sont les problèmes principaux pour les SDF?

In your opinion, what are the main problems facing homeless people?

Simple Answer

Je crois que le plus grand problème est qu'ils ne peuvent pas trouver un emploi pour pouvoir payer un logement.

I think the biggest problem is that they cannot find a job to be able to afford accommodation.

Extended Answer

Je pense que les problèmes des SDF sont complexes. Si on est au chômage, on n'a pas les moyens de payer un logement. Cependant, il n'est pas possible de trouver un emploi sans domicile fixe. Il s'agit d'un cercle vicieux.

I think homeless people's problems are complicated. If people are unemployed, they can't afford to pay for accommodation. However, it is not possible to find a job without a permanent address. It's a vicious circle.

socialement exclu(e)	*socially excluded*
déprimé(e)	*depressed*
vulnérable	*vulnerable*

Grammar — on doit... / il faut...

Use 'on doit...' (from 'devoir') or 'il faut...' (from 'falloir') to say 'we must'. The verb which follows is in the infinitive.

On doit aider les pauvres.
We must help the poor.

Il faut empêcher les guerres.
We must prevent wars.

You can also use the verb 'devoir' to say that someone needs to do something.

Les politiciens doivent donner la priorité à la question de l'inégalité sociale.
Politicians must prioritise the issue of social inequality.

READING — What happened to 'peace and love'...?

Translate this passage into English. [7 marks]

Il y a beaucoup de problèmes sociaux dans ma région, comme le chômage. En plus, il y a des gens qui vivent dans la rue. Hier, j'ai vu des SDF et ils étaient mal nourris. À mon avis, il faut faire quelque chose pour aider ces gens. On doit combattre l'inégalité.

Clive didn't have social problems — he was just misunderstood.

Global Events

Don't worry if you're running out of steam by now — it's renewable. Plus, this section's almost done. Just a few bits and bobs about international events, and then you can have a well-earned cup of tea...

Être spectateur / spectatrice — *To be a spectator*

assister à	to attend	l'événement (m)	event
fêter	to celebrate	le festival (de musique)	(music) festival
bénéficier	to benefit	les Jeux (m) olympiques	Olympic Games
collecter des fonds	to raise money	la coupe du monde	world cup

Question

As-tu déjà assisté à un événement international?

Have you already attended an international event?

Simple Answer

Oui, j'ai assisté à un concert de charité pour les victimes du tremblement de terre en Asie.

Yes, I attended a charity concert for the victims of the earthquake in Asia.

Extended Answer

Oui, je suis allé(e) voir le Tour de France, mais je n'ai pas encore assisté aux Jeux olympiques.

Yes, I've been to see the Tour de France, but I haven't attended the Olympic Games yet.

Grammar — 'déjà' (*already*)

'Déjà' (*already*) goes <u>before</u> the past participle when it's used with the perfect tense (see p.80-81).

J'ai <u>déjà</u> mangé.   *I've <u>already</u> eaten.*

It's used in front of <u>adjectives</u> and <u>adverbs</u>, too.

Il est <u>déjà</u> fatigué.   *He's <u>already</u> tired.*

Elle est <u>déjà</u> là.   *She's <u>already</u> there.*

Grammar — 'ne...pas encore' (*not...yet*)

'Ne...pas encore' means 'not...yet'. Just like a normal negative, the 'ne' and 'pas' go <u>either side of the verb</u> (see p.86). In the <u>perfect tense</u>, they go around the bit of '<u>avoir</u>' or '<u>être</u>':

Je <u>n'</u>ai <u>pas encore</u> mangé.   *I've <u>not</u> eaten <u>yet</u>.*

Il <u>n'</u>est <u>pas encore</u> fatigué.   *He's <u>not</u> tired <u>yet</u>.*

Elle <u>n'</u>est <u>pas encore</u> là.   *She's <u>not</u> there <u>yet</u>.*

Les campagnes mondiales — *Global campaigns*

Je fête la Journée mondiale de l'enfance. Il y a trop d'enfants dans le monde qui doivent travailler et qui ne peuvent pas aller à l'école.

I celebrate Universal Children's Day. There are too many children in the world who have to work and can't go to school.

Consacrer des journées aux campagnes mondiales ne change pas le problème — je les trouve ridicules.

Dedicating days to global campaigns doesn't change the problem — I find them ridiculous.

> doesn't benefit anybody — ne bénéficie à personne

Les campagnes mondiales rappellent aux gens les problèmes de société.

Global campaigns remind people about problems in society.

> good causes — les bonnes causes (f)

Je crois qu'on devrait avoir plus de publicité pour promouvoir les campagnes mondiales.

I believe that we should have more advertising to promote global campaigns.

> funding — d'aide (f) financière

My favourite celebration? World Book Day...

*Traduis le passage suivant **en français**. [12 marks]*

For his birthday, I gave my dad two tickets for a Rugby World Cup match. We're going to go to the match together. We like to watch sport. In 2012, we went to the Olympic Games and it was amazing. There was a pleasant atmosphere with people from many different countries.

Luc misunderstood the Olympic water polo event.

Words for People and Objects | Nouns

Nouns are words for people and objects. This is important in French because all nouns have a gender.

Every noun in French is masculine or feminine

1) Whether a noun is <u>masculine</u> or <u>feminine</u> affects loads of things. The words for '<u>the</u>' and '<u>a</u>' are <u>different</u> and, if that wasn't enough, <u>adjectives</u> change to match the gender too.

For more on how adjectives change to fit the gender, see p.61.

2) '<u>Le</u>' in front of a noun means it's <u>masculine</u>. '<u>La</u>' in front means it's <u>feminine</u>.

> le livre (m) intéressant   *the interesting book*

> la matière (f) intéressante   *the interesting subject*

3) When you <u>learn</u> a <u>noun</u>, learn the <u>article</u> too — don't think 'chien = dog', think '<u>le</u> chien = the dog'.

Koko was keen to remind them that he was 'le chien' not 'le cheval'.

Sometimes you can guess which gender a word is

If you have to <u>guess</u> whether a noun is <u>masculine</u> or <u>feminine</u>, use these <u>rules of thumb</u>:

It's probably <u>masculine</u> if... | ...it <u>ends in</u>: -age, -al, -er, -eau, -ing, -in, -ment, -ou, -ail, -ier, -et, -isme, -oir, -eil | ...<u>or</u> it's a | *male person, language, day, month or season.*

It's probably <u>feminine</u> if... | ...it <u>ends in</u>: -aine, -ée, -ense, -ie, -ise, -tion, -ance, -elle, -esse, -ière, -sion, -tude, -anse, -ence, -ette, -ine, -té, -ure | ...<u>or</u> it's a | *female person.*

These rules don't work every time — there are some exceptions.

Nouns can also be made plural

1) Nouns in French are <u>usually</u> made <u>plural</u> by adding an '<u>s</u>' — the <u>same</u> as in English.

> le chat *the cat* → les chats *the cats*

2) When you make a noun <u>plural</u>, instead of '<u>le</u>' or '<u>la</u>' to say '<u>the</u>', you have to use '<u>les</u>' — see p.60.

3) Some nouns can't be made plural by sticking an '<u>s</u>' on the end — they have <u>irregular plural forms</u>:

Noun ending	Example	Meaning	Irregular plural ending	Example
-ail	le travail	work	-aux	les travaux
-al	le journal	newspaper	-aux	les journaux
-eau	le bureau	office	-eaux	les bureaux
-eu	le jeu	game	-eux	les jeux
-ou	le chou	cabbage	-oux	les choux →

Only a handful of nouns follow this rule — e.g. 'genou' (*knee*), 'bijou' (*jewel*) — most nouns ending in 'ou' are <u>regular</u>.

4) Some nouns <u>don't change</u> in the plural form. These are usually nouns that end in <u>-s</u>, <u>-x</u> or <u>-z</u>.

> la croix *the cross* → les croix *the crosses*

> la souris *the mouse* → les souris *the mice*

Using the correct gender will help boost your marks...

Add 'le' or 'la' to these words and then put the whole thing into its plural form.

1. cadeau *(present)*   **3.** citron *(lemon)*   **5.** voiture *(car)*

2. piscine *(swimming pool)*   **4.** cheval *(horse)*   **6.** pâtisserie *(cake shop)*

| Articles | **'The', 'A' and 'Some'** |

'The' and 'a' are some of the most common words in a language, so it's a good idea to revise them well...

Un, une — *A*

The word for 'a' depends on the gender of the noun (see p.59).

'Un' and 'une' are indefinite articles.

'Un' is used with masculine words...   un café (m)   *a coffee*

...and 'une' is used with feminine ones.   une tasse (f)   *a cup*

Le, la, l', les — *The*

These are definite articles.

1) The word for 'the' is different depending on the gender and number of the noun:

Masculine singular	Feminine singular	Before vowels / 'h' (sometimes)	Masc. or fem. plural
le	la	l'	les

2) For words starting with a vowel, 'le' or 'la' is shortened to 'l''. This makes them easier to say.

l'avion (m)   *the aeroplane*   l'émission (f)   *the programme*

3) Some words starting with an 'h' also take 'l'' instead of 'le' or 'la'. Sadly there's no rule for when this happens — you just have to learn it.

l'homme (m)   *the man*

'De' and 'à' change before 'le' and 'les'

1) 'De' (*of / from*) and 'à' (*to / at*) are prepositions (see p.74).

2) Be careful when you use them before a definite article (le/la/l'/les). They combine with 'le' and 'les' to make new words.

	le	la	l'	les
à +	au	à la	à l'	aux
de +	du	de la	de l'	des

Je reste à **+** le collège. → Je reste au collège.   *I'm staying at school.*
Je viens de **+** le Canada. → Je viens du Canada.   *I come from Canada.*
Je vais à **+** les États-Unis. → Je vais aux États-Unis.   *I'm going to the United States.*

Du, de la, de l', des — *'Some' or 'any'*

1) If you want to say 'some' or 'any', use 'de' with the correct definite article (see the table above). These are called partitive articles.

2) In negative sentences (see p.86), you only use 'de', regardless of the gender or whether it's singular or plural.

Je n'ai pas de pain.   *I haven't got any bread.*

Je n'ai pas de pantalon.   *I haven't got any trousers.*

3) You also just use 'de' after most quantities — such as 'beaucoup de' (*lots of*) or 'un peu de' (*a bit of*).

J'ai un peu de fromage.   *I have a bit of cheese.*

Personally, I prefer French articles about cheese...

Fill in the gaps with the correct article.

1. L'homme a un peu ..... pain.
2. Les étudiants viennent ..... Maroc.
3. Je vais ..... pays de Galles.
4. Nous avons ..... bananes.
5. Ils n'ont pas ..... raisins.
6. Il va ..... bibliothèque.

Words to Describe Things

Adjectives are very useful, but they're a little bit tricky in French...

Adjectives describe things — here are some common ones

beau / belle	beautiful	affreux / affreuse	awful	nouveau / nouvelle	new
triste	sad	long(ue)	long	lent(e)	slow
normal(e)	normal	facile	easy	pratique	practical
intéressant(e)	interesting	difficile	difficult	amusant(e)	funny

French adjectives 'agree' with the thing they're describing

1) In English, adjectives don't <u>change form</u> — even when the word being described is plural, e.g. <u>big</u> boots.

2) In French, most adjectives <u>change</u> to match the <u>gender</u> and <u>number</u> of the word they're <u>describing</u>.

3) You often add an '-e' to the adjective if the word being described is <u>feminine</u> (see p.59).
   But <u>don't</u> do this if the word <u>already ends</u> in 'e'.

le livre intéressant	*the interesting book*		la vie intéressante	*the interesting life*

4) Add an '-s' to the adjective if the word being described is <u>plural</u> (see p.59).
   This means that with <u>feminine plurals</u>, you're adding '-es'.

les livres intéressants	*the interesting books*		les vies intéressantes	*the interesting lives*

Some adjectives don't follow these rules

Adjectives with <u>certain endings</u> follow <u>different</u> rules:

Ending	Important examples	Masculine singular	Feminine singular	Masculine plural	Feminine plural
-x	heureux *(happy)*, sérieux *(serious)*, ennuyeux *(boring)*, dangereux *(dangerous)*	heureux	heureuse	heureux	heureuses
-on, -en, -el, -il	bon *(good)*, mignon *(sweet)*, cruel *(cruel)*, gentil *(kind)*	bon	bonne	bons	bonnes
-er	premier *(first)*, dernier *(last)*, fier *(proud)*, cher *(expensive)*, étranger *(foreign)*	premier	première	premiers	premières
-f	sportif *(sporty)*, actif *(active)*, vif *(lively)*, négatif *(negative)*	sportif	sportive	sportifs	sportives
-c	blanc *(white)*, sec *(dry)*	blanc	blanche	blancs	blanches

These double the last letter + add 'e' in the feminine.

'Sèche' (f. sing.) and 'sèches' (f. pl.) have an accent added to them.

Adjectives — très sérieux, et un peu ennuyeux, mais utiles...

Translate these phrases into **French**, *making sure the adjectives agree.*

1. The proud mother.
2. A sad girl.
3. The slow cat.
4. A blue house.
5. The lively dogs.
6. The white cars.
7. A kind woman.
8. An expensive jacket.

Words to Describe Things

Adjectives add details to what you've written, which will get you those extra marks. So they're pretty useful...

Some adjectives don't follow the rules

1) These adjectives are <u>irregular</u>.

2) Some <u>change</u> before <u>masculine singular</u> nouns starting with a <u>vowel</u> because it's <u>easier</u> to say.

3) Some adjectives <u>never change</u>, e.g. '<u>marron</u>' (brown) and '<u>orange</u>' (orange).

Masculine singular	Before a masc. sing. noun starting with a vowel	Fem. sing.	Masc. plural	Fem. plural
vieux (old)	vieil	vieille	vieux	vieilles
beau (beautiful)	bel	belle	beaux	belles
nouveau (new)	nouvel	nouvelle	nouveaux	nouvelles
fou (mad)	fol	folle	fous	folles
long (long)	long	longue	longs	longues
tout (all)	tout	toute	tous	toutes
rigolo (funny)	rigolo	rigolote	rigolos	rigolotes

Most adjectives go after the word they're describing...

1) In French, <u>most</u> adjectives follow the <u>noun</u> (the word they're describing).

> J'ai une voiture rapide.   *I have a fast car.*

2) You can also <u>use adjectives</u> in sentences with <u>verbs</u> such as '<u>être</u>' (to be) and '<u>devenir</u>' (to become). The adjective still needs to <u>agree</u> with the noun though.

> Ils sont prêts maintenant.   *They are ready now.*
>
> Elle devient grande.   *She is becoming tall.*

Brrumm...

Adjectives are always masculine singular after 'ce', e.g. 'c'est nouveau' (it's new).

...but there are some odd ones which go before

'Grand(e)' goes after the noun when it's describing a person.

1) These adjectives almost always go <u>before</u> the noun:

bon(ne)	*good*	nouveau / nouvel(le)	*new*	grand(e)	*big / tall*
mauvais(e)	*bad*	beau / bel(le)	*beautiful*	haut(e)	*high*
jeune	*young*	premier / première	*first*	joli(e)	*nice / pretty*
vieux / vieil(le)	*old*	petit(e)	*small / short*	faux / fausse	*false*

Adjectives have to agree regardless of whether they come before or after the noun.

> J'ai une petite maison, avec un joli jardin et une belle vue.
> *I have a small house, with a pretty garden and a beautiful view.*

2) Some adjectives <u>change meaning</u> depending on whether they go <u>before</u> or <u>after</u> a word. For example, 'propre' means '<u>own</u>' before a noun but '<u>clean</u>' after it. '<u>Ancien</u>' is another example:

> l'ancien château *the former castle*   le château ancien ⟶ *the old castle*

Only people silly put adjectives in the place wrong...

Without looking at the page above, pick the sentences that have the adjective(s) in the right place.

1. C'est un chien jeune.
2. Le long train est bleu.
3. Elle est une fille sportive.
4. Tu as lu un ennuyeux livre.
5. J'ai une voiture rouge nouvelle.
6. Vous avez la meilleure maison.

Words to Describe Things

They're no ordinary adjectives on this page — they're possessives, indefinites and demonstratives. Fancy.

Words like 'my' and 'your' show who an object belongs to

1) <u>Possessive adjectives</u> show that something <u>belongs</u> to someone. They go <u>before the noun</u>.

| notre cousin | *our cousin* |

	My	Your (inf. sing.)	His / her / its	Our	Your (formal, pl.)	Their
Masculine singular	mon	ton	son	notre	votre	leur
Feminine singular	ma	ta	sa	notre	votre	leur
Plural	mes	tes	ses	nos	vos	leurs

2) They <u>match</u> the <u>thing being described</u> — <u>NOT</u> the <u>person</u> it belongs to. The <u>different</u> forms are in this table.

3) So, for example, it's <u>always</u> '<u>mon</u> père' *(my father)* even if a <u>girl</u> is talking.

| Voici mon père et ma mère. |
| *Here is my dad and my mum.* |

This means that 'son', 'sa' or 'ses' could all mean either 'his' or 'her'. You can usually tell which one it's meant to be by using the context.

4) <u>Before vowels</u>, or words starting with '<u>h</u>' that take '<u>l</u>', you use the <u>masculine</u> possessive adjective — even if the noun is <u>feminine</u>. It's <u>easier to say</u>.

| Mon amie s'appelle Ana. | *My friend's called Ana.* |

Quelque, chaque — *Some, each*

1) '<u>Quelque</u>' *(some)* and '<u>chaque</u>' *(each)* are <u>indefinite adjectives</u>. They <u>don't</u> have a set of <u>different</u> forms for masculine, feminine or plural.

'Quelque chose' is a fixed phrase that uses 'quelque'. It means 'something'.

2) 'Quelque' <u>doesn't</u> have a <u>feminine</u> form, but it <u>does</u> add an '-s' when it changes from <u>singular</u> to <u>plural</u>.

| J'ai acheté quelques bonbons au magasin qui est à quelque distance de chez moi. |
| *I bought some sweets at the shop which is some distance from my house.* |

3) 'Chaque' <u>never</u> changes whether it's describing something <u>masculine</u> or <u>feminine</u>.

| Je lis chaque nuit. | *I read every night.* |

Ce, cet, cette, ces — *This, these*

1) To say '<u>this</u>' or '<u>these</u>', you need the right form of '<u>ce</u>':

Masculine singular	Feminine singular	Masc. words that take 'l"	Masculine or feminine plural
ce	cette	cet	ces

Choose the one that matches the noun you're describing.

2) These are <u>demonstrative adjectives</u> — they're used when you use '<u>this</u>' as a <u>describing word</u>.

| Ce film est terrible. | *This film is terrible.* | | Cet homme est grand. | *This man is tall.* |

These words are short... but they'll make your French sweeter...

Complete these sentences using the correct translation of the words in brackets.

1. ...... père n'aime pas ...... nouvelle voiture. (my, his)
2. ...... amis ne vont pas à ...... lycée. (your (sing. inf.), our)
3. ...... hôtel est grand. (this)
4. ...... cuisinière a ...... légumes. (this, some)

Words to Describe Actions

Words that describe actions are called adverbs. Like adjectives, they're useful for adding more detail to your French and gaining you marks. Nifty...

Adverbs describe how something's being done

1) In English, you don't say 'I run <u>slow</u>' — you add '<u>-ly</u>' on the end to say 'I run <u>slowly</u>'. '<u>Slowly</u>' is an <u>adverb</u>.

2) In French, you add '<u>-ment</u>' on the <u>end</u> of an <u>adjective</u> to make an <u>adverb</u>.
But <u>first</u> you have to make sure it's in the <u>feminine form</u> (see p.61-62).

adroit *(skilful)* ⟶ adroite *(feminine form)* **+** -ment ⟶ adroitement *(skilfully)*

3) Unlike adjectives, <u>adverbs</u> don't have to <u>agree</u> — they're <u>describing</u> an <u>action</u>, not the <u>person</u> doing it.

Elle court adroitement.
She runs skilfully.

Nous courons adroitement.
We run skilfully.

There are some small exceptions

1) Some adjectives <u>don't</u> follow the rules above.

2) If an adjective ends in '<u>-ant</u>' or '<u>-ent</u>', the '<u>nt</u>' is replaced with '<u>-mment</u>'.

fréquent *(frequent)* ⟶ fréque- + -mment ⟶ fréquemment *(frequently)*
récent *(recent)* ⟶ réce- + -mment ⟶ récemment *(recently)*

> 'Présentement' and 'lentement' follow the normal rule and use their feminine adjective forms + '-ment'.

3) With <u>some</u> adjectives ending in '<u>-e</u>', the '<u>e</u>' changes to '<u>é</u>' when they become <u>adverbs</u>.

énorme *(enormous)*   énormément *(enormously)*

précise *(precise)*   précisément *(precisely)*

4) If an adjective's <u>masculine</u> form ends in a <u>vowel</u>, you can just add '<u>-ment</u>' to it to make an <u>adverb</u> — you <u>don't</u> need to use the <u>feminine</u> form.

poli *(polite)*   poliment

5) '<u>Gentiment</u>' *(gently, kindly)* is <u>completely irregular</u>. It comes from '<u>gentil</u>' *(gentle, kind)*.

Some adverbs don't use '-ment'

Some <u>adverbs</u> are quite <u>different</u> from their <u>adjectives</u>.

bon(ne)	*good*	⟶	bien	*well*
mauvais(e)	*bad*	⟶	mal	*badly*
rapide	*fast*	⟶	vite	*fast*

Nous jouons bien au tennis.   *We play tennis well.*
Elle écrit mal.   *She writes badly.*
Tu parles vite.   *You talk fast.*

Remember, adverbs don't have to agree — phew...

Turn these adjectives into adverbs.

1. triste *(sad)*

2. négatif *(negative)*

3. sérieux *(serious)*

4. fier *(proud)*

5. absolu *(absolute)*

6. lent *(slow)*

7. mauvais *(bad)*

8. constant *(constant)*

Words to Describe Actions

Adverbs don't just describe how something's being done — you can use them to specify the time and place it's happening as well. Read on for more...

Adverbs can describe when something's being done

1) <u>Adverbs of time</u> describe <u>when</u>, or <u>how frequently</u>, something happens.

tous les jours	*every day*	il y a...	*...ago*	immédiatement	*immediately*
normalement	*normally*	récemment	*recently*	en même temps	*at the same time*
souvent	*often*	avant	*before*	tôt	*early*
quelquefois	*sometimes*	déjà	*already*	tard	*late*
jamais	*never*	maintenant	*now*	bientôt	*soon*

2) You can also form <u>phrases</u> to describe the <u>day</u>, <u>month</u>, <u>season</u> or <u>year</u> something happens using the adjectives '<u>dernier</u>' *(last)* and '<u>prochain</u>' *(next)*. They can go at the <u>start</u> or <u>end</u> of a <u>sentence</u>.

> Je vais partir lundi prochain.
> *I'm going to leave next Monday.*

> L'année dernière, je suis allé(e) en Italie.
> *Last year, I went to Italy.*

See p.84 for more on the future tense and p.80-83 for more on the past tenses.

3) Words to describe <u>different days</u> can be used as adverbs.

hier	*yesterday*	avant-hier	*the day before yesterday*
aujourd'hui	*today*	après-demain	*the day after tomorrow*
demain	*tomorrow*		

Some adverbs describe location

<u>Adverbs of place</u> usually come <u>after</u> the <u>verb</u> in a phrase or sentence.

ici	*here*
là	*there*
là-bas	*over there*
partout	*everywhere*
quelque part	*somewhere*
loin	*far*
près	*near*

Elle court partout.	*She runs everywhere.*
Il marche loin chaque jour.	*He walks far every day.*
Je fais mes devoirs ici.	*I do my homework here.*
Il gare sa voiture là-bas.	*He parks his car over there.*

If there's a direct object, e.g. 'les devoirs', the adverb always goes after it.

Phrases can be used as adverbs

You can use <u>adverbial phrases</u> in the <u>same</u> way as <u>adverbs</u>. They often come at the <u>beginning</u> of a <u>sentence</u>.

Adverbial phrases are often really handy when you're giving your opinion on something.

> En général, les lapins sont mignons.
> *In general, rabbits are cute.*

par conséquent	*consequently*
en tout cas	*anyway*

tout à fait	*absolutely*
de toute façon	*anyway*

Adverbs — learn them <u>well</u>, revise them <u>often</u> and you'll go <u>far</u>...

*Translate these sentences into **French**. Make sure you use the right adverbs.*

1. I play tennis over there.
2. You (sing.) sing every day.
3. I normally go to town by bus.
4. They're (fem.) going over there.
5. Consequently, I like my subjects.
6. I like this new teacher now.

Words to Compare Things

When you're describing something, it's often useful to be able to compare it to something else. Doing this will also make your language more complex and gain you marks — hurrah! Here's how to do it...

Plus..., le plus... — *More..., the most*

You can do this with most adjectives.

1) In French you <u>couldn't</u> say, for example, 'weird<u>er</u>' or 'weird<u>est</u>' — you have to say '<u>more weird</u>' or '<u>the most weird</u>', using '<u>plus</u>' and '<u>le plus</u>'. Use '<u>que</u>' to say '<u>than</u>'.

Layla est bizarre. *Layla is weird.*	→ Rose est plus bizarre que moi. *Rose is weirder than me.*	→ Paul est le plus bizarre. *Paul is the weirdest.*

2) To say '<u>less</u>' or '<u>the least</u>', you use the word '<u>moins</u>' in the <u>same</u> way as '<u>plus</u>'.

fort *strong*	→ moins fort *less strong*	→ le moins fort *the least strong*

3) If you want to say something is the <u>same</u>, use '<u>aussi...que</u>' *(as...as)*.

Cette émission est aussi passionnante que l'autre. *This programme is as exciting as the other one.*

4) '<u>Plus</u>', '<u>moins</u>' and '<u>aussi</u>' form <u>comparative adjectives</u>. '<u>Le plus</u>' and '<u>le moins</u>' form <u>superlative adjectives</u> — they're saying something is '<u>the most</u>', rather than directly <u>comparing</u> it to something else.

The adjectives still need to agree

1) If you're using <u>comparatives</u> or <u>superlatives</u>, the adjectives still need to <u>agree</u> with the <u>word</u> they're <u>describing</u>.

Elle est plus sportive. *She is more sporty.*

2) If you're saying '<u>the most</u>' or '<u>the least</u>', you have to make '<u>the</u>' agree as well.

Jean et Françoise sont les plus jeunes. *Jean and Françoise are the youngest.*

There are some exceptions

1) There are some <u>odd ones out</u> when it comes to making <u>comparisons</u> — just like in English. Unfortunately, these tend to be words that come up a lot.

2) With these words, you <u>don't</u> use '<u>plus</u>' or '<u>moins</u>':

Lila really was the best at the 'snowflake' pose...

Adjective		Comparative		Superlative	
bon(ne)(s)	*good*	→ meilleur(e)(s)	*better*	→ le/la/les meilleur(e)(s)	*the best*
mauvais(e)(s)	*bad*	→ pire(s)	*worse*	→ le/la/les pire(s)	*the worst*

Ce livre est meilleur que le dernier. *This book is better than the last one.*

Les questions grammaticales sont les pires. *The grammar questions are the worst.*

Superlatives are les meilleurs... I'm sure you agree...

*Translate these phrases into **French**. Remember those pesky adjective agreements...*

1. Navid and Pauline are the strongest.
2. Your grandma is older than my grandad.
3. This shop is the least expensive.
4. Julie is as active as Thérèse.
5. His ideas are the worst.
6. French is the best.

Words to Compare Actions

You can also use adverbs to compare how people do things, or to say they're the best or worst at something.

Comparative adverbs compare actions

1) 'Plus' is used to say someone is doing something 'more...' than someone else. Use 'que' to say 'than'.

| 'Plus' comes before the adverb. | Jean lit plus vite que Souad. | *Jean reads more quickly than Souad.* |

2) You can use 'moins' to say 'less...' — use it in the same way as 'plus'.

Souad lit moins souvent que Danielle. *Souad reads less often than Danielle.*

"Right, let's see who reads five pages first. On your marks, get set, GO!"

3) There are two expressions for when something is done equally. Use 'aussi...que' to say 'as...as' and 'autant que' to say 'as much as'.

Danielle lit aussi vite que Jacques. *Danielle reads as fast as Jacques.*

Danielle lit autant que Jacques. *Danielle reads as much as Jacques.*

Le plus — *The most*

1) 'Le plus...' is a superlative adverb — you use it to say someone does something 'the most...'.

Vivienne chante le plus musicalement.
Vivienne sings the most musically.

2) You always use 'le' because adverbs don't have to agree with the person doing the action — they're describing the action itself. This is different from adjectives.

Ils conduisent le plus dangereusement.
They drive the most dangerously.

'Bien' and 'mal' are the odd ones out

1) 'Bien' *(well)* and 'mal' *(badly)* don't follow the rules. You just need to learn their comparative and superlative forms.

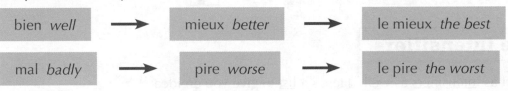

| bien *well* | → | mieux *better* | → | le mieux *the best* |
| mal *badly* | → | pire *worse* | → | le pire *the worst* |

2) 'Beaucoup' *(lots / a lot)* and 'peu' *(little)* are also irregular — they're a bit confusing because they change to 'plus' and 'moins'.

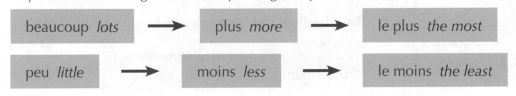

| beaucoup *lots* | → | plus *more* | → | le plus *the most* |
| peu *little* | → | moins *less* | → | le moins *the least* |

Use comparatives to make sure you write as well as possible...

Translate the words in brackets to fill in the gaps in these sentences.

1. Thomas joue du piano ...... *(the best)*
2. François va à l'étranger ...... *(the most frequently)*
3. Lucie court ...... Emmanuel. *(more than)*
4. Je regarde la télévision ...... *(the least often)*
5. Tu ris ...... moi. *(as much as)*
6. Je chante ...... toi. *(worse than)*

Words to Say How Much

Intensifiers and quantifiers change the meaning of adjectives and adverbs slightly, so you can give more precise descriptions and impress the examiners.

Intensifiers strengthen what you're saying

1) Words such as 'trop' *(too)* and 'assez' *(quite)* can add detail to your sentences. They're called intensifiers.

trop	*too*	assez	*quite*
très	*very*	peu	*not very*

2) You can use them to emphasise an adjective, or to say what something's like or what you think of it.

3) Intensifiers can be used with adjectives — they always go before them.

> Camille est trop sérieuse.
> *Camille is too serious.*

> La géographie est peu intéressante.
> *Geography is not very interesting.*

Yeah, geography's not very interesting. I mean, volcanoes are sooo boring...

4) You can use intensifiers with adverbs. They go before the adverb.

> J'écris très vite. *I write very fast.*

> Ils courent assez lentement. *They run quite slowly.*

Quantifiers help you say how many or how much

1) Quantifiers let you say roughly how much of something you have, without being specific, e.g. 'lots' or 'not many'.

trop de	*too many, too much*
beaucoup de	*lots of, many*
assez de	*enough*
peu de	*little, not much, not many*
un peu de	*a little, a little bit of*

2) Many are the same words as above, followed by 'de'.

> J'ai assez de chaussures. *I have enough shoes.*

3) With quantifiers, 'de' doesn't change to agree with the noun, but it changes to 'd'' before a vowel.

> Nous avons peu d'argent. *We have little money.*

> Il a trop d'examens. *He has too many exams.*

Adverbs can be intensifiers

1) Some adverbs can act as intensifiers as well. Here's a list to give you an idea:

particulièrement	*particularly*
vraiment	*really*
incroyablement	*incredibly*
énormément	*enormously*
exceptionnellement	*unusually*

> Ce film est vraiment passionnant. *This film is really exciting.*

2) The adjectives still have to agree but the adverbs don't.

> La montagne est incroyablement haute.
> *The mountain is incredibly high.*

Intensifiers will make your French incredibly good...

Correct these sentences — find incorrectly written quantifiers / intensifiers and wrong genders / agreements.

1. Elle est trèse vive.
2. Ils ont une peu d'eau.
3. Le musicien est vraiment doué.

4. C'est assez d'intéressant.
5. Tu as beaucoup des chaussettes.
6. L'homme a trop chocolat.

I, Me, You, We, Them

I'm sure you're thrilled by the idea of learning lots of pronouns. They're useful words though — they'll help your French sound less repetitive. You use them all the time in English — probably without realising...

Subject pronouns replace the subject of the sentence

1) <u>Subject pronouns</u> are words like '<u>I</u>' and '<u>you</u>':

Yes, that's the *Royal Nous*, thank you very much!

I	je
You (informal, singular)	tu
He / she / it / one / we	il / elle / on
We	nous
You (formal, plural)	vous
They	ils / elles

'Il' means 'he', or 'it' for a masculine noun. 'Elle' means 'she', or 'it' for a feminine noun.

'On' is a bit like 'one' in English. It often means 'we', e.g. 'on doit recycler' *(we should recycle)*.

Use 'vous' in formal situations, e.g. when talking to your teacher, or when you're talking to more than one person. Use 'tu' when talking to one person in an informal situation.

'Ils' is for a group of masculine nouns, or a mixture of masculine and feminine. 'Elles' is for a group of feminine nouns.

2) Subject pronouns can <u>replace</u> the <u>subject</u> (the person or thing <u>doing</u> the action in a sentence). Using them means you <u>don't</u> have to <u>keep saying</u> the same noun over and over again.

Mon frère est musicien. Il est fana de musique rock.

My brother is a musician. He is a fan of rock music.

'My brother' can be replaced with 'he' to sound less repetitive.

There are different pronouns for the direct object...

Remember, when 'le' or 'la' is followed by a word beginning with a vowel, it becomes 'l''.

The <u>direct object</u> is the <u>person</u> or <u>thing</u> that the action is <u>being done to</u> — direct object pronouns <u>replace</u> the <u>noun</u> used as the direct object:

Me	**You** (inf sing.)	**Him / her / it**	Us	**You** (formal, pl.)	Them
me	te	le / la	nous	vous	les

Il voit son amie. ➡ Il la voit.
He sees his friend. ➡ *He sees her.*

...and for the indirect object

<u>Indirect objects</u> are things that are <u>affected</u> by the <u>action</u> being done, but not <u>directly</u>. They often have '<u>to</u>' or '<u>for</u>' before them in English:

Me	**You** (informal singular)	**Him / her / it**	Us	**You** (formal, plural)	Them
me	te	lui	nous	vous	leur

Il donne le cadeau à son amie.
He gives the present to his friend.

Il lui donne le cadeau.
He gives her the present.

You are my pronoun — no-one could ever replace you...

Replace the words in bold with the correct pronoun from the brackets.

1. Hélène (lui / la / les) donne le livre **à son ami**.
2. Emilie (Elle / Tu / La) aime les chiens.
3. Tu peux (leur / elles / les) voir **les tortues**?
4. Avez-vous le livre? Non, elle (il / l' / le) a **le livre**.
5. **Moi et mon amie** (Nous / Elles / La) allons au cinéma.
6. Non, **les tortues** (les / elles / ils) ne sont pas ici.

| Pronouns | # Something, There, Any |

There are even pronouns for unspecified things, e.g. 'everyone'. There are a couple of tricky little ones on this page too, so have a good read and then try the questions at the bottom of the page to test yourself.

Use indefinite pronouns for unspecified things

Indefinite pronouns refer to general, unspecific things, such as 'everyone' and 'something'.

quelqu'un	*someone*	plusieurs	*several*
tout le monde	*everyone*	tout	*all / everything*
quelque chose	*something*	chacun(e)	*each one*

> Tout le monde aime le chocolat.
> *Everyone likes chocolate.*

Y — *There*

1) 'Y' can mean 'there'. It replaces the noun for a location which has already been mentioned.

> Elle va à la banque. *She's going to the bank.* → Elle y va. *She's going there.*

This is often used to talk about weather. See p.36.

2) It's also used in some common expressions.

> Allons-y! *Let's do it! / Let's go!*   Vas-y! *Do it! / Go on!*   Il y a... *There is / There are...*

3) It means 'it' or 'them' after verbs followed by 'à'.

> Je pense à l'idée. *I'm thinking about the idea.* → J'y pense. *I'm thinking about it.*

En — *Of it, of them, some, any*

1) 'En' has a few meanings — depending on the context, it can mean 'of it', 'of them', 'some' or 'any'.

> As-tu peur des guêpes? Oui, j'en ai peur. *Are you scared of wasps? Yes, I'm scared of them.*

> As-tu des oranges? Oui, j'en ai. *Have you got any oranges? Yes, I have some.*

> As-tu des poires? Non, je n'en ai pas. *Have you got any pears? No, I don't have any.*

2) It means 'it' or 'them' after verbs followed by 'de'.

> Tu as besoin d'aide. *You need help.* → Tu en as besoin. *You need it.*

Des bonbons? J'en ai besoin. — Sweets? I need some.

Choose the correct sentences and have a go at rewriting the ones that are wrong.

1. Il y a une cuisine si vous en avez besoin.
2. Toutes le monde sait que c'est vrai.
3. A-t-elle des livres? Oui, elle y a.
4. J'y réfléchis.
5. Tu connais le château? J'en suis allé(e).
6. Il y en a plusieurs.

Position and Order of Object Pronouns Pronouns

To give you a break from learning pronouns, some of this page is about the order they go in instead...

Object pronouns always go before the verb

1) If there's <u>more than one pronoun</u>, they go in a <u>certain</u> order:

ne	me te se nous vous	le la les	lui leur	y	en	verb	pas

In negative sentences, 'ne' goes before the object pronouns and 'pas' goes after the verb. See p.86 for more about negatives. ←

> Elle me le donne.
> *She gives it to me.*

2) With <u>compound</u> tenses, which use 'avoir' or 'être' before the main verb, the pronouns go <u>before both verbs</u>.

> Elle me l'a donné. *She gave it to me.*

The perfect (p.80-81) and pluperfect (p.89) are compound tenses.

3) Certain verbs (vouloir, pouvoir, devoir) are often used with the <u>infinitive</u> of another verb. The <u>object pronouns</u> go <u>between</u> them.

> Je peux le lui donner. *I can give it to him / to her.*

My friend gave me a chameleon. The chameleon wasn't very happy about it.

Use pronouns to emphasise who you're talking about

1) <u>Emphatic pronouns</u> make it really <u>clear</u> who you're talking about.

2) You need them...

Me	moi
You (informal singular)	toi
Him / her / one	lui / elle / soi
Us	nous
You (formal, plural)	vous
Them (m / f)	eux / elles

- if the words are <u>on their own</u>, or <u>after</u> 'c'est'.

> Qui parle? Moi! C'est moi! *Who's speaking? Me! It's me!*

- to <u>compare</u> people or things — the emphatic pronoun goes after 'que' (than).

> Il est plus petit que toi. *He's smaller than you.*

- for <u>giving instructions</u>. (See p.88 for more on how to do this.)

> Écoutez-moi! *Listen to me!*   Donne-lui ton portable! *Give him your mobile!*

- <u>after prepositions</u> such as '<u>for</u>' or '<u>with</u>'.

> Tu le fais pour elle. *You do it for her.*   Je suis allé avec eux. *I went with them.*

3) You can add '<u>-même</u>' on the end of an <u>emphatic pronoun</u> to say '<u>-self</u>'. Add an '<u>s</u>' if it's <u>plural</u> ('<u>-mêmes</u>').

> On le fait soi-même. *One does it oneself.*

Don't forget that by itself, 'même' means 'even', e.g. 'même si' (even if).

> Elles l'ont écrit elles-mêmes. *They wrote it themselves.*

You! You there — learn the order of the object pronouns...

*Unscramble the words in these sentences and then translate them into **English**.*

1. donne. lui Il le
2. ai l' qui C'est écouté. moi
3. l' toi- Tu as écrit même.
4. nous. êtes allés Vous y avec
5. t' Elle dit. a
6. vais en parler. Je lui

Relative and Interrogative Pronouns

These help link bits of a sentence together so you're not stuck with lots of short phrases. Read on for more...

'Qui' and 'que' are relative pronouns

1) Relative pronouns introduce extra information about something you've mentioned in your sentence.

2) 'Qui' is used if you're referring to the subject of the sentence — the person or thing doing the action.

> La femme qui a volé le portefeuille.   *The woman who stole the wallet.*

3) 'Que' is used to refer to the object of the sentence — the person or thing that something's being done to.

> Le portefeuille que la femme a volé.   *The wallet that the woman stole.*

You can use 'qui' and 'que' to ask questions

See p.4-5 on questions.

1) In questions, 'qui' and 'que' are interrogative pronouns. 'Qui' means 'who', and 'que' means 'what'.

2) They can be the subject of a question. 'Que' changes to 'qu'est-ce qui' when it's the subject.

> Qui parle?   *Who is speaking?*   Qu'est-ce qui se passe?   *What is happening?*

3) You can also use 'qui' and 'que' as the object of the question.

> Qui connaissez-vous?   *Who do you know?*   Que savez-vous?   *What do you know?*

4) 'Qui' and 'que' can be used after prepositions (words such as 'with' or 'for' — see p.74-75). 'Que' changes to 'quoi' after a preposition but 'qui' stays the same.

> Tu parles avec qui?   *Who are you talking to?*   De quoi parles-tu?   *What are you talking about?*

Dont — *Of which, whose, about which...*

You only need to recognise 'dont' — you don't have to use it.

'Dont' has several meanings and can be used in different ways:

- To replace 'de' when 'de' is used with a verb. For example, 'parler de' (to talk about).

> L'araignée dont on a parlé.   *The spider we talked about. (The spider about which we talked.)*

- To say 'whose'. 'Dont' replaces the 'de' used to show possession.

> La chef dont les repas sont délicieux.
> *The chef whose meals are delicious.*

Literally 'The chef of whom the meals are delicious'.

- To talk about something that's part of a group.

> J'ai trois films dont un est une comédie.   *I've got three films, of which one is a comedy.*

Make sure you learn the difference between 'qui' and 'que'.

Translate these sentences, making sure you're using the correct pronoun.

1. The man who is sporty.
2. The pizza that I like eating.
3. I've got five pencils which are red.
4. Who do you run with?
5. The car that she drives is slow.
6. What are you thinking about?

Possessive and Demonstrative Pronouns | Pronouns

There are pronouns for showing who owns something, as well as for saying 'this one' and 'that one'.

Possessive pronouns show something belongs to someone

1) Possessive pronouns replace a noun that belongs to someone — they're words like 'mine' and 'yours'. You need to be able to recognise them for the exam — but you don't have to use them.

> Le ballon rouge est ici. C'est le mien.   *The red ball is here. It's mine.*

2) They agree with the gender and number of the noun being replaced — have a look at the table:

	Mine	**Yours** (informal singular)	**His / her / its**	**Our**	**Yours** (formal, plural)	**Their**
Masculine singular	le mien	le tien	le sien	le nôtre	le vôtre	le leur
Feminine singular	la mienne	la tienne	la sienne	la nôtre	la vôtre	la leur
Plural (m / f)	les miens / miennes	les tiens / tiennes	les siens / siennes	les nôtres	les vôtres	les leurs

> Il y a trois bananes — ce sont les miennes.   *There are three bananas — they're mine.*

Celui, celle, ceux, celles — *This, these, those*

> ⌇ Don't worry — you don't have to use ⌇
> ⌇ these, just know what they mean. ⌇

1) 'Celui', 'celle', 'ceux' and 'celles' are demonstrative pronouns. They mean 'this', 'this one' 'those' or 'the one(s)'.

Masculine singular	celui
Feminine singular	celle
Masculine plural	ceux
Feminine plural	celles

> J'aime ce gâteau, mais celui qu'on a mangé hier était meilleur.
> *I like this cake, but the one we ate yesterday was better.*

2) They're used with '-ci' on the end to mean 'this one' or 'this one here'. Adding '-là' on the end changes the meaning to 'that one' or 'that one there'.

> Il y a deux gâteaux. J'aime celui-ci, mais celui-là est meilleur.
> *There are two cakes. I like this one, but that one there is better.*

'Celui-ci' and 'celui-là' are used to point things out. ←

Ceci, cela, ça — *This, that, that*

1) 'Ceci', 'cela' and 'ça' are also demonstrative pronouns. They're used for more general things, not when you're pointing something out.

2) You need to be able to use these ones, so take a look at these examples:

> Ceci est intéressant.
> *This is interesting.*

> Cela n'est pas vrai!
> *That isn't true!*

> Je n'aime pas faire ça.
> *I don't like doing that.*

> ⌇ 'Ça' is a more ⌇
> ⌇ informal way ⌇
> ⌇ to say 'that'. ⌇

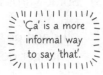

I reckon these demonstrative pronouns are possessed...

Translate the words in brackets to fill in the gaps.

1. Le stylo là est ...... *(yours, informal)*
2. Celle-là est ...... *(hers)*
3. ...... n'est pas drôle! *(that)*
4. Ces chiens sont ...... *(ours)*
5. Où as-tu vu ...... ? *(that)*
6. C'est ...... *(yours, formal)*

Prepositions

Prepositions may not be much to look at, but size is no guarantee of power. These fellas are some of the most useful words in the French language — and, luckily, they're also some of the easiest to pronounce.

À — 'to', 'in' or 'at'

1) <u>Prepositions</u> are short words like 'to' and 'from'. They let you add <u>extra information</u> to sentences.

2) '<u>À</u>' can mean '<u>to</u>', '<u>in</u>' or '<u>at</u>'. It changes to '<u>au</u>' and '<u>aux</u>' when it's followed by 'le' and 'les' (see p.60).

> Je vais au magasin.
> *I'm going to the shop.*

> Je suis à la maison.
> *I'm at home.*

> J'habite aux États-Unis.
> *I live in the United States.*

3) Some <u>verbs</u> are <u>followed</u> by '<u>à</u>' when they go before a <u>noun</u>. Here are some examples:

(s')intéresser à	*to be interested in*	rendre visite à	*to visit (someone)*
jouer à	*to play (a game)*	penser à	*to think about*

'En' doesn't mean 'on'

1) '<u>En</u>' can mean '<u>in</u>' or '<u>to</u>'. It's used instead of '<u>à</u>' for <u>feminine</u> countries and countries starting with a <u>vowel</u>.

> Clare habite en France.   *Clare lives in France.*

> Je vais en Iran en mai.   *I'm going to Iran in May.*

> For something happening in a specific season, month or year, you usually use 'en'.

2) You should use '<u>en</u>' to say <u>how long</u> an action takes:

> Elle a lu l'article en cinq minutes.   *She read the article in five minutes.*

3) '<u>En</u>' is also used to describe what something is <u>made of</u>.

> une veste en cuir   *a leather jacket*

De — 'of' or 'from'

> French doesn't have apostrophes to show belonging — it uses 'de' instead.

1) '<u>De</u>' often means '<u>of</u>'.

> une tasse de thé   *a cup of tea*

> Je porte la robe de ma mère.   *I'm wearing my mother's dress.*

2) '<u>De</u>' can also mean '<u>from</u>'. It changes to '<u>du</u>', '<u>de la</u>' or '<u>des</u>' when it's next to a <u>definite article</u> (see p.60).

> Jean revient de la plage (f).   *Jean is coming back from the beach.*

3) Some <u>verbs</u> are <u>followed by 'de'</u> when they go <u>before a noun</u>. Learn these important examples:

Il s'agit de	*it's about*	avoir besoin de	*to need*	jouer de	*to play (an instrument)*
changer de	*to change*	avoir envie de	*to want*	partir de	*to leave*

Now I get why Muhammad 'Au-lit' was so tired all the time...

*Translate these phrases into **French** using the correct prepositions.*

1. I play football.   **3.** It's about a young boy.   **5.** I play the clarinet.   **7.** He's going to the bank.

2. She visits Manu.   **4.** a woollen jumper   **6.** They live in France.   **8.** You (sing, inf.) come from Wales.

Prepositions

Just for your enjoyment, here are some more handy prepositions...

Chez Natalie — *At Natalie's*

These prepositions are <u>really important</u> for your exams — try to learn them all.

avec	*with*	à cause de	*because of*	chez	*at the house of*
sans	*without*	au lieu de	*instead of*	grâce à	*thanks to*

Lots of prepositions relate to time

For more on telling the time, see p.2.

1) Prepositions of <u>time</u> tell you <u>when</u> something happened <u>in relation to</u> something else.

avant	*before*	depuis	*since / for*
après	*after*	jusqu'à	*until*
pour	*for*	pendant	*during / for*

> Florence a fini avant les autres.
> *Florence finished before the others.*

2) '<u>Pendant</u>', '<u>depuis</u>' and '<u>pour</u>' are a little bit tricky because they can all be translated as '<u>for</u>'.

3) Use '<u>pendant</u>' for actions that have <u>already happened</u>, or <u>will happen</u> in the future, but <u>aren't happening</u> now.

> J'ai travaillé dans un hôtel pendant deux ans.   *I worked in a hotel for two years.*

See p.79 and p.83 for more about 'depuis'.

4) Use '<u>depuis</u>' for actions that <u>began in the past</u>, but are <u>still continuing</u> today.

> J'habite dans le Cumbria depuis trois mois.   *I've lived in Cumbria for three months.*

5) '<u>Pour</u>' (*for*) is used very similarly to in English, but with time, it's <u>only used</u> in the <u>future tense</u>.

> Martine va aller en Suisse pour une semaine.   *Martine is going to go to Switzerland for a week.*

Use prepositions to describe position

1) Some prepositions describe the <u>location</u> of <u>something</u> or <u>someone</u>.

sur	*on*	dans	*in*	devant	*in front of*
sous	*under*	derrière	*behind*	à côté de	*next to*

Alec was worried he'd given away his position.

2) '<u>Dans</u>' (*in*) is normally used to describe when something is <u>actually inside</u> something else.

'En' also means 'in', but it can't mean 'inside' — see p.75.

> Mon passeport est dans ma valise.   *My passport is in my suitcase.*

3) '<u>Dans</u>' is also used to say how much time will pass before an event. E.g. 'dans cinq minutes' (*in five minutes*).

Depuis or not depuis — that is the question...

Choose the correct preposition to complete each of the sentences below.

1. Je suis (*à / chez*) Paul avec Dima.

2. Le magasin est (*sous / dans*) le pont.

3. Je vais aller en vacances (*pendant / pour*) deux semaines.

4. Je travaille à la pharmacie (*depuis / pendant*) six mois.

Conjunctions

Joining Words

Conjunctions link words together. They help make your French sound more natural and more sophisticated, too — because nothing says sophistication like accurate French conjunctions...

Use conjunctions to make longer sentences

This is the longest sentence ever...

1) Here are some <u>common</u> conjunctions:

mais	*but*	ou bien	*or else*	ainsi	*therefore / so*
et	*and*	puis	*then*	ensuite	*then / next*
ou	*or*	donc	*therefore / so*	ni...ni	*neither...nor*

A clause is a group of words that has a subject and a verb. See the next page for more on verbs.

2) Some conjunctions <u>link</u> two <u>clauses</u> or <u>sentences</u> together. They make the sentences sound more <u>natural</u>.

J'ai un petit job.	**donc**	Je mets de l'argent de côté chaque mois.	J'ai un petit job, donc je mets de l'argent de côté chaque mois.
I have a part-time job.	***therefore***	*I save some money every month.*	*I have a part-time job, therefore I save some money every month.*

Les fleurs sont bleues claires et l'herbe est verte.   *The flowers are light blue and the grass is green.*

3) 'Ou' (<u>or</u>) is used to give <u>more than one</u> option.

Amélie veut être infirmière.	**ou**	Amélie veut être ingénieur.	Amélie veut être infirmière ou ingénieur.
Amélie wants to be a nurse.	**or**	*Amélie wants to be an engineer.*	*Amélie wants to be a nurse or an engineer.*

Make sure you don't get mixed up between 'ou' (or) and 'où' (where).

Some conjunctions add extra information to a sentence

1) Some conjunctions can also add <u>extra detail</u> to a <u>sentence</u>.

2) Often these conjunctions introduce a <u>reason</u> for something happening, a <u>contradiction</u> or a <u>condition</u>.

parce que	*because*	pendant que	*while*	comme	*like*
puisque	*since*	par contre	*on the other hand*	y compris	*including*
quand	*when*	lorsque	*when / as soon as*	si	*if*
cependant	*however*	par exemple	*for example*	même si	*even if*

Je déteste le tabac parce que c'est mauvais pour la santé.
I hate smoking because it's bad for your health.

Conjunctions can go at the beginning of sentences, too.

Même s'ils sont délicieux, je ne les veux pas.   *Even if they're delicious, I don't want them.*

Even after all these clauses, Santa's still my firm favourite...

Match the French conjunctions below with their English definitions.

1. therefore	**3.** however	**5.** including	**a)** pendant que	**c)** y compris	**e)** cependant
2. or else	**4.** while	**6.** since	**b)** ou bien	**d)** ainsi	**f)** puisque

Verbs in the Present Tense

You need to know the present tense inside out and back to front — it crops up all over the place. It also provides the foundations for some trickier tenses later on, so learning it properly now is well worth it.

Verbs are action words

1) A verb is a word that describes an action. 'Eat', 'sing' and 'jump' are all examples of English verbs.

2) Actions can take place in different times — or tenses — the past, present or future.

3) To put a verb in a tense, you need to know its infinitive, e.g. 'être' (*to be*). They're in this form in the dictionary.

The present describes something happening now

1) Use the present tense to describe something that's occurring now.

You can use the French present tense to say that something 'is happening' or that something 'happens'.

Je mange une pomme.   *I am eating an apple. / I eat an apple.*

2) You should also use the present tense to describe something that happens regularly.

Le lundi, je fais du jogging.   *I go jogging on Mondays.*

3) Verbs in the present tense have different endings, but you always start by finding the verb's stem.

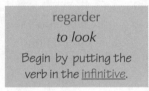
regarder
to look
Begin by putting the verb in the infinitive.

—

-er
Remove the last two letters of the infinitive.

=

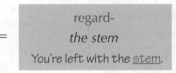
regard-
the stem
You're left with the stem.

Infinitive	Stem
parler	parl-
finir	fin-
vendre	vend-

4) Then you add the correct endings to the stem (see below).

Add the right endings to the verb's stem

The 'il'/'elle'/'on' form of the present tense for '-re' verbs doesn't have an ending.

In French, there are three groups of verbs — verbs ending in '-er', '-ir' and '-re':

'-er' endings

I	je	-e
you (inf. sing)	tu	-es
he/she/it/one	il/elle/on	-e
we	nous	-ons
you (pl., formal)	vous	-ez
they (m/f)	ils/elles	-ent

'-ir' endings

I	je	-is
you (inf. sing)	tu	-is
he/she/it/one	il/elle/on	-it
we	nous	-issons
you (pl., formal)	vous	-issez
they (m/f)	ils/elles	-issent

'-re' endings

I	je	-s
you (inf. sing)	tu	-s
he/she/it/one	il/elle/on	—
we	nous	-ons
you (pl., formal)	vous	-ez
they (m/f)	ils/elles	-ent

E.g. 'regarder'   (*to watch*)
'regard-'   (the stem)
+ '-ons'   ('nous' ending)
nous regardons   (we watch)

E.g. 'finir'   (*to finish*)
'fin-'   (the stem)
+ '-issent'   ('elles' ending)
elles finissent   (they finish)

E.g. 'vendre'   (*to sell*)
'vend-'   (the stem)
+ nothing   ('elle' ending)
elle vend   (she sells)

Regular presents are always the best...

Have a go putting the verbs below into the present tense. The subject is given in brackets.

1. parler (je)
2. établir (il)
3. remplir (nous)
4. répondre (tu)
5. entendre (elles)
6. commencer (vous)
7. perdre (vous)
8. grossir (ils)
9. allumer (je)
10. vendre (on)

Irregular Verbs in the Present Tense

Irregular verbs don't follow a set pattern. This means that there aren't any concrete rules you can apply to them — they're a rebellious lot. The only way to keep these guys in line is to learn them off by heart.

Some of the most useful verbs are irregular

Lots of important verbs are irregular — this means that they don't follow the usual rules. Here are some of the most common ones that you need to know for your exams:

avoir — to have

I have	j'ai
you (inf. sing.) have	tu as
he/she/it/one has	il/elle/on a
we have	nous avons
you (pl., formal) have	vous avez
they have	ils/elles ont

Make sure you know the difference between 'a' from 'avoir' and the preposition 'à' (see p.74).

être — to be

I am	je suis
you (inf. sing.) are	tu es
he/she/it/one is	il/elle/on est
we are	nous sommes
you (pl., formal) are	vous êtes
they are	ils/elles sont

faire — to make / do

I make	je fais
you (inf. sing.) make	tu fais
he/she/it/one makes	il/elle/on fait
we make	nous faisons
you (pl., formal) make	vous faites
they make	ils/elles font

Remember, you don't usually pronounce the last letter of a word in French if it's a consonant. This means that some endings (e.g. 'fais' and 'fait') are spelt differently but sound exactly the same.

aller — to go

I go	je vais
you (inf. sing.) go	tu vas
he/she/it/one goes	il/elle/on va
we go	nous allons
you (pl., formal) go	vous allez
they go	ils/elles vont

devoir — must / to have to

I must	je dois
you (inf. sing.) must	tu dois
he/she/it/one must	il/elle/on doit
we must	nous devons
you (pl., formal) must	vous devez
they must	ils/elles doivent

'Devoir' is a verb, but 'les devoirs' is a noun meaning 'homework'.

vouloir — to want

I want	je veux
you (inf. sing.) want	tu veux
he/she/it/one wants	il/elle/on veut
we want	nous voulons
you (pl., formal) want	vous voulez
they want	ils/elles veulent

pouvoir — to be able to / can

I can	je peux
you (inf. sing.) can	tu peux
he/she/it/one can	il/elle/on peut
we can	nous pouvons
you (pl., formal) can	vous pouvez
they can	ils/elles peuvent

Don't mix up 'savoir' and 'connaître' — 'savoir' means to know something. To say that you know somebody, use 'connaître'.

savoir — to know

I know	je sais
you (inf. sing.) know	tu sais
he/she/it/one knows	il/elle/on sait
we know	nous savons
you (pl., formal) know	vous savez
they know	ils/elles savent

Phew — this page is so intense...

Each verb below is spelt incorrectly — using the verb tables above, rewrite each of the phrases correctly.

1. nous doivons
2. je veut
3. vous êtez
4. tu doix
5. elle vat
6. ils faient
7. elles pouvent
8. on saix
9. ils avont
10. nous faions

More About the Present Tense

I don't know about you, but I don't feel like we've exhausted the present tense quite yet... encore, encore!

Verbs sometimes stay in their infinitive

1) When one verb <u>follows</u> another in a sentence or phrase, the <u>first verb</u> needs to be in the right form, but the <u>second verb</u> is <u>always</u> in the <u>infinitive</u>.

> Je veux aider les autres. *I want to help other people.*
>
> 'Je veux' is the <u>first verb</u> in the sentence — it's in the <u>first person singular</u> form of the present tense. Because '<u>aider</u>' comes <u>directly after</u> 'je veux', it's in the <u>infinitive</u> form.

Four hours later, Léna had to admit her story was not helping the children to sleep.

2) Some <u>verbs</u> can be followed <u>directly</u> by an <u>infinitive</u>, but a few verbs need a <u>preposition</u> in between.

commencer à	*to begin*	essayer de	*to try*
réussir à	*to succeed*	décider de	*to decide*
apprendre à	*to learn*	(s')arrêter de	*to stop (oneself)*
arriver à	*to succeed in / to manage*	menacer de	*to threaten*

When 'venir de' is followed by an infinitive, its definition changes — it means 'to have just done something'.

'Arriver <u>à</u>' + an <u>infinitive</u> means 'to succeed' in doing something.

> J'essaie de faire plus de sport. *I'm trying to do more sport.*

> J'apprends à conduire la voiture de mon père. *I'm learning to drive my dad's car.*

'Depuis' can be used with the present tense

For when to use the imperfect with 'depuis', see p.83.

1) 'Depuis' means '<u>since</u>' or '<u>for</u>' (see p.75).

2) If the <u>action</u> you're talking about is <u>still going on</u> today, use the <u>present tense</u>.

> Il habite à Belfast depuis 1997. *He's lived in Belfast since 1997.*

Even though the action began in the past, the person is still living in Belfast — so you need the present tense.

> Je travaille comme serveur depuis six mois. *I've worked as a waiter for six months.*

Swap your subject and verb to form a question

Look at p.4-5 for more on how to ask questions.

1) To form a <u>question</u>, invert (or swap over) the <u>subject pronoun</u> and the <u>verb</u>.

2) When you do this, you <u>always</u> need to add a <u>hyphen</u> (-) between the <u>verb</u> and <u>subject pronoun</u>.

If the last letter of the verb and the first letter of the subject pronoun are both vowels, separate them by adding a 't'. This just makes it easier to pronounce — the 't' doesn't mean anything.

> Elle a mal au ventre. → A-t-elle mal au ventre?
> *She has a stomach ache.* → *Has she got a stomach ache?*

To infinitives, and beyond...

*Translate these sentences into **French**. Make sure you invert the subject and the verb for the questions.*

1. I'm starting to understand.
2. I want to eat some pizza.
3. I've been studying French for 2 years.
4. I've played football since 1999.
5. Do you like plums?
6. Do you play the piano?

Perfect Tense | # Talking About the Past

Now you've got the hang of the present tense, it's time to look at the past — that's if you can remember what life was like before revision, of course. The perfect tense can be tricky, so read carefully.

Use the perfect tense for completed actions

1) Use the <u>perfect tense</u> to describe an action that <u>happened</u> and <u>finished</u> in the <u>past</u>.

2) In French, it has <u>three</u> parts — a <u>subject</u>, the <u>present tense</u> of '<u>avoir</u>' or '<u>être</u>' and a <u>past participle</u>.

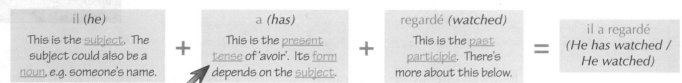

il *(he)*		a *(has)*		regardé *(watched)*		il a regardé
This is the <u>subject</u>. The subject could also be a <u>noun</u>, e.g. someone's name.	+	This is the <u>present tense</u> of 'avoir'. Its <u>form</u> depends on the <u>subject</u>.	+	This is the <u>past participle</u>. There's more about this below.	=	*(He has watched / He watched)*

3) You don't always need the 'have' part in English, but you <u>must</u> have it in French.

Most verbs use 'avoir' in the perfect tense

1) Use the <u>present tense</u> of '<u>avoir</u>' to make the '<u>have</u>' part of the perfect tense:

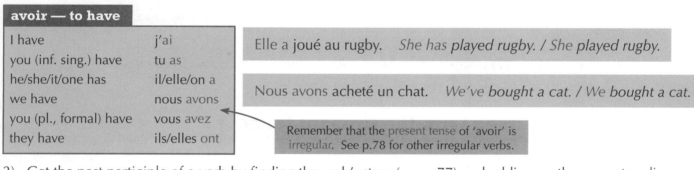

avoir — to have	
I have	j'ai
you (inf. sing.) have	tu as
he/she/it/one has	il/elle/on a
we have	nous avons
you (pl., formal) have	vous avez
they have	ils/elles ont

Elle a joué au rugby. *She has played rugby. / She played rugby.*

Nous avons acheté un chat. *We've bought a cat. / We bought a cat.*

Remember that the present tense of 'avoir' is irregular. See p.78 for other irregular verbs.

2) Get the <u>past participle</u> of a verb by finding the verb's <u>stem</u> (see p.77) and adding on the <u>correct ending</u>.

3) Verbs ending in '<u>-er</u>', '<u>-ir</u>' and '<u>-re</u>' each have a <u>different</u> ending:

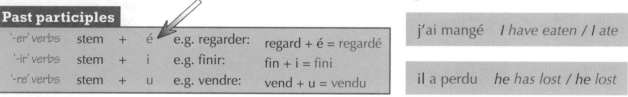

Past participles					
'-er' verbs	stem	+	é	e.g. regarder:	regard + é = regardé
'-ir' verbs	stem	+	i	e.g. finir:	fin + i = fini
'-re' verbs	stem	+	u	e.g. vendre:	vend + u = vendu

j'ai mangé *I have eaten / I ate*

il a perdu *he has lost / he lost*

Past participles agree with some direct objects

1) Past participles taking '<u>avoir</u>' only <u>change form</u> if there's a <u>direct object</u> or <u>direct object pronoun</u> (see p.69) <u>before</u> the verb.

2) When this happens, the <u>past participle</u> acts a bit like an adjective and <u>agrees</u> in <u>gender</u> and <u>number</u>.

Les voix (f) que j'ai entendues. *The voices that I heard.*

The object comes before the verb, so the verb needs to agree with it. 'Voix' is feminine and plural, so 'entendues' has an 'e' and an 's' on the end.

J'ai fini cette page. — A perfect sentence if I ever saw one...

Change these phrases from the present to the perfect tense.

1. je parle
2. il élargit
3. nous finissons
4. tu vends
5. on grandit
6. elles mangent
7. je réponds
8. vous cherchez

Talking About the Past

That's the easiest bit done and dusted. Now it's time to sit up straight, roll up your sleeves and discover why the perfect tense isn't so perfect after all. It's nothing you can't handle — just take it one step at a time.

'Vivre' becomes 'vécu'

1) Some really important verbs have <u>irregular past participles</u>. This means that they <u>don't use</u> the same endings as regular verbs (see p.80).

Look out for the past participle of 'être' — it's spelt exactly the same way as the noun 'été' (summer).

2) These are the most important ones:

Irregular past participles

avoir (*to have*)	→ eu	faire (*to do / make*)	→	fait
boire (*to drink*)	→ bu	lire (*to read*)	→	lu
connaître (*to know someone*)	→ connu	mettre (*to put*)	→	mis
devoir (*to have to / must*)	→ dû	prendre (*to take*)	→	pris
dire (*to say / tell*)	→ dit	savoir (*to know something*)	→	su
écrire (*to write*)	→ écrit	venir (*to come*)	→	venu
être (*to be*)	→ été	vivre (*to live*)	→	vécu

Some verbs take 'être' instead of 'avoir'

To see how the present tense of 'être' is formed, see p.78.

1) A few verbs use <u>'être'</u> instead of <u>'avoir'</u> to form the <u>perfect tense</u>.

aller	*to go*	partir	*to leave*	naître	*to be born*	tomber	*to fall*
venir	*to come*	sortir	*to go out*	mourir	*to die*	retourner	*to return*
revenir	*to come back*	descendre	*to go down*	devenir	*to become*	entrer	*to go in*
arriver	*to arrive*	monter	*to go up*	rester	*to stay*	rentrer	*to go back*

2) Just like <u>'avoir'</u> verbs, the correct <u>present tense form</u> of 'être' is needed.

Luc est allé à l'épicerie. *Luc went to the grocer's.*

Il s'est habillé. *He got dressed.*

All reflexive verbs (see p.85) take 'être' in the perfect tense.

Verbs that take 'être' have to agree

1) <u>All verbs</u> that take <u>'être'</u> in the perfect tense <u>have to agree</u> with their <u>subject</u>.

2) The <u>past participle</u> gains an '<u>s</u>' if the subject is <u>plural</u>, an '<u>e</u>' if it's <u>feminine</u> and '<u>es</u>' if it's <u>feminine and plural</u>.

Hélène and Nousha always saw eye to eye.

When a reflexive verb is in the perfect tense, the present tense of 'être' always goes between the reflexive pronoun and the past participle.

Les filles sont parties il y a une heure. *The girls left an hour ago.*

Ils se sont lavés dans la rivière. *They washed themselves in the river.*

It's so nice to see these 'être' verbs getting along so well...

*Translate these phrases into **French**. Remember to check if they take 'être' or 'avoir'.*

1. they (fem.) put
2. we've read
3. you (sing.) said
4. I went
5. she arrived
6. we had to
7. they (masc.) returned
8. I washed myself

Imperfect Tense

Talking About the Past

Like English, French has more than one past tense — time is a complicated notion, after all. The imperfect tense is really useful though, and dead easy to form. Once you've got the hang of it, you won't look back.

Get the stem from the present tense 'nous' form

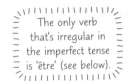
The only verb that's irregular in the imperfect tense is 'être' (see below).

1) To form the imperfect tense, you have to find the stem of the verb you want and add on the correct ending.

2) To get the stem, find the present tense 'nous' form of the verb and take off the '-ons'.

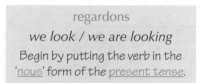

regardons
we look / we are looking
Begin by putting the verb in the 'nous' form of the present tense.

—

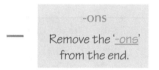

-ons
Remove the '-ons' from the end.

=

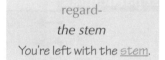

regard-
the stem
You're left with the stem.

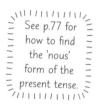
See p.77 for how to find the 'nous' form of the present tense.

3) When you've got the stem, add on the ending you need. The endings are the same for all verbs:

Imperfect tense endings		
I	je	-ais
you (inf. sing.)	tu	-ais
he/she/it/one	il/elle/on	-ait
we	nous	-ions
you (pl., formal)	vous	-iez
they (m/f)	ils/elles	-aient

Verb	Stem	Imperfect form	
aller	all-	j'	allais
attendre	attend-	tu	attendais
venir	ven-	il/elle/on	venait
faire	fais-	nous	faisions
parler	parl-	vous	parliez
avoir	av-	ils/elles	avaient

'Être', 'avoir' and 'faire' crop up a lot

1) Some verbs crop up more than others, so it's a good idea to become really familiar with them.

2) 'Être' is irregular in the imperfect tense — its stem is 'ét-'. It uses the regular endings, though:

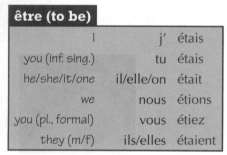

être (to be)		
I	j'	étais
you (inf. sing.)	tu	étais
he/she/it/one	il/elle/on	était
we	nous	étions
you (pl., formal)	vous	étiez
they (m/f)	ils/elles	étaient

C'était formidable.   *It was great.*

'C'était' (*it was*) is the past tense of 'c'est' (*it is*). C'était + an adjective is useful for descriptions.

Nous étions épuisés.   *We were exhausted.*

La pièce était bondée.   *The room was overcrowded.*

3) All the other verbs are regular — they form the imperfect tense following the normal rules.

4) Make sure you learn 'avoir' and 'faire' inside out. They're used in lots of handy phrases.

Il y avait...   *There was... / There were...*

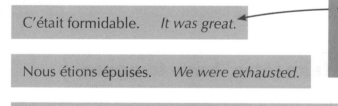

Il faisait froid.   *It was cold.*

Another tense, another stem, more endings...

These phrases are a mixture of the imperfect and present tense. List all of the phrases that are in the imperfect.

1. nous venions
2. j'attends
3. elle faisait
4. vous veniez
5. j'ai
6. nous remplissons
7. elles vendent
8. tu étais

Talking About the Past

Now you know how to form the imperfect tense, it's a good idea to learn when to use it.

Use the imperfect for descriptions in the past

1) Use the <u>imperfect tense</u> to <u>describe something</u> or <u>someone</u> in the past.

It was so hot, Xavier's only option was to chill with his seals.

| Il était une heure. | *It was one o'clock.* | Il faisait chaud. | *It was hot.* |

| Yann était heureux de la voir. | *Yann was happy to see her.* |

2) The imperfect tense also describes an <u>action</u> that '<u>was happening</u>' in the past. It's different to the perfect tense (see p.80-81) because the action <u>isn't complete</u>.

| J'attendais le train. | *I was waiting for the train.* |

The person hadn't finished waiting for the train, so the action is incomplete.

| Il parlait à l'avocat. | *He was talking to the lawyer.* |

Imperfect	Perfect
I was going	I went
she was running	she ran
we were waiting	we waited

3) When one action <u>interrupts</u> another action in a past tense sentence, the <u>first action</u> is left <u>unfinished</u>. This means that it needs to be in the <u>imperfect tense</u>.

| Je lisais quand le téléphone a sonné. | *I was reading when the telephone rang.* |

The second action is in the perfect tense.

Use the imperfect for what used to happen

You can use the imperfect for something you used to do regularly, or something you used to do in general.

You also use the <u>imperfect tense</u> to talk about what you <u>used to do</u>.

| J'allais au cinéma tous les jeudis. | *I used to go to the cinema every Thursday.* |

This verb is describing someone.

| Quand j'avais dix ans, je jouais de la guitare. | *When I was ten, I used to play the guitar.* |

Imperfect + 'depuis' — *had been*

See p.79 for when to use 'depuis' with the present tense.

'Depuis' means '<u>for</u>' or '<u>since</u>' (see p.75). In French, when you want to say that something '<u>had been</u>' happening 'for' or 'since' a <u>certain time</u>, use the <u>imperfect tense</u> with '<u>depuis</u>'.

This could also mean 'It had been raining since two o'clock.'

| Il pleuvait depuis deux heures. | *It had been raining for two hours.* |

| Il attendait depuis six heures du matin. | *He had been waiting since six o'clock in the morning.* |

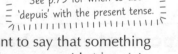

Once upon a time, I used to have a life...

Decide whether the verbs below should be in the perfect or the imperfect tense, then translate each sentence.

1. I ran.　　3. You (sing.) were laughing.　5. It was terrifying.　7. I used to play basketball.
2. They have eaten.　4. He was annoying.　　6. She cried.　　8. I was tidying up when she arrived.

| **Immediate and Proper Future Tenses** | # Talking About the Future |

You need to be able to talk about things that'll happen in the future, too. Don't worry — there are no crystal balls involved, just some good old-fashioned verb conjugations. Everything you need to know is on this page.

Use 'I'm going' + infinitive

The <u>immediate future</u> is the <u>easiest</u> future tense — it uses the <u>present tense</u> form of '<u>aller</u>' and <u>an infinitive</u>.

je vais (*I am going*)		danser (*to dance*)		Je vais danser.
This is the <u>present tense</u> of 'aller' (see p.78). You <u>change</u> this to say 'you are going', 'he is going' etc.	**+**	The next verb goes in the <u>infinitive</u> (see p.77).	**=**	(*I am going to dance.*) A sentence about the future.

Il va déménager la semaine prochaine.   *He's going to move house **next week**.*

La forêt et ses animaux vont disparaître.   *The forest and its wildlife are going to disappear.*

'I will' — the proper future tense

1) Using the proper <u>future tense</u> in French is the same as saying '<u>will</u>' in English, e.g. 'I will bake'.

2) To form the <u>future tense</u>, you need find the verb's <u>infinitive</u> (see p.77) and add on the correct <u>endings</u>. The endings are <u>the same</u> for <u>all verbs</u>:

Future tense endings

I	je	-ai	we	nous	-ons
you (inf. sing.)	tu	-as	you (pl., formal)	vous	-ez
he/she/it/one	il/elle/on	-a	they (m/f)	ils/elles	-ont

These endings might look familiar because they're similar to the present tense of 'avoir'.

3) Verbs <u>ending</u> in '<u>-re</u>' are a bit different — you drop the <u>final '-e</u>' from the <u>infinitive</u> to get the stem.

Verb	Stem
regarder (*to look*)	regarder-
finir (*to finish*)	finir-
vendre (*to sell*)	vendr-

je regarderai   *I will look*   il finira   *he will finish*

Ils vendront les fruits.   *They will sell the fruit.*

Some important verbs have irregular stems

Some <u>important verbs</u> are <u>irregular</u> in the future tense — their <u>stems</u> aren't in the infinitive form:

Verb	Stem	Verb	Stem	Verb	Stem	Verb	Stem	Verb	Stem
aller	ir-	*avoir*	aur-	*venir*	viendr-	*voir*	verr-	*pouvoir*	pourr-
être	ser-	*faire*	fer-	*vouloir*	voudr-	*devoir*	devr-	*recevoir*	recev-

The stems are the only irregular part of these verbs — they all use the normal endings listed above.

After my exams — je vais aller au lit, je vais dormir et je dormirai...

Put each of these present tense phrases into the immediate and proper future tenses.

1. il va	**3.** nous finissons	**5.** elles disent	**7.** tu peux	**9.** ils sont
2. j'ai	**4.** tu regardes	**6.** vous faites	**8.** elle vient	**10.** on vend

Reflexive Verbs and Pronouns

It's time to say goodbye to tenses and hello to reflexive verbs and pronouns. Lots of people get put off by the sight of these, but they're actually really simple — you just need to know a few rules.

Reflexive verbs have an extra part

Reflexive pronouns	
myself	me
yourself (inf. sing.)	te
himself/herself/itself/oneself	se
ourselves	nous
yourselves (pl., formal)	vous
themselves, each other (m/f)	se

1) Reflexive verbs describe actions that you do to yourself, like washing yourself or getting yourself up.

2) These verbs look different because they've got an extra part — a pronoun that means 'self', e.g. 'se laver' (to wash oneself). The pronoun changes form depending on who's doing the action.

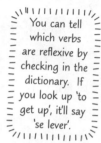

You can tell which verbs are reflexive by checking in the dictionary. If you look up 'to get up', it'll say 'se lever'.

Je me lave — *I wash myself / have a wash*

1) Reflexive verbs can end in '-er', '-ir' or '-re'. They form tenses in exactly the same way as other verbs:

For the present, imperfect and proper future tenses, the reflexive pronoun always goes between the subject and the verb.

se laver — to wash oneself

I wash myself	je me lave	*one washes oneself*	on se lave
you (inf. sing.) wash yourself	tu te laves	*we wash ourselves*	nous nous lavons
he washes himself	il se lave	*you (pl., formal) wash yourselves*	vous vous lavez
she washes herself	elle se lave	*they wash themselves*	ils/elles se lavent

2) Reflexive verbs are really important — you'll need to use them to talk about your hobbies and your daily routine. Make sure you learn these useful examples:

se lever	*to get up*	se détendre	*to relax*	s'appeler	*to be called*
se coucher	*to go to bed*	se sentir	*to feel*	se plaindre	*to complain*
s'intéresser à	*to be interested in*	se disputer	*to argue*	s'amuser	*to enjoy oneself*

Reflexives keep their pronouns in all tenses

1) All reflexive verbs take 'être' in the perfect tense — this means they agree with their subject (see p.81).

2) The reflexive pronoun (me, te, se, etc.) always goes between the subject and the present tense of 'être'.

Je me suis levé(e) à sept heures ce matin.
I got up at seven o'clock this morning.

Elle s'est lavée.
She washed herself.

'Lavée' has an 'e' on the end here because its subject (elle) is feminine.

3) In the immediate future tense (see p.84), the reflexive infinitive needs the pronoun that matches its subject.

Je vais me coucher.   *I'm going to go to bed.*

Ils vont se plaindre.   *They're going to complain.*

Reflexive verbs just think about themselves — they're so selfish...

Translate these phrases into **French**. *Make sure you put the reflexive pronouns in the right places.*

1. we're going to bed
2. you (pl.) argue
3. they (fem.) get up
4. he's interested in
5. you (sing.) enjoyed yourself
6. I'm going to relax
7. she felt
8. we're going to complain

Negative Forms

You've reached the page where you can grumble and moan. Take all your stress out on two of the most important French words ever — 'ne' and 'pas'. (Don't worry — they're only little but they can take it.)

'ne...pas' — *not*

*Luc's dinner definitely
didn't agree with him.*

1) In English, you change a sentence to mean <u>the opposite</u> by adding '<u>not</u>'. In French, you add <u>two words</u> — '<u>ne</u>' and '<u>pas</u>'. They go <u>either side</u> of the <u>verb</u>.

je suis d'accord	→ je ne suis pas d'accord
I agree	→ *I do not agree*

'Suis' is the verb. The 'ne' goes before it, and the 'pas' goes after it.

2) For verbs in the <u>perfect tense</u> (see p.80-81), put the '<u>ne</u>' and '<u>pas</u>' <u>around</u> the bit of '<u>avoir</u>' or '<u>être</u>'.

Je n'ai pas aimé l'école primaire.
I did not like the primary school.

Elle n'est pas encore arrivée.
She hasn't arrived yet.

To say 'not yet', add the word 'encore' directly after the 'pas' in a normal negative sentence.

3) To make an <u>infinitive negative</u>, put the '<u>ne</u>' and the '<u>pas</u>' in <u>front</u> of it.

Elle préfère ne pas parler de son talent. *She prefers not to talk about her talent.*

'ne...jamais' — *never*

There are <u>other negatives</u> that work in the <u>same way</u> as 'ne...pas'. Here are some of the most common ones:

ne...jamais	*never*	ne...personne	*nobody / anyone*	
ne...rien	*nothing*	ne...ni...ni	*neither...nor*	
ne...plus	*no more / no longer*	ne...que	*only / nothing but*	

These negatives position themselves around the verb in the same way as 'ne...pas'.

Je ne vais plus à York.
I don't go to York any more.

Je ne vais jamais à York.
I never go to York.

Je ne vais ni à York ni à Belfast.
I neither go to York nor Belfast.

Il n'y a rien ici.
There's nothing here.

Je n'en ai plus.
I don't have any more of them.

'Y' and 'en' always go between the 'ne' and the verb.

Articles change to 'de' after a negative

After a <u>negative</u>, indefinite articles ('<u>un</u> / <u>une</u>') and partitives ('<u>du</u>', '<u>de la</u>', '<u>des</u>' — see p.60) usually become '<u>de</u>'.

Elle n'a plus de pain. *She doesn't have any more bread.*

'Ne...que' doesn't follow this rule — it keeps its articles. E.g. 'Je n'ai que du café.' (*I only have coffee.*)

The 'de' is only shortened if the next word begins with a vowel or an 'h' which takes 'l'. E.g. 'd'animaux', 'd'hôpital'.

Je ne veux pas d'argent. *I don't want any money.*

This page is overly negative — chin up...

*Translate these sentences into **French** using the negative phrases you've learnt on this page.*

1. I never eat meat.
2. He doesn't have a dog.
3. You (sing.) only drink water.
4. They (masc.) don't like anyone.
5. We don't live together any more.
6. You (pl.) never go there.

Would, Could and Should

Conditional

The conditional is a bit of a mish-mash of different tenses. On the plus side, you already know half of it...

The conditional = future stem + imperfect endings

Be careful — the imperfect 'je' ending ('-ais') sounds just like the future 'je' ending ('-ai'). This can make the future and conditional tenses tricky to tell apart.

1) The <u>conditional</u> is where you'd say '<u>would</u>', '<u>could</u>' or '<u>should</u>' in English.

2) Forming the conditional is pretty straightforward — you take the verb's <u>stem</u> from the <u>future tense</u> and add on the <u>endings</u> you learnt for the <u>imperfect tense</u>.

je regarderai *(I will look)*
This is the first person singular <u>future tense</u> of 'regarder' (see p.84). The verb is <u>regular</u>, so its stem is its <u>infinitive</u> — 'regarder'.

+

je regardais *(I was looking)*
This is the first person singular <u>imperfect tense</u> of 'regarder' (see p.82). Its ending is '<u>-ais</u>'.

=

je regarderais *(I would look)*
This is the first person singular <u>conditional</u> of 'regarder'.

Verb	Future stem	Imperfect ending	Conditional
manger (to eat)	je mangerai	je mangeais	je mangerais (*I would eat*)
finir (to finish)	je finirai	je finissais	je finirais (*I would finish*)
vendre (to sell)	je vendrai	je vendais	je vendrais (*I would sell*)
être (to be)	je serai	j'étais	je serais (*I would be*)

Remember that '-re' verbs drop the '-e' off their infinitive to get their future / conditional stem.

Some verbs, like 'être', have irregular stems (see p.84).

3) '<u>Si</u>' + <u>the imperfect tense</u> is always followed by a verb in the <u>conditional</u>.

Si j'étais riche, je voyagerais autour du monde. *If I was rich, I'd travel around the world.*

4) To say '<u>could</u>' in French, use the conditional form of '<u>pouvoir</u>' (*to be able to*) followed by <u>an infinitive</u>. To say '<u>should</u>', use the conditional form of '<u>devoir</u>' (*to have to*) followed by <u>an infinitive</u>.

Elle pourrait aller en France. *She could go to France.*

Tu devrais te plaindre. *You should complain.*

'Je voudrais' and 'j'aimerais' — *I would like*

These two verbs are really useful in the <u>conditional</u> — you can use them lots in your <u>speaking assessment</u>:

vouloir (to want)	
I would like	je voudrais
you (inf. sing.) would like	tu voudrais
he/she/it/one would like	il/elle/on voudrait
we would like	nous voudrions
you (pl., formal) would like	vous voudriez
they (m/f) would like	ils/elles voudraient

Both of these verbs are often followed by an infinitive. Look at p.79 for more on infinitives.

aimer (to like)	
I would like	j'aimerais
you (inf. sing.) would like	tu aimerais
he/she/it/one would like	il/elle/on aimerait
we would like	nous aimerions
you (pl., formal) would like	vous aimeriez
they (m/f) would like	ils/elles aimeraient

Je voudrais aller à l'hôpital. *I'd like to go to the hospital.*

J'aimerais du lait. *I would like some milk.*

The conditional — I'd do it if I could...

Put these verbs into the conditional. The subject has been given to you in brackets.

1. améliorer (tu)
2. élargir (il)
3. rendre (nous)
4. faire (je)
5. aller (elles)
6. venir (vous)
7. être (on)
8. avoir (elle)
9. se laver (ils)
10. chercher (vous)

| Imperative | # Giving Orders |

Learning to order other people about is a pretty important life skill, whatever language you're speaking in. Putting verbs in their imperative lets you do just that — it's really useful and very easy to form.

Imperatives use the present tense

1) <u>Imperatives</u> are words that give an <u>order</u>. They tell someone <u>to do something</u>, or <u>suggest</u> doing something together, e.g. 'sit down' or 'let's eat'.

For when to choose 'tu' or 'vous', see p.69.

2) In French, imperatives are formed using the <u>present tense</u> of the '<u>tu</u>', '<u>nous</u>' and '<u>vous</u>' parts of a verb:

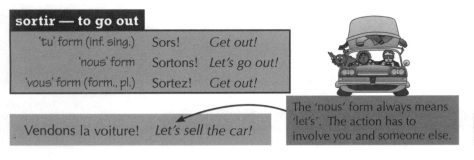

sortir — to go out		
'tu' form (inf. sing.)	Sors!	*Get out!*
'nous' form	Sortons!	*Let's go out!*
'vous' form (form., pl.)	Sortez!	*Get out!*

'Tu', 'nous' and 'vous' never appear with an imperative verb — otherwise they would be in the present tense.

Vendons la voiture! *Let's sell the car!*

The 'nous' form always means 'let's'. The action has to involve you and someone else.

Écoutez ceci! *Listen to this!*

Take off the '-s' from the 'tu' form of '-er' verbs

Regular '-er' verbs in the 'tu' form of the present tense normally end in '-es', e.g. 'tu parles'.

1) Watch out for '<u>tu</u>' forms that <u>end</u> in '<u>-es</u>' — you have to <u>lose</u> the <u>final</u> '<u>-s</u>' from the present tense. This means you have to be careful with <u>regular</u> '<u>-er</u>' <u>verbs</u>.

Arrête de me parler! *Stop talking to me!*   Regarde Jean-Paul! *Look at Jean-Paul!*

2) Some verbs have <u>irregular</u> imperatives. They're nothing like the present tense, so you have to <u>learn</u> them.

Imperative form	être — to be	avoir — to have	savoir — to know	aller — to go
tu (*you inf. sing.*)	sois	aie	sache	va
nous (*we*)	soyons	ayons	sachons	allons
vous (*form., pl.*)	soyez	ayez	sachez	allez

Only the 'tu' form of 'aller' has an irregular imperative.

Negative imperatives use 'ne...pas' normally

1) To make an imperative verb <u>negative</u>, put '<u>ne</u>' <u>before</u> the verb and '<u>pas</u>' <u>after</u> it (see p.86).

Ne vendez pas la voiture! *Don't sell the car!*   N'écoute pas! *Don't listen!*

François learned to mask his negative emotions.

2) Imperative <u>reflexive verbs</u> (see p.85) have an <u>emphatic pronoun</u> (see p.71) that goes <u>after</u> the verb.

Tu te lèves. → Lève-toi!
You get up. → *Get up!*

The emphatic pronoun is always joined to the verb by a dash (-).

Tu ne te lèves pas. → Ne te lève pas!
You don't get up. → *Don't get up!*

3) When <u>reflexive verbs</u> are <u>imperative</u> and <u>negative</u>, they use their <u>normal pronouns</u> (me, te, etc.). The '<u>ne</u>' goes <u>before</u> the pronoun, and the '<u>pas</u>' goes <u>after</u> the verb.

Learning this stuff is pretty imperative...

*Translate these phrases into **French**.*

1. Finish your homework! (pl.)
2. Let's organise a party!
3. Listen! (sing.)
4. Let's eat!
5. Don't go! (sing.)
6. Don't run! (pl.)
7. Go to bed! (sing.)
8. Don't argue! (pl.)

| ‘Had done’ and ‘-ing’ | Pluperfect, Present Participle, Perfect Infinitive |

It may sound like a made-up tense, but the pluperfect tense is real and you need to know how to use it. It's fairly straightforward, though — plus, you can learn about the present participle once you're done...

J'avais fait — *I had done*

1) The pluperfect tense is for saying what you had done. It's like the perfect tense — which describes what you have done — but it deals with actions further in the past.

For more about the perfect tense, see p.80-81. For the imperfect tense, look at p.82-83.

2) The pluperfect is made up of the imperfect version of ‘avoir’ or ‘être’ + a past participle.

il (*he*)		avait (*had*)		regardé (*watched*)
This is the subject. The subject could also be a noun, e.g. someone's name.	**+**	This is the imperfect tense of ‘avoir’. Its form depends on the subject.	**=**	This is the past participle of ‘regarder’ (see p.80).

| J'avais écrit une lettre. *I had written a letter.* | Elles s'étaient disputées. *They had argued.* |

Verbs taking ‘avoir’ don't agree with their subject, but verbs taking ‘être’ always do.

With reflexive verbs, the word order is exactly the same as it would be for the perfect tense — the reflexive pronoun goes before the bit of ‘avoir’ or ‘être’.

‘Doing’, ‘saying’ and ‘thinking’ are present participles

1) To form the present participle, get the imperfect stem of the verb (see p.82) and add ‘-ant’:

Verb	Imperfect stem	Present participle
regarder	regard-	regardant (*watching*)
finir	finiss-	finissant (*finishing*)
vendre	vend-	vendant (*selling*)
faire	fais-	faisant (*doing / making*)

Careful — to say you're ‘doing something’, e.g. ‘I am laughing’, you should use the present tense (see p.77-79). If you use two verbs together, e.g. ‘I like writing’, you use the present tense with an infinitive (see p.79).

| Renonçant à l'idée, Clare est retournée chez elle. | Giving up on the idea, Clare returned home. |

2) ‘En’ + the present participle usually means ‘while doing something’ or ‘by doing something’.

| Il lit le journal en déjeunant. *He reads the paper whilst having lunch.* |

3) Some verbs have irregular stems in the present participle.

Verb	Irregular stem
avoir (*to have*)	ay-
être (*to be*)	ét-
savoir (*to know*)	sach-

| Il a réussi en sachant les faits. *He succeeded by knowing the facts.* |

Après avoir mangé — *After having eaten*

‘Avoir’ / ‘être’ + ‘past participle’ means ‘having done something’. This is called the perfect infinitive.

| Il regrette d'avoir joué au foot. *He regretted having played football.* | Après être arrivées, elles... *After having arrived, they...* |

Because ‘arriver’ takes ‘être’, it needs to agree with its subject.

No wonder the imperfect tense has an inferiority complex...

Translate the following phrases into **French**.

1. I had played
2. we had argued
3. you (pl.) had arrived
4. they (fem.) had been
5. whilst helping
6. by staying
7. after having left
8. after having destroyed

The Passive

Passive sentences in French are structured just like passive sentences in English, so they're dead easy to recognise. But for that theory to work, you need to know what all this passive stuff is in the first place...

La tasse est cassée — *The cup is broken*

André was a passive dog through and through.

1) In most sentences, there's a person or thing <u>doing</u> the verb, e.g. '<u>The fly bit</u> the man'. These are <u>active sentences</u>. In a <u>passive</u> sentence, the person or thing has <u>something done to it</u>, e.g. '<u>The man was bitten</u> by the fly'.

2) The <u>present passive</u> is made up of a <u>person</u> or <u>thing</u> followed by the <u>present tense</u> of '<u>être</u>' + a <u>past participle</u>.

> Il est aidé par ses parents.   *He is helped by his parents.*

See p.80-81 for more on past participles.

3) The <u>past participle</u> has to <u>agree</u> with the <u>person</u> or <u>thing</u> that is having the <u>action done to it</u>.

> La télé réalité est regardée par beaucoup de gens.
> *Reality TV is watched by lots of people.*

This is passive — 'reality TV' is having something done to it. 'Regardée' has an 'e' so it agrees with 'la télé'.

In the past and the future, only the 'être' bit changes

1) The passive voice can also be <u>in the past</u> or <u>future</u> tenses. It's formed in <u>the same way</u> as it is in <u>the present</u> — the only thing that changes is <u>the tense</u> of '<u>être</u>'.

2) The <u>perfect passive</u> tells you about a passive event that happened in the <u>past</u>. It's formed using the <u>perfect tense</u> of '<u>être</u>' (see p.81) and a <u>past participle</u>.

> La photo a été prise.   *The photo was taken.*

You don't need to be able to form the passive — you just have to know how to recognise it.

3) The <u>imperfect passive</u> describes a passive action that '<u>was happening</u>'. It's formed using the <u>imperfect tense</u> of 'être' (see p.82) and a <u>past participle</u>.

> Le livre était écrit pendant la guerre.   *The book was being written during the war.*

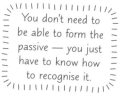

4) The <u>future passive</u> is made up of the <u>future tense</u> of '<u>être</u>' and a <u>past participle</u>.

> Tu seras puni(e).   *You will be punished.*

> Les déchets seront jetés.   *The rubbish will be thrown away.*

French often uses 'on' instead of the passive

The passive isn't used very much in French. French speakers often use '<u>on</u>' (*one*) with an <u>active sentence</u> instead.

'One didn't see' sounds quite formal in English, so you'd normally use the passive voice instead.

> On n'a pas vu l'homme.   *One didn't see the man. / The man wasn't seen.*

The grammar section will soon be finished...

Identify all of the passive sentences in the list below.

1. L'homme est heurté par la voiture.
2. La fille perd le ballon.
3. Le match est intéressant.
4. La pomme sera mangée par mon oncle.
5. On regarde la télé.
6. La tasse a été cassée.

Impersonal Verbs and the Subjunctive

Right, you're almost there now — just one last page until you're granted grammar freedom. The subjunctive is the crème de la crème of French grammar, but luckily you only have to recognise it in the exam.

Impersonal verbs only work with 'il'

1) <u>Impersonal verbs</u> always have '<u>il</u>' as their subject. Here are some common examples:

il faut	*you must / it is necessary to*	il est nécessaire de	*it's necessary to*
il s'agit de	*it's about*	il pleut / neige	*it's raining / snowing*
il semble	*it seems*	il fait chaud / froid	*it's hot / cold*

Il s'agit d'une mère et ses enfants.   *It's about a mother and her children.*

Il semble injuste d'ignorer la décision.   *It seems unfair to ignore the decision.*

> You often use impersonal verbs to talk about the weather. For more about the weather, see p.36.

2) '<u>Il faut</u>' and '<u>il est nécessaire de</u>' are always followed by an <u>infinitive</u>:

> See p.79 to learn more about infinitives.

Il faut aller au lycée tous les jours.
You must go to school every day.

Il est nécessaire de lutter contre le réchauffement de la Terre.
It's necessary to fight against global warming.

You may see the subjunctive instead of the infinitive

1) The subjunctive <u>doesn't have</u> an <u>equivalent</u> in English. You don't have to use it in your exams, but you do have to be able to <u>recognise common verbs</u> in the subjunctive:

avoir	être	faire	aller	pouvoir
j'aie	je sois	je fasse	j'aille	je puisse
tu aies	tu sois	tu fasses	tu ailles	tu puisses
il/elle/on ait	il/elle/on soit	il/elle/on fasse	il/elle/on aille	il/elle/on puisse
nous ayons	nous soyons	nous fassions	nous allions	nous puissions
vous ayez	vous soyez	vous fassiez	vous alliez	vous puissiez
ils/elles aient	ils/elles soient	ils/elles fassent	ils/elles aillent	ils/elles puissent

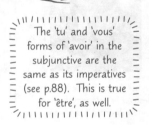

> The 'tu' and 'vous' forms of 'avoir' in the subjunctive are the same as its imperatives (see p.88). This is true for 'être', as well.

2) Certain expressions need to be followed by the <u>subjunctive</u> rather than the <u>infinitive</u>, e.g. '<u>il faut que</u>'.

Il faut que tu fasses la vaisselle.
You must do the washing up.

Il est nécessaire que vous soyez sages.
It is necessary that you're well behaved.

> The subjunctive is often used after 'que'.

3) The subjunctive is also used with certain <u>constructions</u>. '<u>Bien que</u>' (*although*), '<u>avant que</u>' (*before*) and '<u>pour que</u>' (*so that*) are all followed by the subjunctive too.

Bien qu'elle ait deux enfants...
Although she has two children...

Avant que vous partiez...
Before you leave...

Pour qu'il fasse ses devoirs...
So that he does his homework...

Impersonal verbs — such an unfriendly end to the section...

List all phrases below that contain a verb in the subjunctive.

1. Il faut commencer.
2. Le livre que tu veux.
3. avant que vous alliez
4. bien qu'elles soient
5. Il me semble ridicule.
6. pour que nous puissions
7. le stylo que j'ai
8. bien qu'il puisse

The Listening Exam

Ah. Your reward for conquering all that grammar is a section about those pesky exams... Sorry about that. But there is some good news — these pages are crammed full of advice to help you tackle them head on.

There are four exams for GCSE French

1) Your <u>Edexcel French</u> GCSE is assessed by <u>four</u> separate exams — <u>Listening</u>, <u>Speaking</u>, <u>Reading</u> and <u>Writing</u>.

2) Each exam is worth <u>25%</u> of your final mark. You'll get a grade between <u>1</u> and <u>9</u> (with 9 being the highest).

3) You won't sit all of the papers at the same time — you'll probably have your speaking exam <u>a couple of weeks before</u> the rest of your exams.

The Listening Exam has two sections

If you're sitting foundation tier papers, the format of your exams will be slightly different, but this advice will still be useful.

1) For the <u>listening paper</u>, you'll listen to various <u>recordings</u> of people speaking in French and answer questions on <u>what you've heard</u>.

2) The paper is <u>45 minutes</u> long (including 5 minutes reading time) and is split into <u>Section A</u> and <u>Section B</u>.

3) Section A is the <u>shorter</u> section — the questions will be multiple choice, with the instructions in <u>French</u>. Section B is <u>longer</u>, but the questions are in <u>English</u> and your answers will be, too.

Read through the paper carefully at the start of the test

1) Before the recordings begin, you'll be given five minutes to <u>read through</u> the paper.

2) Use this time to <u>read each question</u> carefully. Some are multiple choice, and others require you to write some short answers — make sure you know what <u>each one</u> is asking you to do.

3) In particular, look at the questions in Section A, which are written in <u>French</u>. Try to <u>work out</u> what the questions mean. There's a list of <u>exam-style</u> French question words and phrases on the <u>inside front cover of this book</u> to help you prepare for this.

Michel read 'whole model' instead of 'role-model' — it went downhill from there.

4) Reading the <u>question titles</u>, and the <u>questions themselves</u>, will give you a good idea of the topics you'll be asked about. This should help you <u>predict</u> what to listen out for.

5) You <u>can write</u> on the exam paper, so <u>scribble down</u> anything that might be <u>useful</u>.

Make notes while listening to the recordings

1) You'll hear each audio track <u>twice</u>, and then there'll be <u>a pause</u> for you to write down your answer.

2) While you're listening, it's a good idea to <u>jot down</u> a few details — e.g. <u>dates</u>, <u>times</u>, <u>names</u> or <u>key words</u>. But make sure you <u>keep listening</u> while you're writing down any notes.

Listen to the speaker's tone, too — this will hint at their mood, e.g. angry or excited.

3) Listen <u>right to the end</u>, even if you think you've got the answer — sometimes the person will change their mind or <u>add an important detail</u> at the end.

4) <u>Don't worry</u> if you can't understand every word that's being said — just <u>listen carefully</u> both times and try to <u>pick out the vocabulary</u> you need to answer the question.

Don't worry, I'm all ears...

If you've heard a track twice, and you're still not sure of the answer, scribble one down anyway — you never know, it might be the right one. You may as well write something sensible just in case — it's worth a shot.

The Speaking Exam

The Speaking Exam can seem daunting, but remember — no one is trying to catch you out, so try to stay calm.

There are three parts to the Speaking Exam

During your preparation time, you can make notes to take in with you for the first two tasks. You can't keep the notes for the conversation.

1) Your speaking exam will be conducted and recorded by your teacher.

2) The exam is in three parts. Before you start, you'll get 12 minutes to prepare for the first two sections:

① Role play (~2 min.)	② Picture-based task (~3 min.)	③ Conversation (~6 min.)
You'll get a card with a scenario on it. It'll have five bullet points — two will be notes on what to say, in French. The '!' means you'll be asked an unknown question, and '?' shows you have to ask a question about the words next to it. See p.5 for an example.	Before the exam, you'll receive a photo and five bullet points relating to it (there's an example on p.17 for you to have a look at). Your teacher will ask you questions based on the prompts on the picture card, as well as one question you haven't seen.	You and your teacher will have a conversation. The conversation will have two parts. In the first part, you'll talk about the theme that you've chosen. Then, you'll discuss another theme that hasn't been covered in the second task.

3) The role play card will tell you if you should use 'tu', but otherwise, use 'vous' to talk to your teacher.

Try to be imaginative with your answers

You need to find ways to show off the full extent of your French knowledge. You should try to:

1) Use a range of tenses — e.g. for a question on daily routine, think of when something different happens.

| Mais demain ce sera différent car je jouerai au snooker après les cours. | *But tomorrow it will be different because I will play snooker after lessons.* |

If you can't remember a word, just say something suitable that you do know instead, e.g. swap 'snooker' for 'hockey', or 'nephew' for 'sister'.

2) Talk about other people, not just yourself — it's fine to make people up if that helps.

| J'aime le foot, mais mon neveu le déteste. | *I like football, but my nephew hates it.* |

3) Give loads of opinions and reasons for your opinions.

| À mon avis, il faut faire plus de recyclage parce qu'on produit trop de déchets. | *In my opinion, we must do more recycling because we produce too much rubbish.* |

If you're really struggling, ask for help in French

1) If you get really stuck trying to think of a word or phrase, you can ask for help — as long as it's in French.

2) For example, if you can't remember how to say 'homework' in French, ask your teacher. You won't get any marks for vocabulary your teacher's given you though.

| Comment dit-on 'homework' en français? | *How do you say 'homework' in French?* |

3) If you don't hear something clearly, just ask:

| Pouvez-vous répéter, s'il vous plaît? | *Could you repeat that, please?* |

You could also ask this if you're desperately in need of time to think of an answer.

What animal always aces speaking exams? 'Le chat'...

Given that you're only human, you're bound to have a few slip-ups in the speaking exam. Don't panic, it's completely natural. What's important is how you deal with a mistake — just correct yourself and move on.

The Reading Exam

After all that listening and speaking, the reading exam offers some nice peace and quiet. Apart from the voice inside your head that screams "WHAT ON EARTH DOES THAT WORD MEAN?!" (Or maybe that's just me...)

Read the questions and texts carefully

1) The higher tier reading paper is 1 hour long, and has three sections.

2) In Sections A and B, you'll be given a variety of French texts and then asked questions about them. The texts could include blog posts, emails, newspaper reports, adverts and literary texts. Section A has questions and answers in English, and Section B has questions and answers in French.

3) Section C is a translation question — you'll have to translate a short passage of text from French into English. See p.96 for more tips on tackling translation questions.

4) In Sections A and B, scan through the text first to get an idea of what it's about. Then read the questions that go with it carefully, making sure you understand what information you should be looking out for.

5) Next, go back through the text. You're not expected to understand every word, so don't get distracted by trying to work out what everything means — focus on finding the information you need.

> The inside front cover of this book has a list of common French question words, phrases and instructions.

Don't give up if you don't understand something

1) Use the context of the text to help you understand what it might be saying. You might be able to find some clues in the title of the text or the type of text.

2) Knowing how to spot different word types (e.g. nouns, verbs) can help you work out what's happening in a sentence. See the grammar section (p.59-91) for more.

3) You can guess some French words that look or sound the same as English words, e.g. le problème — *problem*, la musique — *music*, dangereux — *dangerous*.

> Look for words that look like ones you know, e.g. 'le sac de couchage'. 'Le sac' means 'bag', and 'se coucher' means 'to sleep', so you can guess it means 'sleeping bag'.

4) Be careful though — you might come across some 'false friends'. These are French words that look like an English word, but have a completely different meaning:

sensible	*sensitive*	mince	*slim*	la journée	*day*	le car	*coach*	les affaires (f)	*things*
grand(e)	*big*	joli(e)	*pretty*	la cave	*cellar*	le médecin	*doctor*	les baskets (f)	*trainers*
large	*wide*	le genre	*type / kind*	la veste	*jacket*	le crayon	*pencil*	attendre	*to wait*

Keep an eye on the time

1) There are quite a few questions to get through in the reading exam, so you need to work at a good speed.

2) If you're having trouble with a particular question, you might want to move on and come back to it later.

Xavier and his colleagues never underestimated the importance of thyme.

3) Don't forget that the last question in the paper (Section C) is a translation — this is worth more marks than any other question, so you should leave plenty of time to tackle it.

4) Make sure you put an answer down for every question — lots of the questions are multiple choice, so even if you can't work out the answer, it's always worth putting down one of the options.

Friend or faux?

Don't forget, the questions in Section B will be in French. Don't panic if you don't understand them — search for any familiar vocabulary and use any answer lines or boxes to help you guess what you have to do.

The Writing Exam

The Writing Exam is a great way of showing off what you can do — try to use varied vocabulary, include a range of tenses, and pack in any clever expressions that you've learnt over the years.

There'll be three tasks in the Writing Exam

1) The higher tier writing paper is 1 hour and 20 minutes long and has three tasks.

2) Each task is worth a different number of marks, so you should spend more time on the higher-mark tasks.

① Informal writing (20 marks)

There will be two tasks to choose from. You'll be asked to write about 80-90 words in French, based on four bullet points. You'll need to write about each bullet point and give opinions. The scenario for the task will be informal, so use the 'tu' form.

② Formal writing (28 marks)

There will also be two tasks to choose from. You'll need to write about 130-150 words in French, based on four bullet points. Make sure you include some opinions and justify your reasons. You'll need to be more formal in this task, so use the 'vous' form.

③ Translation (12 marks)

You'll be given an English passage to translate into French. The passage could be on any topic you've studied. Make sure you leave plenty of time for this task. There's more advice for doing translations on p.96.

Read the instructions carefully, and spend some time planning

1) Read the instructions for questions 1 and 2 carefully — you'll need to make sure you cover all of the bullet points. You can often use words from the question in your answer too.

Try to use varied vocab and a range of tenses.

2) Spend a few minutes for each question planning out your answer. Decide how you're going to cover everything that's required and in what order you're going to write things.

3) Write the best answer you can, using the French that you know — it doesn't matter if it's not true.

Check through your work thoroughly

Checking your work is really important — even small mistakes can cost marks. Take a look at this checklist:

- Are all the verbs in the right tense?
  Demain, je travaillais dans le jardin. ✘   Demain, je travaillerai dans le jardin. ✔

- Are the verb endings correct?
  Tu n'aime pas les framboises? ✘   Tu n'aimes pas les framboises? ✔

All of the points on this checklist are covered in the grammar section — see p.59-91.

- Do your adjectives agree with their nouns?
  La cuisine est grand. ✘   La cuisine est grande. ✔

- Are your adjectives in the right place?
  Il porte une rose chemise. ✘   Il porte une chemise rose. ✔

- Do your past participles agree?
  Ils sont parti. ✘   Ils sont partis. ✔

- Have you spelt everything correctly, including using the right accents?
  Ele ecoute de la music avec ma mere. ✘   Elle écoute de la musique avec ma mère. ✔

And lastly, don't forget your pen...

When you're nervous and stressed, it's dead easy to miss out something the question has asked you to do. For tasks one and two, try to write about the bullet points in order, and tick them off as you go along.

The Translation Tasks

When you're studying French, you do little bits of translation in your head all the time. For the translation questions, you just need to apply those skills — one sentence at a time — to a couple of short passages.

In the Reading Exam, you'll translate from French to English

1) The final question of the reading paper will ask you to translate a <u>short French passage</u> (about 50 words) <u>into English</u>. The passage will be on a <u>topic you've studied</u>, so most of the vocabulary should be familiar.

2) Here are some <u>top tips</u> for doing your translation:

- Read the whole text <u>before you start</u>. Make some <u>notes in English</u> to remind you of the main ideas.

- Translate the text <u>one sentence at a time</u>, rather than word by word — this will avoid any of the French word order being carried into the English.

Elle achète la pomme rouge.	*She buys the apple red.* ✘	*She buys the red apple.* ✔
Thomas l'a mangée.	*Thomas it ate.* ✘	*Thomas ate it.* ✔

- Keep an eye out for <u>different tenses</u> — there will definitely be a variety in the passage.

- <u>Read through</u> your translation to make sure it sounds <u>natural</u>. Some words and phrases don't translate literally, so you'll need to make sure that your sentences sound like <u>normal English</u>:

> Watch out for adverbs that might suggest a change in tense, e.g. hier — *yesterday,* demain — *tomorrow,* à l'avenir — *in the future.*

La semaine dernière, elle a fait du camping.	*The week last, she did some camping.* ✘	*Last week, she went camping.* ✔

3) Make sure you've translated <u>everything</u> from the original text — you'll lose marks if you miss something.

In the Writing Exam, you'll translate from English to French

1) In the writing paper, you will have to translate <u>a short English passage</u> (about 50 words) <u>into French</u>.

2) Here are <u>some ideas</u> for how you could approach the translation:

- <u>Read</u> through the <u>whole text</u> before you get started so you know exactly what the text is about.

- Tackle the passage <u>one sentence at a time</u> — work slowly and carefully through each one.

- <u>Don't</u> translate things <u>literally</u> — think about what each English sentence means and try to write it in the <u>most French way</u> you know. Don't worry — the translation is likely to include similar sentences to the ones you've learnt.

- Work on the <u>word order</u> — remember that most French adjectives follow the noun. If the sentence is <u>negative</u>, check you've got 'ne' in the <u>right place</u> (see p.86).

> Don't try to write a perfect translation first time — do it roughly first, and then write it up properly, crossing out any old drafts. Remember to keep an eye on the time.

3) Once you've got something that you're happy with, go back through and <u>check that you've covered everything</u> that was in the English.

4) Now <u>check</u> your French text thoroughly using the <u>list from p.95</u>.

Thankfully, none of that got lost in translation...

Élise's translations got the seal of approval.

Congratulations — you've made it to the end of the book. 96 pages is no mean feat, so give yourself a pat on the back. Make sure you still read this page properly though, and take the translation advice on board.

Vocabulary

Section 1 — General Stuff

Conjunctions (p.76)

à cause de	*because of*
à part	*apart from*
ainsi	*therefore / so*
alors	*so / therefore / then*
aussi	*also*
car	*because*
cependant	*however*
c'est-à-dire	*that is to say*
comme	*as / like*
d'un côté / de l'autre côté	*on the one hand / on the other hand*
donc	*therefore / so*
enfin / finalement	*finally*
ensuite	*then / next*
et	*and*
évidemment	*obviously*
lorsque	*when / as soon as*
mais	*but*
même si	*even if*
ni...ni	*neither...nor*
ou	*or*
ou bien	*or else*
par contre	*on the other hand*
parce que	*because*
par exemple	*for example*
pendant que	*while*
pourtant	*however*
puis	*then*
puisque	*seeing that / since*
quand	*when*
sans doute	*undoubtedly / without doubt*
si	*if*
tout d'abord	*first of all*
y compris	*including*

Comparisons (p.66 & 67)

aussi...que	*as...as*
plus / moins	*more / less*
plus que / moins que	*more than / less than*
bon(ne) / meilleur(e) / le/la meilleur(e)	*good / better / the best*
mauvais(e) / pire / le/la pire	*bad / worse / the worst*
bien / mieux / le/la mieux	*well / better / the best*
mal / plus mal / le/la plus mal	*badly / worse / the worst*
beaucoup / plus / le/la plus	*lots / more / the most*
peu / moins / le/la moins	*few / less / the least*

Prepositions (p.74-75)

à	*to / in / at*
à côté de	*next to*
à travers	*across / through*
après	*after*
au bord de	*at the side / edge of*
au bout de	*at the end of (length, rather than time)*
au-dessous de	*beneath / below*
au-dessus de	*above / over*
au fond de	*at the back of / at the bottom of*
au lieu de	*instead of*
au milieu de	*in the middle of*
autour de	*around*
avant	*before*
avec	*with*
chez	*at the house of*
contre	*against*
dans	*in*
de	*of / from*
depuis	*since / for*
derrière	*behind*
devant	*in front of*
en	*in / to*
en dehors de	*outside (of)*
en face de	*opposite*
entre	*between*
jusqu'à	*up to / until*
loin de	*far from*
malgré	*despite / in spite of*
parmi	*amongst*
pendant	*during*
pour	*for / in order to*
près de	*near*
sans	*without*
selon	*according to*
sous	*under*
sur	*on*
vers	*towards*

Negatives (p.86)

ne...aucun(e)	*not any / not a single*
ne...jamais	*never*
ne...ni...ni	*neither...nor*
ne...pas	*not*
ne...personne	*nobody / no one*
ne...plus	*no more / no longer*
ne...que	*only / nothing but*
ne...rien	*nothing*
pas encore	*not yet*

Numbers (p.1)

zéro	*zero*
un	*one*
deux	*two*
trois	*three*
quatre	*four*
cinq	*five*
six	*six*
sept	*seven*
huit	*eight*
neuf	*nine*
dix	*ten*
onze	*eleven*
douze	*twelve*
treize	*thirteen*
quatorze	*fourteen*
quinze	*fifteen*
seize	*sixteen*
dix-sept	*seventeen*
dix-huit	*eighteen*
dix-neuf	*nineteen*
vingt	*twenty*
vingt et un	*twenty-one*
vingt-deux	*twenty-two*
trente	*thirty*
quarante	*forty*
cinquante	*fifty*
soixante	*sixty*
soixante-dix	*seventy*
soixante et onze	*seventy-one*
soixante-douze	*seventy-two*
quatre-vingts	*eighty*
quatre-vingt-un	*eighty-one*
quatre-vingt-dix	*ninety*
quatre-vingt-onze	*ninety-one*
quatre-vingt-dix-huit	*ninety-eight*
cent	*one hundred*
mille	*one thousand*
dix mille	*ten thousand*
cent mille	*one hundred thousand*
un million	*one million*
premier / première	*first*
deuxième	*second*
troisième	*third*
quatrième	*fourth*
cinquième	*fifth*
sixième	*sixth*
septième	*seventh*
huitième	*eighth*
neuvième	*ninth*
dixième	*tenth*
quatre-vingt-dix-neuvième	*ninenty-ninth*
une dizaine	*about ten*
des dizaines	*lots / dozens*
une douzaine	*a dozen*
une vingtaine	*about twenty*
un nombre de	*a number of*

Times and Dates (p.2-3)

lundi	*Monday*
mardi	*Tuesday*
mercredi	*Wednesday*
jeudi	*Thursday*

vendredi	*Friday*	et demie	*half past*	**Weights and Measures**	
samedi	*Saturday*	la fin	*end*	assez	*enough / quite*
dimanche	*Sunday*	hier	*yesterday*	bas(se)	*low*
janvier	*January*	il y a	*ago*	la boîte	*box / tin / can*
février	*February*	le jour	*day*	la bouteille	*bottle*
mars	*March*	la journée	*day*	court(e)	*short*
avril	*April*	le lendemain	*the next day*	le demi	*half*
mai	*May*	longtemps	*for a long time*	un demi-litre	*half a litre*
juin	*June*	maintenant	*now*	encore de	*more*
juillet	*July*	le matin	*morning*	étroit(e)	*narrow*
août	*August*	moins le quart	*quarter to*	un gramme	*a gram*
septembre	*September*	le mois	*month*	gros	*fat*
octobre	*October*	normalement	*normally*	haut(e)	*high*
novembre	*November*	la nuit	*night*	un kilogramme	*a kilogram*
décembre	*December*	parfois	*sometimes*	large	*wide*
l'hiver (m)	*winter*	le passé	*past*	un litre	*a litre*
le printemps	*spring*	pendant	*during*	maigre	*skinny / thin*
l'été (m)	*summer*	plus tard	*later*	mince	*slim / thin*
l'automne (m)	*autumn*	presque	*almost / nearly*	la moitié	*half*
à la fois	*at the same time*	prochain(e)	*next*	le morceau	*piece*
à l'avenir	*in the future*	la quinzaine / les	*fortnight*	moyen / moyenne	*medium / average*
à l'heure	*on time*	quinze jours (m)		le nombre	*number*
à temps partiel	*part-time*	quelquefois	*sometimes*	le paquet	*packet*
à temps plein	*full-time*	rarement	*rarely*	pas mal de	*quite a few*
l'an (m)	*year*	récemment	*recently*	peser	*to weigh*
l'année (f)	*year*	la semaine	*week*	plein de	*full of / lots of*
après	*after*	seulement	*only*	la pointure	*size (for shoes)*
après-demain	*the day after tomorrow*	le siècle	*century*	la portion	*portion*
		le soir	*evening*	le quart	*quarter*
l'après-midi (m / f)	*afternoon*	soudain	*suddenly*	suffisamment	*sufficiently*
l'aube (f)	*dawn*	souvent	*often*	la taille	*size (for clothes)*
au début	*at the start*	suivant(e)	*following*	tout(e)	*all*
aujourd'hui	*today*	(être) sur le point	*(to be) about to*	la tranche	*slice*
auparavant	*formerly / in the past*	de		tranché(e)	*sliced*
avant	*before*	tard	*late*	les trois-quarts (m)	*three quarters*
avant-hier	*the day before yesterday*	tôt	*early*	trop	*too much*
		toujours	*always / still*		
bientôt	*soon*	tous les jours	*every day*	**Materials**	
le coucher du soleil	*sunset*	tout à coup	*suddenly / all of a sudden*	l'argent (m)	*silver*
d'abord	*at first / firstly*			le béton	*concrete*
d'habitude	*usually*	tout de suite	*immediately*	le bois	*wood*
de bonne heure	*early*	vite	*quickly*	le cuir	*leather*
de l'après-midi	*in the afternoon*	le week-end	*weekend*	le fer	*iron*
de nouveau	*again*			la laine	*wool*
de temps en temps	*from time to time*	**Colours and Shapes**		l'or (m)	*gold*
le début	*start*	blanc / blanche	*white*	la soie	*silk*
déjà	*already*	bleu(e)	*blue*	le verre	*glass*
dès que	*as soon as*	châtain	*light brown*		
demain	*tomorrow*	clair(e)	*light*	**Access**	
dernier / dernière	*last*	foncé(e)	*dark*	complet / complète	*full*
du matin	*in the morning*	gris(e)	*grey*	l'entrée (f)	*entry / entrance*
du soir	*in the evening*	jaune	*yellow*	fermé(e)	*closed*
en attendant	*whilst waiting (for)*	marron	*brown*	fermer	*to close*
en avance	*in advance*	noir(e)	*black*	interdit(e)	*forbidden*
en ce moment	*at the moment*	noisette	*hazel*	libre	*free / vacant / unoccupied*
en retard	*late*	orange	*orange*		
en train de (faire...)	*in the process of (doing)*	pourpre	*purple*	occupé(e)	*taken / occupied / engaged*
		rose	*pink*		
en même temps	*at the same time*	rouge	*red*	ouvert(e)	*open*
encore une fois	*once more*	vert(e)	*green*	ouvrir	*to open*
enfin	*at last / finally*	carré(e)	*square*	la sortie	*exit*
environ	*about*	rond(e)	*round*		
et quart	*quarter past*				

Vocabulary

Questions (p.4-5)

Combien ?	How much / How many?
Comment ?	How?
Est-ce que ?	expression put before a verb that makes a sentence into a question
lequel / laquelle	Which one?
Où ?	Where?
Pourquoi ?	Why?
Quand ?	When?
Que ?	What?
Quel / Quelle ?	Which?
Qu'est-ce que ?	What?
Qu'est-ce qui ?	What?
Qu'est-ce que c'est ?	What is it?
Qui ?	Who?
Quoi ?	What?
À quelle heure ?	At what time?
Que veut dire... ?	What does... mean?
Quelle heure est-il ?	What time is it?

Being Polite (p.6-7)

à bientôt	see you soon
à demain	see you tomorrow
à tout à l'heure	see you soon / later
allô	hello (on phone)
amitiés	best wishes
au revoir	goodbye
Au secours !	Help!
bienvenue	welcome
bonjour	hello
Bonne chance !	Good luck!
bonne idée	good idea
bonne nuit	good night
bonnes vacances	have a good holiday
bonsoir	good evening
ça va bien, merci	(I am) fine, thanks
ça ne va pas bien	(I am) not well
comme ci, comme ça	so-so / OK
Comment ça va ?	How are you? (informal)
Comment allez-vous ?	How are you? (formal)
d'accord	OK / fine
de rien	you're welcome
désolé(e)	sorry
enchanté(e)	pleased to meet you
Et toi ?	And you? (informal)
Et vous ?	And you? (formal)
excusez-moi	excuse me (formal)
Félicitations !	Congratulations!
j'aimerais...	I would like...
je me sens...	I feel...
je ne sais pas	I don't know
je voudrais...	I would like...
merci (beaucoup)	thank you (very much)
pardon	excuse me (informal)
pas mal	not bad
Puis-je... ?	May I.... ?

Puis-je te présenter... ?	May I introduce... ? (informal)
Puis-je vous présenter... ?	May I introduce...? (formal)
quel dommage	what a shame
salut	hi
Santé !	Cheers!
s'il te plaît	please (informal)
s'il vous plaît	please (formal)
Super !	Great!
voici...	this is... / here is...

Opinions (p.8-10)

à mon avis	in my opinion
absolument	absolutely
adorer	to love
agaçant(e)	annoying
aimer	to like / to love
aimer bien	to like
affreux / affreuse	awful
agréable	pleasant
amical(e)	friendly
amusant(e)	funny
l'avantage (m)	advantage
barbant(e)	boring
bien entendu	of course
bien sûr	of course, certainly
bon(ne)	good
ça dépend	it depends
ça m'énerve	it gets on my nerves
ça me fait rire	it makes me laugh
ça me fait pleurer	it makes me cry
ça me plaît	I like it
ça m'est égal	I don't care
ça ne me dit rien	it means nothing to me / I don't fancy that / I don't feel like it
ça suffit	that's enough
car	because
casse-pieds	annoying
certainement	certainly
cher / chère	expensive
chouette	great
compliqué(e)	complicated
content(e)	happy
croire	to believe
désagréable	unpleasant
désirer	to want
détester	to hate
dire	to say / to tell
doué(e)	gifted / talented
drôle	funny
embêtant(e)	annoying
en général	in general
enchanté(e)	delighted
ennuyeux / ennuyeuse	boring
espérer	to hope
Es-tu d'accord ?	Do you agree?
étonné(e)	astonished / amazed
facile	easy
faible	weak

fantastique	fantastic
formidable	great
franchement	frankly
généralement	generally
génial(e)	brilliant
grâce à	thanks to
grave	serious
habile	clever
l'inconvénient (m)	disadvantage
intéressant(e)	interesting
s'intéresser à	to be interested in
inutile	useless
incroyable	incredible
inquiet / inquiète	worried
marrant(e)	funny
en avoir marre (de)	to be fed up (with)
mauvais(e)	bad
merveilleux / merveilleuse	marvellous
mignon / mignonne	cute
moche	ugly
(moi) non plus	(me) neither
nouveau / nouvelle	new
nul / nulle	rubbish
par contre	on the other hand
parfait(e)	perfect
passionnant(e)	exciting
la peine	the bother
penser	to think
personnellement	personally
peut-être	perhaps
pourtant	however
pratique	practical
préférer	to prefer
promettre	to promise
Quel est ton avis sur... ?	What is your opinion of...?
ridicule	ridiculous
rigolo / rigolote	funny
sage	well-behaved
selon moi...	in my opinion...
sembler	to seem
sensass	sensational
super	great
supporter	to put up with
sympa / sympathique	nice (person)
utile	useful
vouloir	to wish / to want
vraiment	really / truly

Correctness

avoir raison	to be right
avoir tort	to be wrong
corriger	to correct
l'erreur (f)	error / mistake
la faute	fault / mistake
il (me) faut	you (I) must
juste	correct
obligatoire	compulsory
sûr(e)	certain / sure
se tromper	to make a mistake

Vocabulary

Abbreviations

le CES (collège d'enseignement secondaire)	secondary school
l'HLM (habitation à loyer modéré) (f)	council / social housing
le SDF (sans domicile fixe)	homeless person
le TGV (train à grande vitesse)	high-speed train
le VTT (vélo tout terrain)	mountain bike

Dialogues and Messages

à l'appareil	speaking / on the line
à l'attention de	for the attention of
appelle-moi / appelez-moi	call me (formal / informal)
le bip sonore	tone
le combiné	receiver (telephone)
composer le numéro	dial the number
envoi de	sent by
le faux numéro	wrong number
l'indicatif (m)	area code
un instant	one moment
je reviens tout de suite	I'll be right back
je vous écoute	I'm listening
je vous le / la passe	I will put you through
le mail / le courriel	email
la messagerie vocale	voicemail
ne quittez pas	stay on the line
patientez	wait
suite à	further to / following

Section 2 — About Me

You and Your Family (p.11-12)

adopté(e)	adopted
aîné(e)	elder
l'anniversaire (m)	birthday
s'appeler	to be called
avoir...ans	to be...years old
le beau-frère	brother-in-law
le beau-père	step-father
le bébé	baby
la belle-mère	step-mother
la belle-sœur	sister-in-law
le cousin / la cousine	cousin
le demi-frère	half-brother / step-brother
la demi-sœur	half-sister / step-sister
divorcé(e)	divorced
d'origine...	of... origin
la famille proche	close relatives
la famille élargie	extended family
la fille	daughter / girl
le fils	son
le fils / la fille unique	only child
le frère	brother
la grand-mère	grandmother
le grand-père	grandfather
les grands-parents (m)	grandparents
le jumeau / la jumelle	twin
la maison de retraite	old people's home
la maman	mum
la mamie / mémé	grandma / granny
la mère	mother
mort(e)	dead
mourir	to die
la naissance	birth
naître	to be born
né(e) le...	born on the...
le neveu	nephew
la nièce	niece
le nom	surname
nous sommes...	there are... of us
l'oncle (m)	uncle
le papa	dad
le papy / pépé	grandad
le parent / la parente	relative
le / la partenaire	partner
le père	father
le / la petit(e) ami(e)	boyfriend / girlfriend
la petite-fille	granddaughter
le petit-fils	grandson
plus âgé(e)	older
plus jeune	younger
le prénom	first name
la sœur	sister
la tante	aunt

Describing People (p.13-14)

aimable	kind
l'apparence (f)	appearance
autoritaire	bossy
avoir l'air	to look (e.g. angry)
la barbe	beard
bavard(e)	chatty / talkative
beau / bel / belle	handsome / beautiful
bête	stupid / silly
les bijoux (m)	jewellery
blond(e)	blonde
bouclé(e)	curly
le bouton	spot / pimple
brun(e)	brown
le caractère	personality
les cheveux (m)	hair
la cicatrice	scar
clair(e)	light
compréhensif / compréhensive	understanding
court(e)	short (hair)
de mauvaise humeur	bad-tempered
de taille moyenne	of medium height
égoïste	selfish
équilibré(e)	well-balanced
l'esprit (m)	mind
étonnant(e)	amazing
étrange	strange
fâché(e)	angry
fiable	reliable
fier / fière	proud
foncé(e)	dark
fou / fol / folle	mad, crazy
frisé(e)	curly
gêner	to annoy
généreux / généreuse	generous
gentil / gentille	kind, nice
le grain de beauté	mole (on skin)
grand(e)	tall
gros / grosse	fat
heureux / heureuse	happy
honnête	honest
insupportable	unbearable
jaloux / jalouse	jealous
jeune	young
la jeunesse	youth
joli(e)	pretty
laid(e)	ugly
long / longue	long
les lunettes (f)	glasses
méchant(e)	naughty
mi-long / mi-longue	medium length
mince	slim
ondulé(e)	wavy
paresseux / paresseuse	lazy
pénible	annoying
la personnalité	personality
petit(e)	short
raide	straight
roux / rousse	ginger
le sens de l'humour	sense of humour
sensible	sensitive
sportif / sportive	sporty
sûr(e) de soi	self-confident
sympa	kind / nice
têtu(e)	stubborn
timide	shy
tranquille	quiet / calm
travailleur / travailleuse	hard-working
triste	sad
vaniteux / vaniteuse	conceited
vieux / vieil / vieille	old
vif / vive	lively
les vrais jumeaux (m) / les vraies jumelles (f)	identical twins
les yeux (m)	eyes

Pets (p.15)

affectueux / affectueuse	affectionate
allergique à	allergic to
le chat	cat
le cheval	horse
le chien	dog
le cochon d'Inde	guinea pig
effronté(e)	cheeky
fidèle	loyal / faithful
le hamster	hamster
le lapin	rabbit
mignon(ne)	cute
l'oiseau (m)	bird
le poil	animal hair
le poisson rouge	goldfish
le poisson tropical	tropical fish
le serpent	snake
la tortue	tortoise

Style and Fashion (p.16)

la bague	ring
les boucles d'oreille (f)	earrings
la casquette	cap
le collier	necklace
le collant	tights
la confiance en soi	self-confidence
le costume	suit
en coton	made of cotton
en cuir	made of leather
d'occasion	second-hand

se faire coiffer	to have one's hair done
se faire couper les cheveux	to have one's hair cut
habillé / vêtu de	dressed in
en laine	made of wool
large	loose
le maquillage	make-up
se maquiller	to put on make-up
la mode	fashion
le parfum	perfume
à points	spotted
porter	to wear
rayé(e)	striped
le rouge à lèvres	lipstick
serré(e)	tight
le tatouage	tattoo
teint	dyed (hair)
en velours	made of velvet

Relationships (p.17-19)

l'amitié (f)	friendship
l'amour (m)	love
casse-pieds	a pain in the neck
célibataire	single
la confiance	trust
connaître	to know (a person)
le copain / la copine	friend / mate
se disputer	to argue
ensemble	together
s'entendre (avec)	to get on (with)
épouser	to marry
être fâché(e)	to be angry

se faire des amis	to make friends
la femme	wife / woman
la fête familiale	family celebration
les fiançailles (f)	engagement
gâter	to spoil
gâté(e)	spoilt
injuste	unfair
joyeux / joyeuse	happy
le mari	husband
le mariage	marriage
se marier	to get married / to marry
le / la meilleur(e) ami(e)	best friend
mépriser	to despise
se mettre en colère	to get angry
le modèle	role model
les noces (f)	wedding
partager	to share
le / la partenaire	partner
participer à	to take part in
passer du temps avec	to spend time with
le petit ami	boyfriend
la petite amie	girlfriend
les rapports (m)	relationships
le sentiment	feeling
séparé(e)	separated
se rendre compte	to realise
sortir	to go out
soutenir	to support
le surnom	nickname
traîner avec	to hang out with

Section 3 — Daily Life

Everyday Life (p.20)

aider	to help
l'argent (m) de poche	pocket money
le bricolage	DIY (do it yourself)
se brosser les dents	to brush your teeth
se coucher	to go to bed
les courses (f)	shopping
cuisiner	to cook
devoir	to have to
se doucher	to shower
faire le lit	to make the bed
la fleur	flower
garder	to look after
s'habiller	to get dressed
le jardinage	gardening
laver	to wash
se laver	to wash (yourself)
la lessive	laundry
se lever	to get up
mettre la table	to lay the table
nettoyer	to clean
passer l'aspirateur	to vacuum

la pelouse	lawn
prendre le petit-déjeuner	to eat breakfast
propre	clean, tidy
ranger	to tidy
la tâche	task
la vaisselle	washing-up

Food (p.21)

avoir faim	to be hungry
avoir soif	to be thirsty
l'agneau (m)	lamb
l'ail (m)	garlic
allergique à	allergic to
amer / amère	bitter
l'ananas (m)	pineapple
l'artichaut (m)	artichoke
l'assiette (f)	plate / dish
le beurre	butter
le bifteck	steak
le bœuf	beef
les bonbons (m)	sweets
la boulette	meatball
la brochette	kebab
le canard	duck

la cerise	cherry
le champignon	mushroom
les chips (m)	crisps
le chou	cabbage
le chou-fleur	cauliflower
les choux de Bruxelles	brussels sprouts
le citron	lemon
la confiture	jam
la côtelette (de porc / d'agneau)	(pork / lamb) chop
la crêpe	pancake
le croque-monsieur	toasted ham and cheese sandwich
cuisiner	to cook
le déjeuner	lunch
la dinde	turkey
le dîner	evening meal
épicé(e)	spicy
les épinards (m)	spinach
l'espèce (f)	type / kind
essayer	to try
fait(e) maison	homemade
la fraise	strawberry
la framboise	raspberry

le fromage	cheese
le fromage de chèvre	goat's cheese
les frites (f)	chips
les fruits (m)	fruit
les fruits (m) de mer	seafood
fumé	smoked
le gâteau	cake
la glace	ice cream
le goût	taste
goûter	to taste
les haricots (m) verts	green beans
le jambon	ham
le lait	milk
les légumes (m)	vegetables
manger	to eat
les nouilles (f)	noodles
la noix	nut
nourrissant(e)	nourishing
la nourriture	food
l'œuf (m)	egg
l'oignon (m)	onion
le pain	bread
le pamplemousse	grapefruit
les pâtes (f)	pasta
la pêche	fishing / peach
le petit-déjeuner	breakfast
les petits pois (m)	peas
piquant(e)	spicy
le plat cuisiné	ready meal
la poire	pear
les poireaux (m)	leeks
le poisson	fish
le poivre	pepper
le poivron	pepper (vegetable)
la pomme	apple
la pomme de terre	potato
le potage	soup
le poulet	chicken
la prune	plum
les raisins (m)	grapes
le repas	meal
le riz	rice
rôti(e)	roast
salé(e)	salty
la sauce vinaigrette	salad dressing
la saucisse	sausage
le saucisson	cold sliced meat
le saumon	salmon
le sel	salt
le steak haché	burger
le sucre	sugar
sucré(e)	sweet
le thon	tuna
végétalien(ne)	vegan
végétarien(ne)	vegetarian
la viande	meat
la viande hachée	mince
le yaourt	yoghurt

Shopping (p.22-23)

abîmé(e)	damaged
les baskets (f)	trainers
besoin (m) (avoir... de)	need (to need)
la boîte	box / tin / can
le blouson	coat / jacket
bon marché	cheap
les bottes (f)	boots
Ça me va.	It suits me.
la caisse	till
la carte bancaire	bank card
la ceinture	belt
le centre commercial	shopping centre
C'est combien, s'il vous plaît ?	How much is it, please?
le caleçon	leggings
le chapeau	hat
les chaussettes (f)	socks
les chaussures (f)	shoes
la chemise	shirt
cher / chère	expensive
le choix	choice
la chose	thing
les courses (f)	shopping
la cravate	tie
défectueux / défectueuse	faulty
dépenser	to spend (money)
l'écharpe (f)	scarf
endommagé(e)	damaged
en espèces	with cash
en ligne	online
essayer	to try on
l'étiquette (f)	label
faire la queue	to queue
se faire rembourser	to get a refund
le foulard	scarf
les gants (m)	gloves
le gilet	waistcoat
le grand magasin	department store
la grande surface	superstore
gratuit(e)	free (of charge)
l'imperméable (m)	raincoat
le jean	jeans
la jupe	skirt
un kilogramme	a kilogram
le lèche-vitrine (faire du)	window shopping (to go window shopping)
un litre	litre
livrer	to deliver
le magasin	shop
le maillot (de sport)	sports shirt
le manteau	coat
la marque	make / label / brand
la mode	fashion
la moitié	half
le morceau	piece
le pantalon	trousers

un paquet	packet
perdre	to lose
peser	to weigh
le polo	polo shirt
le portefeuille	wallet
le porte-monnaie	purse
la portion	portion
pouvoir	to be able
pratique	convenient
le prix	price
les provisions (f)	food shopping
le pull	jumper
le pull à capuche	hoodie
le pyjama	pyjamas
le quart	quarter
le rayon	department
réduire	to reduce
réduit(e)	reduced
je regarde	I'm browsing
rembourser	to refund
la robe	dress
le sac à main	handbag
les soldes (m)	sale
le survêtement / le jogging	tracksuit
le sweat	sweatshirt
la taille	size
le ticket de caisse	receipt
la tranche	slice
tranché(e)	sliced
le tricot	sweater / jumper
le vendeur / la vendeuse	shop assistant
vendre	to sell
la veste	jacket
les vêtements (m)	clothes
la vitrine	shop window

Technology (p.24-27)

à cause de	because of
l'abonné (m) / l'abonnée (f)	subscriber
acheter	to buy
afficher	to post
au lieu de	instead of
l'avantage (m)	advantage
le bloggeur	blogger
chercher	to look for
le clavier	keyboard
cliquer	to click
le compte	account
la console de jeux	games console
le courrier électronique	email
la cyber-intimidation	cyberbullying
dangereux / dangereuse	dangerous
le désavantage	disadvantage
les détails (m) personnels	personal details
l'écran (m) tactile	touch screen
l'écrivain (m)	author

effacer	to delete
en ligne	online
enregistrer	to record
envoyer	to send
être accro à	to be addicted to
faire attention	to be careful
faire des recherches	to do research
le fichier	file
le forum	chat room
la fraude	fraud
le genre	type / kind
grâce à	thanks to
l'imprimante (f)	printer
imprimer	to print
l'inconvénient (m)	disadvantage / drawback
l'internaute (m)	internet user
Internet (m)	Internet
le jeu	game
le lecteur DVD	DVD player
le lecteur MP3	MP3 player
le logiciel	software
le mail / le courrier électronique	e-mail
mettre	to put
mettre en ligne	to upload
le moniteur	monitor
le mot de passe	password
naviguer (sur)	to browse
numérique	digital
l'ordinateur (m)	computer
l'ordinateur (m) portable	laptop
la page d'accueil	welcome page
la page internet	internet page
partager	to share
passer du temps	to spend time
la pile	battery
le portable	mobile (phone)
pratique	practical
recevoir	to receive
remplir	to fill (in)
le réseau social	social network
rester en contact	to stay in contact
le risque	risk
sauvegarder	to save
le site internet / web	website
les sites sociaux	social media sites
la souris	mouse
surfer sur Internet	to surf the internet
la tablette	tablet
taper	to type
tchatter	to talk online
télécharger	to download
le texto	text message
la toile / le web	web
la touche	key
le traitement de texte	word processing
la vie privée	private life

Section 4 — Free-Time Activities

Celebrations and Festivals (p.28-29)

l'Aïd (f) al-Fitr	Eid al-Fitr
athée	atheist
Bonne année !	Happy New Year!
Bon anniversaire !	Happy birthday!
Bonne chance !	Good luck!
la bougie	candle
la bûche de Noël	yule log
le cadeau	present
le Carême	Lent
célébrer	to celebrate
chanter	to sing
chrétien(ne)	Christian
commercial(e)	commercial
la couronne	crown
la danse	dance
le défilé	procession
la dinde	turkey
l'église (f)	church
l'événement (m)	event
Félicitations !	Congratulations!
la fête	festival / celebration / party
la fête des mères / pères	Mother's / Father's Day
la fête des rois	Epiphany / Twelfth Night
la fête du travail	May Day
la fête nationale	Bastille Day
fêter	to celebrate
les feux (m) d'artifice	fireworks
la fève	charm
la foi	faith
la galette des rois	cake for Epiphany
le gâteau des rois	cake for Epiphany
la Hanouka	Hanukkah

historique	historical
impressionnant(e)	impressive
jouer un tour	to play a trick
le Jour de l'An	New Year's Day
le jour férié	bank holiday
Joyeux Noël !	Merry Christmas!
juif / juive	Jewish
le lundi de Pâques	Easter Monday
la messe	mass
la mosquée	mosque
musulman(e)	Muslim
l'oie (f)	goose
le pain calendal	Christmas loaf
Pâques	Easter
la Pentecôte	Whitsuntide
la plaisanterie	joke
le poisson d'avril	April Fools' Day
Poisson d'avril !	April Fool!
prier	to pray
le ramadan	Ramadan
la reine	queen
religieux / religieuse	religious
la réunion	meeting
le réveillon	meal eaten after midnight in France
le roi	king
la Saint Valentin	Valentine's Day
la Saint-Sylvestre	New Year's Eve
le sapin de Noël	Christmas tree
sentimental(e)	sentimental
la synagogue	synagogue
la Toussaint	All Saints Day
les vacances	holidays
la veille de Noël	Christmas Eve
le vendredi saint	Good Friday

Books and Reading (p.30)

la bande dessinée (BD)	comic book
collectionner	to collect
les connaissances (f)	knowledge
le journal	newspaper
la lecture	reading
la liseuse électronique	e-reader
le livre	book
le livre électronique	e-book
le magazine	magazine
le plaisir	pleasure / amusement
la revue	magazine
le roman	novel
le roman policier	detective story
romantique	romantic

Music, Film and TV (p.31-32)

s'abonner	to subscribe
l'acteur (m) / l'actrice (f)	actor / actress
les actualités (f)	news
l'ado (m / f)	adolescent
apprendre à	to learn to
l'argent (m)	money
la bande-annonce	trailer
la batterie	drums
le billet	ticket
célèbre	famous
la chaîne de télé	TV channel
la chanson	song
chanter	to sing
le chanteur / la chanteuse	singer
la chorale	choir
les clips (m)	music videos
la comédie musicale	musical comedy (a musical)

commencer	to start
le concert	concert
la dance	dance music
débuter	to begin
le dessin animé	cartoon
diffuser	to broadcast
divertissant(e)	entertaining
le documentaire	documentary
écouter de la musique	to listen to music
les effets (m) spéciaux	special effects
l'émission (f)	programme
entraînant(e)	catchy
faire partie de	to take part in
le feuilleton	soap opera
le film d'action / d'aventure	action film
le film d'amour / romantique	romantic film
le film d'animation	animated film
le film comique	comedy film
le film de guerre	war film
le film d'horreur / d'épouvante	horror film
le film policier	detective film
le film de science-fiction	science fiction film
le film / l'histoire (f) de suspense	thriller (film / book)
la flûte	flute
le genre	genre / type / kind
le groupe	band
la guitare	guitar
l'histoire (f)	storyline
les informations (f)	news
s'intéresser à	to be interested in
l'intrigue (f)	plot
le jeu télévisé	game show
jouer (d'un instrument)	to play (an instrument)
le musicien / la musicienne	musician
la musique folk	folk music
la musique pop	pop music
la musique rock	rock music
l'orchestre (m)	orchestra
le personnage	character

la publicité	advert(s)
regarder	to watch
relaxant(e)	relaxing
rencontrer	to meet
répéter	to rehearse / practise
se reposer	to rest
la séance	performance
la série	series
la série historique	period drama
les sous-titres (m)	subtitles
le spectacle	show (e.g. theatre)
le tarif réduit	reduced price
la télé réalité	reality TV
la télévision satellite	satellite TV
le temps libre	free time
la vedette	film star
le violon	violin
voir	see

Sport (p.33)

à l'intérieur	inside
à l'extérieur	outside
les arts martiaux (m)	martial arts
l'athlétisme (m)	athletics
l'aviron (m)	rowing
le badminton	badminton
le basket	basketball
la boxe	boxing
le canoë-kayak	canoeing
captivant(e)	engaging
le centre sportif	sports centre
le cheval	horse
le club des jeunes	youth club
compétitif / compétitive	competitive
courir	to run
la course	race
les échecs (m)	chess
l'entraînement (m)	sports practice
s'entraîner	to train
l'équipe (f)	team
l'équitation (f)	horse riding
l'escalade (f)	rock climbing
l'escrime (f)	fencing
l'événement (m)	event

faire de la gymnastique	to do gymnastics
faire du vélo	to cycle
faire une randonnée	to go on a walk / hike
gagner	to win
fana de	a fan of
le foot / football	football
le hockey	hockey
le jeu de société	board game
le lieu (avoir lieu)	place (to take place)
marquer un but / un essai	to score a goal / a try
se motiver	to motivate oneself
la musculation	body building
nager	to swim
la natation	swimming
le netball	netball
le parapente	paragliding
participer (à)	to take part (in)
le patin à glace	ice skating
la patinoire	ice rink
la pêche	fishing
perdre	to lose
la piscine	swimming pool
la planche à voile	wind-surfing
la plongée sous-marine	scuba diving
pratiquer un sport	to do a sport
la promenade	walk
régulièrement	regularly
le rugby	rugby
le skate	skateboarding
le ski (nautique)	(water) skiing
sportif / sportive	sporty
les sports (m) d'hiver	winter sports
les sports (m) extrêmes	extreme sports
le stade	stadium
le surf	surfing
le tennis	tennis
le terrain de sport	sports field
le tir à l'arc	archery
la tournée	tour
le tournoi	tournament
tricher	to cheat
la voile	sailing
le volley	volleyball

Section 5 — Where You Live

Where You Live (p.34-35)

à la campagne	in the countryside
à la montagne	in the mountains
au bord de la mer	by the sea
au premier / deuxième étage (m)	on the first / second floor
animé	lively
l'appartement (m)	flat
l'arbre (m)	tree
l'armoire (f)	wardrobe
la banlieue	suburb

la banque	bank
le bâtiment	building
la bibliothèque	library
la bijouterie	jeweller's shop
la boucherie	butcher's
la boulangerie	bakery
le bowling	bowling alley
le bruit	noise
bruyant	noisy
le bureau	office / study / desk
calme	quiet

le canapé	sofa
la cave	cellar
célèbre	famous
le centre commercial	shopping centre
le centre-ville	town centre
la chaise	chair
la chambre	bedroom
le champ	field
la charcuterie	delicatessen
le cinéma	cinema

la circulation	traffic
la colline	hill
les commerces (m)	shops
le commissariat	police station
la cuisine	kitchen / cooking
déménager	to move house
démodé	old-fashioned
les distractions (f)	things to do
l'embouteillage (m)	traffic jam
emménager	to move in
l'endroit (m)	place
l'escalier (m)	staircase
l'espace (m) vert	park / green space
l'étage (m)	floor / storey
la fenêtre	window
la ferme	farm
la fermeture	closure
le four	oven
le foyer	home
la gare	railway station
la gare routière	bus station
les gens (m)	people
la grande ville	city
le grenier	loft
l'habitant (m)	inhabitant
l'HLM (f)	council housing
l'hôpital (m)	hospital
l'hôtel (m) de ville	town hall
l'immeuble (m)	block of flats
le lac	lake
la librairie	bookshop
le lit	bed
le loyer	rent
la lumière	light
la mairie	town hall
la maison (individuelle / jumelée / mitoyenne)	house (detached / semi-detached / terraced)
le marché	market
le métro	underground railway
les meubles (m)	furniture
la moquette	carpet
multiculturel/le	multicultural
le mur	wall

le musée	museum
tout(e) neuf / neuve	brand new
le parc	park
la pâtisserie	cake shop
pauvre	poor
la pièce	room
la piste cyclable	cycle path
pittoresque	picturesque
le placard	cupboard
la place	square
le pont	bridge
la poste	post office
le quartier	area
la quincaillerie	ironmonger's / hardware shop
quitter	to leave
le rez-de-chaussée	ground floor
le risque	risk
sale	dirty
la salle à manger	dining room
la salle de bains	bathroom
le salon	living room / lounge
la sécurité	safety
le sous-sol	basement
la station-service	service station
le supermarché	supermarket
surchargé	overcrowded
le tabac	newsagent's
le théâtre	theatre
les transports (m) en commun	public transport
travailler	to work
se trouver	to be situated
l'usine (f)	factory
la vie	life
le village	village
la ville	town
vivre	to live
le voisin / la voisine	neighbour
la zone piétonne	pedestrian zone

Weather (p.36)

agité(e)	turbulent
l'averse (f)	shower
briller	to shine

le brouillard	fog
la brume	mist
la chaleur	heat
chaud(e)	hot
le ciel	sky
clair(e)	bright
le climat	climate
couvert(e)	overcast
doux / douce	mild
l'éclair (m)	lightning
l'éclaircie (f)	bright spell
ensoleillé(e)	sunny
faire beau	to be fine (weather)
faire mauvais	to be bad (weather)
froid(e)	cold
geler	to freeze
grêler	to hail
la glace	ice
humide	humid / wet
la météo	weather report
mouillé(e)	wet
neiger	to snow
le nuage	cloud
nuageux / nuageuse	cloudy
l'ombre (m)	shade, shadow
l'orage (m)	storm
orageux / orageuse	stormy
pleuvoir	to rain
la pluie	rain
les prévisions météo (f)	weather forecast
sec / sèche	dry
le soleil	sun
la température basse	low temperature
la température élevée	high temperature
la température moyenne	average temperature
la tempête	storm
le temps	weather
le tonnerre	thunder
tremper	to soak
variable	changeable
le vent	wind

Section 6 — Travel and Tourism

Where to Go (p.37)

à la montagne	in the mountains
à l'étranger	abroad
l'Afrique (f)	Africa
africain(e)	African
l'Algérie (f)	Algeria
algérien(ne)	Algerian
l'Allemagne (f)	Germany
allemand(e)	German
les Alpes (f)	the Alps
l'Amérique (f) du Sud	South America
américain(e)	American
l'Angleterre (f)	England
anglais(e)	English

l'Asie (f)	Asia
asiatique	Asian
l'Autriche (f)	Austria
autrichien(ne)	Austrian
la Belgique	Belgium
belge	Belgian
la Bourgogne	Burgundy
le Brésil	Brazil
brésilien(ne)	Brazilian
la Bretagne	Brittany
le Canada	Canada
canadien(n)	Canadian
la Chine	China
chinois(e)	Chinese

la Corse	Corsica
la côte	coast
le Danemark	Denmark
danois(e)	Danish
le département	administrative area of France
Douvres	Dover
l'Écosse (f)	Scotland
écossais(e)	Scottish
l'Espagne (f)	Spain
espagnol(e)	Spanish
les États-Unis (m)	United States
l'Europe (f)	Europe
européen(ne)	European

la France	France
français(e)	French
la frontière	border / frontier
la Grande-Bretagne	Great Britain
britannique	British
la Grèce	Greece
grec(que)	Greek
la Guyane	French Guiana
l'île (f)	island
l'Inde (f)	India
indien(ne)	Indian
l'Irlande (f)	Ireland
irlandais(e)	Irish
l'Italie (f)	Italy
italien(ne)	Italian
le Japon	Japan
japonais(e)	Japanese
Londres	London
la Manche	English Channel
le Maroc	Morocco
marocain(e)	Moroccan
la Méditerranée	Mediterranean
la mer	sea
le monde	world
la Normandie	Normandy
Paris	Paris
les Pays-Bas (m)	Netherlands
néerlandais	Dutch
le pays de Galles	Wales
gallois(e)	Welsh
la Picardie	Picardy
la plage	beach
le Royaume-Uni	United Kingdom
la Réunion	Reunion
la Russie	Russia
russe	Russian
le Sénégal	Senegal
la Suisse	Switzerland
suisse	Swiss
la Tunisie	Tunisia
tunisien(ne)	Tunisian
la Turquie	Turkey
turc / turque	Turkish

Preparation (p.38-39)

l'accueil (m)	welcome / reception
l'agence (f) de voyages	travel agency
l'aire (f) de jeux	play area
l'ascenseur (m)	lift
l'auberge (f) de jeunesse	youth hostel
les bagages (m)	luggage
le camping	campsite
le camping-car	campervan
la caravane	caravan
casser	to break
la chambre	room
la chambre d'hôte	bed and breakfast
la chambre de famille	family room

la chambre pour deux personnes	double room
chercher	to look for
la clé	key
la climatisation	air conditioning
la colonie de vacances	holiday / summer camp
la demie-pension	half board
déranger	to disturb
descendre	to go down
donner sur	to overlook
le dortoir	dormitory
dresser	to put up (tent)
durer	to last
l'échange (m)	exchange
l'emplacement (m)	pitch
en plein air	in the open air
expliquer	to explain
héberger	to lodge / accommodate
l'hôtel (m) (de luxe)	(luxury) hotel
inconnu(e)	unknown
jumelé(e)	twinned
le lavabo	wash basin
lever	to lift
le lit	bed
le lit à deux places	double bed
les lits (m) jumeaux	twin beds
les lits (m) superposés	bunk beds
le logement	accommodation
loger	to stay / to lodge
le passeport	passport
la pension complète	full board
la pièce d'identité	ID
les préparatifs (m)	preparations
prêt(e)	ready
le projet	plan
le / la propriétaire	owner
remercier	to thank
réserver	to book / to reserve
rester	to stay
le sac de couchage	sleeping bag
la salle de séjour	lounge
le séjour	stay / visit
la station balnéaire	seaside resort
la tente	tent
les vacances (f)	holidays
la valise	suitcase
la vue de mer	sea view

Getting There (p.40)

l'aéroport (m)	airport
aller-retour (m)	return ticket
aller-simple (m)	single ticket
l'arrivée (f)	arrival
s'asseoir	to sit down
attendre	to wait (for)
atterrir	to land
l'auto (f)	car
l'autobus (m)	bus
l'autoroute (f)	motorway

l'avion (m)	plane
le bateau	boat
le car	coach
la carte	map
le chemin	way / path
le chemin de fer	railway
conduire	to drive
la correspondance	connection
décoller	to take off
le départ	departure
en provenance de	coming from
en retard	late
s'enregistrer	to check in
l'essence (f)	petrol
le gasoil	diesel
l'horaire (m)	timetable
lentement	slowly
la location de voitures	car rental
louer	to rent / to hire
manquer	to miss
se mettre en route	to set off
la moto	motorbike
partir	to leave
le permis de conduire	driving licence
ralentir	to slow down
le retour	return
retourner	to return
revenir	to come back
la route	way / road
le train	train
le trajet	journey
la traversée	crossing
la voiture	car
le vol	flight
voler	to fly
le voyage	journey / trip
voyager	to travel

What To Do (p.41)

l'aventure (f)	adventure
l'avis (m)	opinion
se baigner	to bathe, swim
le bord de la mer	seaside
la carte postale	postcard
la cathédrale	cathedral
le château	castle
le concours	competition
la crème solaire	sun cream
la culture	culture
se débrouiller	to get by
les distractions (f)	entertainment / things to do
l'événement (m)	event
l'étranger (m) / l'étrangère (f)	stranger / foreigner
explorer	to explore
l'exposition	exhibition
se faire bronzer	to sunbathe
faire du camping	to go camping
faire la connaissance	to get to know

Vocabulary

faire la grasse matinée	to lie in / sleep in	le café	coffee	le porte-monnaie	purse
la foire	fair	la carte	menu	le quai	platform
se garer	to park	le chocolat chaud	hot chocolate	remplacer	to replace
s'habituer à	to get used to	choisir	to choose	réparer	to repair
l'herbe (f)	grass	commander	to order	le retard	delay
le lac	lake	coûter	to cost	le service client	customer services
laver	to wash	le couvert	place setting	tomber en panne	to break down
le loisir	free time (activity)	les cuisses (f) de grenouille	frogs' legs	le vol	robbery / theft
louer	to hire	le dessert	dessert	voler	to steal
les lunettes (f) de soleil	sunglasses	l'eau (f) minérale	mineral water		

Directions (p.44)

le maillot de bain	swimming costume	l'eau (f) plate / gazeuse	still / fizzy water	à droite	on / to the right
marcher	to walk			à gauche	on / to the left
la montagne	mountain	emporter	to take away	le carrefour	crossroads
monter	to go up / ascend	l'escargot (m)	snail	C'est loin d'ici ?	Is it far from here?
le musée	museum	fermé(e)	closed	de chaque côté	on each side
nager	to swim	le hors d'œuvre	starter	de l'autre côté	on the other side
la nature	nature	le menu à prix fixe	fixed price menu	en bas	down(stairs)
l'office (m) de tourisme	tourist office	payer	to pay (for)	en face de	opposite
		prendre	to take	en haut	up(stairs)
paraître	to seem	se plaindre	to complain	environ	about
le parc d'attractions	theme park	le plat principal	main meal / dish	l'est (m)	east
la plage	beach	le pourboire	tip	les feux (m) (de signalisation)	(traffic) lights
plaire	to please	la pression	beer (from the pump)		
le plan de ville	town plan			la grande rue	high street / main street
se présenter	to introduce oneself	le restaurant	restaurant		
se promener	to go for a walk	le serveur / la serveuse	waiter / waitress	ici	here
la randonnée	walk / hike			juste à côté de	right next to
remarquer	to notice	la tasse	cup	jusqu'à	until / as far as
le rendez-vous	meeting	le thé	tea	là	there
les renseignements (m)	information	un verre de...	a glass of	là-bas	over there
		le vin	wine	loin de	far from
se réveiller	to wake up			le nord	north

Practical Stuff (p.43)

la rivière	river			nulle part	nowhere
le sable	sand	le bureau des objets trouvés	lost property office	Où est...?	Where is...?
la salle de jeux	games room			l'ouest (m)	west
le site touristique	tourist attraction	cassé(e)	broken	le panneau	sign
le sommet	summit	le commissariat	police station	par	by
le spectacle	show	composter	to validate (ticket)	partout	everywhere
le tour	tour	le contrôleur / la contrôleuse	ticket inspector	le péage	toll
le tour en bateau	boat tour			la place	square
le tourisme	tourism	défense de / interdit de	(it is) forbidden to...	le pont	bridge
tourner	to turn			pour aller à... ?	how do I get to...?
traduire	to translate	l'endommagement (m)	damage	près de	near to
la visite guidée	guided tour			quelque part	somewhere
le zoo	zoo	la facture	bill (invoice)	le rond-point	roundabout
		les freins (m)	brakes	la rue	street

Eating Out (p.42)

		garantir	to guarantee	situé(e)	situated
l'addition (f)	the bill	laisser	to leave (behind)	le sud	south
l'auberge (f)	inn (traditional)	la livraison	delivery	tout droit	straight ahead
bien cuit(e)	well cooked	le mode d'emploi	instructions for use	tout près	very near
la bière	beer	la perte	loss	toutes directions	all directions
boire	to drink	se plaindre	to complain	traverser	to cross
la boisson	drink	la plainte	complaint	le trottoir	pavement
		le pneu crevé	flat tyre	se trouver	to be situated
		le portefeuille	wallet		

Section 7 — Current and Future Study and Employment

School Subjects (p.45)

l'allemand (m)	German	l'art (m) dramatique	drama	la chimie	chemistry
apprendre	to learn	les arts (m) ménagers	food technology	la couture	sewing
				le dessin	art

Vocabulary

l'espagnol (m)	Spanish	l'école (f) secondaire	secondary school	la retenue	detention
l'EPS (éducation physique et sportive) (f)	PE (physical education)	l'élève (m / f)	pupil	réussir un examen	to pass an exam
		l'emploi (m) du temps	timetable	la salle de classe	classroom
l'étude (f) des médias	media studies	en retard	late	savoir	to know
		en seconde	in year 11	scolaire	school (adj)
le français	French	enseigner	to teach	sécher les cours	to skip lessons
l'histoire-géo (f)	humanities	les études (f)	study	la semaine	week
il ne sert à rien	it's useless	l'étudiant (m)	student	le succès / la réussite	success
l'informatique (f)	ICT	l'examen (m)	examination		
l'instruction (f) civique	personal and social education (PSE)	l'expérience (f)	experiment	le tableau	board
		faire attention	to pay attention	le terrain de sport	sports ground
s'intéresser à	to be interested in	fatigant(e)	tiring	le trimestre	term
la langue	language	les grandes vacances (f)	summer holidays	l'uniforme (m) scolaire	school uniform
les langues vivantes (f)	modern languages	le groupe théâtral	drama group	les vestiaires (m)	changing rooms
le latin	Latin	le gymnase	sports hall		
la littérature anglaise	English literature	l'heure du déjeuner	lunch break	**School Events (p.49)**	
		les incivilités (f)	rudeness	à l'étranger	abroad
la matière (obligatoire)	(compulsory) subject	l'injure (f)	insult	un(e) correspondante	penfriend / pen pal
la physique	physics	l'instituteur (m) / l'institutrice (f)	primary school teacher	l'échange (m) (scolaire)	(school) exchange
préféré(e)	favourite	interdit(e)	forbidden	l'excursion (f) scolaire	school trip
la religion	religious studies	l'internat / le pensionnat (m)	boarding school	le groupe scolaire	school group / party
les sciences (f) naturelles	biology	une journée typique	a typical day	participer à	to take part
la technologie	DT (design technology)	le laboratoire	laboratory	la remise des prix	prize giving
		le laboratoire de langues	language lab	la rencontre parents-professeurs	parents' evening
School Life (p.46-48)		la leçon	lesson	la réunion	meeting
aller à pied	to go on foot	la lecture	reading		
l'ambiance (f)	atmosphere	lire	to read	**Education Post-16 (p.50)**	
bien équipé(e)	well equipped	le lycée	sixth form college	l'année (f) sabbatique	gap year
le bulletin scolaire	school report	mal équipé(e)	badly equipped	l'apprenti(e) (m / f)	apprentice
la calculette	calculator	le maquillage	make up	l'apprentissage (m)	apprenticeship
la cantine	canteen	la maternelle	nursery school	l'avenir (m)	future
le car de ramassage	school bus	le niveau	achievement, performance	avoir envie de	to want to
la chorale	choir	la note	mark / grade	avoir l'intention de	to intend to
le collège	secondary school	oublier	to forget	le bac(calauréat)	A-levels
comprendre	to understand	passer (en classe supérieure)	to move up (to the next form / year)	le but	aim / goal
le contrôle	class test / assessment			le conseiller / la conseillère d'orientation	careers adviser
le couloir	corridor	passer un examen	to sit an exam		
le cours	lesson	la pause	break / pause	le diplôme	qualification
de bonne heure	early	penser	to think	le droit	law (study of)
demander	to ask	permettre	to allow / permit	en première	in year 12
les devoirs (m)	homework	la piscine	swimming pool	en terminale	in year 13
la difficulté	difficulty	porter	to wear / carry	l'enseignement (m) postscolaire	further education
le diplôme	qualification	la pression	pressure		
le directeur	headmaster	le / la professeur	teacher	l'épreuve (f)	test
la directrice	headmistress	le progrès	progress	l'établissement (m)	establishment
distribuer	to give out	le proviseur	head teacher	étudier	to study
doué(e)	gifted / talented	la récré(ation)	break	la faculté	university / faculty
le droit	right	la rédaction	essay	former	to train
échouer	to do badly / fail	redoubler	to repeat a year	laisser tomber	to drop
l'école (f) confessionnelle	religious school	la règle	rule	la liberté	freedom
		le règlement	school rules	la licence	degree
l'école maternelle	nursery school	la rentrée	return to school (after the holidays)	le lycée	sixth form college / grammar school
l'école (f) primaire	primary school				
l'école (f) privée	private school	répéter	to repeat	le lycée professionnel	technical college
l'école (f) publique	state school	la réponse	reply		
		le résultat	result	la médecine	medicine (study of)

les projets pour l'avenir	future plans
le travail bénévole	voluntary work
l'université (f)	university

Career Choices (p.51)

à peine	scarcely
à temps partiel	part-time
à temps plein	full-time
l'agent de police (m)	police officer
l'architecte (m / f)	architect
l'artiste (m / f)	artist
assis(e)	sitting
l'avenir (m)	future
l'avocat(e) (m / f)	lawyer
le babysitting	babysitting
bien payé	well paid
le boulot	job (informal)
le candidat	candidate
le coiffeur / la coiffeuse	hairdresser
le commerce	business
le / la comptable	accountant
compter (sur)	to count (on)
le cuisinier / la cuisinière	cook
le débouché	job opportunity / prospect
debout	standing
le / la dentiste	dentist
le dessinateur / la dessinatrice de mode	fashion designer
disponible	available
élargir	to widen
l'électricien(ne) (m / f)	electrician
l'emploi (m)	job (formal)
l'employé(e) (m / f)	employee
l'employeur (m) / l'employeuse (f)	employer
enrichissant(e)	enriching / rewarding
l'entreprise (f)	firm / enterprise
l'entretien (m)	interview
espérer	to hope
le facteur / la factrice	postman / postwoman

le fermier / la fermière	farmer
le / la fonctionnaire	civil servant
gagner	to earn / win
l'hôtesse (f) de l'air	air hostess
l'idée (f)	idea
l'infirmier (m) / l'infirmière (f)	nurse
l'informaticien(ne) (m / f)	computer scientist
l'ingénieur (m / f)	engineer
l'instituteur (m) / l'institutrice (f)	primary school teacher
l'interprète (m / f)	interpreter
le journal	newspaper
le / la journaliste	journalist
la livre (sterling)	pound (sterling)
le maçon	builder
mal payé	badly paid
le mécanicien / la mécanicienne	mechanic
le médecin	doctor
mettre de l'argent de côté	to save money
le monde du travail	the world of work
le musicien / la musicienne	musician
l'outil (m)	tool
le patron / la patronne	boss
le petit job	part-time job
le pharmacien / la pharmacienne	pharmacist
le plombier	plumber
le policier / la policière	police officer
le / la professeur	teacher
le programmeur	programmer
la retraite	retirement
le rêve	dream
rêver	to dream
le salaire	salary
le steward de l'air	air steward
le traducteur / la traductrice	translator
le travailleur social / la travailleuse sociale	social worker

varié(e)	varied
le vendeur / la vendeuse	shop assistant
venir de	to have just
le / la vétérinaire	vet

Languages for the Future (p.52)

l'assistant(e) (m / f) de langue	language assistant
communiquer	to communicate
discuter	to talk / to discuss
s'exprimer	to express oneself
les langues (f) étrangères	foreign languages
obtenir un métier	to get a job
parcourir le monde	to travel the world
parler couramment	to speak fluently
les possibilités (f) d'avancement	promotion prospects
rencontrer quelqu'un	to meet someone
la société multiculturelle	multicultural society

Applying for Jobs (p.53)

l'annonce (f) de recrutement	job advertisement
bénévolement	voluntarily / without pay
les compétences (f)	skills
les conditions (f) d'emploi	terms of employment
les diplômes requis	the required qualifications
faire un stage	to do work experience
joindre	to attach / enclose
le jour de congé	(a) day's leave
la lettre de motivation	application letter
l'offre (f) d'emploi	job offer
poser sa candidature	to apply for a job
le poste	position
postuler	to apply
les possibilités (f) d'avancement	promotion prospects
qualifié	qualified
remplir un formulaire	to fill in a form

Section 8 — Global Issues

The Environment (p.54-56)

allumer	to switch on
améliorer	to improve
les animaux (m)	animals
augmenter	to increase
le bain	bath
la boîte (en carton)	(cardboard) box
le boîte (en aluminium)	(aluminium) can
la campagne	campaign

la catastrophe naturelle	natural disaster
le centre de recyclage	recycling centre
le charbon	coal
le chauffage central	central heating
climatique	climate (adjective)
le commerce équitable	fair trade
contaminer	to contaminate

la couche d'ozone	ozone layer
cultiver	to grow
le déboisement	deforestation
les déchets (m)	rubbish
décomposer	to decompose
le désastre	disaster
détruire	to destroy
disparaître	to disappear
la douche	shower
l'eau (f) douce	fresh water

l'eau (f) potable	drinking water	la poubelle	dustbin
économiser	to save	les produits (m) bio	green products
écologique	environmentally friendly	protéger	to protect
l'effet (m) de serre	greenhouse effect	ramasser	to pick up
effrayant(e)	frightening	le réchauffement de la Terre	global warming
l'électricité (f)	electricity	recyclable	recyclable
l'emballage (m)	packaging	le recyclage	recycling
empêcher	to prevent	les ressources (f) naturelles	natural resources
en danger	in danger	le risque sanitaire	health hazard
endommager	to damage	le robinet	tap
l'énergie (f) éolienne	wind power	le sac en plastique	plastic bag
les énergies (f) fossiles	fossil fuels	sauver	to save
l'énergie (f) renouvelable	renewable energy	sauvegarder	to keep safe
		la sécheresse	drought
l'énergie (f) solaire	solar power	le souci	worry / concern
l'ennui (m)	problem, worry	survivre	to survive
l'environnement (m)	environment	la terre	earth
l'éolienne (f)	wind turbine	le tremblement de terre	earthquake
l'espace (m) vert	green area	trier	to sort
l'espèce (f)	species	le trou	hole
l'état (m)	state	utiliser	to use
être vert(e)	to be green	la vague	wave
faire du compost	to make compost	le verre	glass
faire du recyclage	to recycle	le volcan	volcano
la famine	famine		
gaspiller	to waste	**Problems in Society (p.57)**	
le gaz carbonique	carbon dioxide	affamé(e)	starving
le gaz d'échappement	exhaust fumes	agresser	to attack
		améliorer	to improve
les habitats (m)	habitats	l'attaque (f)	attack
l'incendie (m)	fire	avoir besoin de	to need
l'inondation (f)	flood	la bande	gang
inonder	to flood	battu(e)	hit
s'inquiéter	to worry	les biens	possessions
instantané(e)	instant	blessé(e)	injured
jeter	to throw (away)	la bonne action	good deed
s'inquiéter	to worry	le chômage	unemployment
le manque (de)	lack (of)	combattre	to combat
la marée	tide	coupable	guilty
les matières (f) premières	raw materials	un défi	a challenge
		déprimé(e)	depressed
menacé(e)	threatened	la dette	debt
menacer	to threaten	la discrimination	discrimination
mener à	to lead to	les droits (m) de l'homme	human rights
le monde	world		
mondial(e)	worldwide	égal(e)	equal
le niveau	level	l'égalité (f)	equality
les ordures (f)	rubbish	l'émeute (f)	riot
l'organisation (f) charitable	charity	l'enquête (f)	enquiry
		entouré(e)	surrounded
l'ouragan (m)	hurricane	éradiquer	to eradicate
le papier	paper	l'espionnage (m)	spying
le paysage	countryside / landscape	la faim	hunger
		gratifiant(e)	rewarding
le pétrole	oil	la guerre	war
la planète	planet	le harcèlement	bullying / harassment
pollué(e)	polluted		
polluer	to pollute	Il vaut la peine.	It's worthwhile.
la pollution	pollution	l'immigration (f)	immigration
potable	drinkable	l'immigré (m)	immigrant

l'inégalité (f) sociale	social inequality
lourd(e)	heavy / serious
lutter	to struggle
malheureux / malheureuse	unfortunate / needy
mal nourri(e)	malnourished
la manifestation	demonstration
mener une campagne	to lead a campaign
mentir	to lie
se moquer de	to make fun of
les morts (f)	deaths / fatalities
mourir	to die
la paix	peace
les pauvres	the poor
la pauvreté	poverty
les personnes (f) défavorisées	disadvantaged people
se plaindre	to complain
le / la politicien(ne)	politician
prioritiser	to prioritise
produire	to provide / to produce
le racisme	racism
reconnaissant(e)	grateful
le réfugié	refugee
le / la sans-abri	homeless person
les SDF	homeless people
la sécurité	security
socialement exclu(e)	socially excluded
supporter	to tolerate / put up with
supprimer	to suppress / eliminate
le témoin	witness
le travail bénévole / volontaire	voluntary work
le troisième âge	old age
tuer	to kill
la victime	victim
vivre	to live
voler	to steal
le voyou	yob / hooligan
vulnérable	vulnerable

Global Events (p.58)

l'aide (f) financière	funding
assister à	to attend
bénéficier	to benefit
la bonne cause	good cause
collecter des fonds	to raise money
la coupe du monde	world cup
l'événement (m)	event
le festival (de musique)	(music) festival
les Jeux (m) olympiques	Olympic Games
la rencontre sportive	sports event
rester en contact	to stay in touch

Answers

The answers to the translation questions are sample answers only, just to give you an idea of one way to translate them. There may be different ways to translate these passages that are also correct.

Section 1 — General Stuff

Page 1 — Numbers
1) Il a trois sœurs. (Il n'a pas de frère.)
2) la première maison de la rue Phillipe
3) C'est la troisième rue après le parc.
4) une vingtaine

Page 3 — Times and Dates
1 a) 6.45 am   c) Tuesdays and Thursdays
  b) 8.30 am   d) 1996

Page 9 — Opinions
1) Maurice le Pain is not very funny.
2) He is really talented.
3) They are always great.
4) Because he is handsome.
5) He is great.

Page 10 — Putting it All Together
1(i) a) son équipe   c) regarder des films
   b) sport
(ii) a) ennuyeux   c) agaçantes
   b) lire

Section 2 — About Me

Page 12 — My Family
In my family, there are three people — my mother, my father and me. Unfortunately, I don't have any brothers or sisters / I have neither brothers nor sisters, so I'm an only child. On the other hand, I have lots of cousins and I see them often. Last weekend, for example, we went to the cinema together and we really enjoyed ourselves.

Page 13 — Describing People
1 i) A and D   ii) C and D

Page 15 — Pets
1 a) He walks his dog for him every week.
  b) Duc is a very young dog.
  c) They are cute. **or** They are affectionate.
  d) cats and dogs

Page 16 — Style and Fashion
1) Sylvie 2) Jérôme 3) Jérôme 4) Pauline

Page 19 — Partnership
1) C   2) B

Section 3 — Daily Life

Page 20 — Everyday Life
I get ten euros of pocket money per / a week. But I have to work to earn this money. I do household chores every day to help my parents. In addition, last Saturday I babysat. I buy lots of music online, but I'm going to try to save up because I would like to go on holiday with my friends.

Page 21 — Food
1 a) B   b) A   c) A   d) B

Page 23 — Shopping
1 a) You can't ask an assistant for advice.
  b) You don't have to queue. **or** You save time.
    or The supermarkets deliver your shopping.
  c) if the clothes will be the right size

Page 25 — Technology
J'ai reçu / eu un nouveau portable pour mon anniversaire. Ma mère me l'a acheté. C'est très utile parce que je peux contacter mes parents et mes amis quand je veux. Je peux aussi télécharger de la musique et des jeux d'Internet. Demain, je l'utiliserai pour acheter un livre en ligne.

Page 26 — Social Media
1) Elle tchatte avec ses amis.
2) Ils sont indispensables.
3) Elle regarde ses photos.

Section 4 — Free-Time Activities

Page 29 — Celebrations and Festivals
1 a) A   b) B   c) B

Page 31 — Music
1(i) a) le violon   b) son professeur
 (ii) a) en groupe   b) répéter

Page 32 — Film and TV
Mon ami(e) et moi sommes allé(e)s au cinéma le week-end dernier. Nous avons regardé un film d'horreur. Je n'avais pas peur, mais mon ami(e) a crié pendant le film. J'aime aller au cinéma. C'est toujours divertissant. Le mois prochain, j'irai voir le nouveau film d'action.

Page 33 — Sport
B, E, F

Section 5 — Where You Live

Page 34 — Talking About Where You Live
1) by the second year
2) one for men and one for women
3) He gave them a job and bread.
4) unemployment and poverty

Page 36 — Weather
1) true   2) true   3) false

Section 6 — Travel and Tourism

Page 37 — Where to Go
1) Elle veut aller en Angleterre. Elle veut voir un match de football.
2) Elle veut passer les vacances au bord de la mer. Elle veut aller chaque jour à la plage.
3) Il veut rester en France. Il veut faire du camping.

Page 38 — Accommodation
1) It seemed as though he hadn't left England.
2) on the ground floor
3) Two from: dried meat / oyster soup / biscuits / cheese
4) Two from: They didn't have to pay for the food. / The restaurant was comfortable. / They were served a lot of food.

Page 40 — How to Get There
Next week, I'm going to go on holiday to the United States. In particular, I would like to see New York. I've reserved / booked a luxury hotel there with a big swimming pool. However, the journey worries me a lot. I'm scared of flying, and I will be on the plane for seven hours.

112

Page 44 — Giving and Asking for Directions
1 a) C   b) A   c) A   d) B

Section 7 — Current and Future Study and Employment

Page 46 — School Routine
1 a) son frère   b) le mardi   c) libres

Page 47 — School Life
1) Vusi   2) Karine   3) Alain

Page 49 — School Events
1) (i) D   (ii) A

Page 50 — Education Post-16
Pour célébrer la fin des examens, j'ai regardé des films avec mes amis. Nous sommes très heureux / heureuses parce que c'est les vacances. En septembre prochain, j'irai au lycée pour faire le bac(calauréat) et j'aimerais / je voudrais obtenir de bons résultats. Cependant, mon / ma meilleur(e) ami(e) veut / a envie de faire un apprentissage.

Page 51 — Career Choices and Ambitions
When I was younger, I wanted to be a baker because I loved to make cakes. Today, I'm still interested in cooking, and I would like to be a chef when I leave school. I have a part-time job in a restaurant kitchen. I don't earn a lot of money, but I hope that the experience will be useful in the future.

Page 52 — Languages for the Future
1) Because she would travel the world.
2) Because if she marries someone from abroad, she will be able to speak to them in their native language.
3) the culture of a country

Section 8 — Global Issues

Page 55 — Environmental Problems
Samit pense que nous devons / qu'il faut protéger la planète. Il croit que le réchauffement de la Terre a causé des problèmes graves, comme des sécheresses et des ouragans. À son avis, les gens gaspillent trop de ressources naturelles. Il pense que, dans le futur / à l'avenir, nous devrons utiliser l'énergie renouvelable au lieu du charbon et du pétrole.

Page 57 — Problems in Society
There are lots of social problems in my area / region, such as unemployment. Also, there are people who live on the street. Yesterday I saw some homeless people and they were malnourished. In my opinion, we must do something to help these people. We must combat inequality.

Page 58 — Global Events
Pour son anniversaire, j'ai donné à mon père deux billets pour un match de la coupe du monde de rugby. Nous allons aller au match ensemble. Nous aimons regarder le sport. En 2012, nous sommes allés aux Jeux olympiques et c'était incroyable / magnifique. Il y avait une ambiance agréable avec des gens de beaucoup de pays différents.

Section 9 — Grammar

Page 59 — Words for People and Objects
1) le cadeau — les cadeaux
2) la piscine — les piscines
3) le citron — les citrons
4) le cheval — les chevaux
5) la voiture — les voitures
6) la pâtisserie — les pâtisseries

Page 60 — 'The', 'A' and 'Some'
1) L'homme a un peu **de** pain.
2) Les étudiants viennent **du** Maroc.
3) Je vais **au** pays de Galles.
4) Nous avons **des** bananes.
5) Ils n'ont pas **de** raisins.
6) Il va **à la** bibliothèque.

Page 61 — Words to Describe Things
1) La mère fière.
2) Une fille triste.
3) Le chat lent.
4) Une maison bleue.
5) Les chiens vifs.
6) Les voitures blanches.
7) Une femme gentille.
8) Une veste chère.

Page 62 — Words to Describe Things
3 and 6 are correct. The others should be:
1) C'est un jeune chien.
2) Le train long est bleu.
4) Tu as lu un livre ennuyeux.
5) J'ai une nouvelle voiture rouge.

Page 63 — Words to Describe Things
1) **Mon** père n'aime pas **sa** nouvelle voiture.
2) **Tes** amis ne vont pas à **notre** lycée.
3) **Cet** hôtel est grand.
4) **Cette** cuisinière a **quelques** légumes.

Page 64 — Words to Describe Actions
1) tristement
2) négativement
3) sérieusement
4) fièrement
5) absolument
6) lentement
7) mauvais
8) constamment

Page 65 — Words to Describe Actions
1) Je joue au tennis là-bas.
2) Tu chantes tous les jours.
3) Normalement, je vais en ville en bus.
4) Elles vont là-bas.
5) Par conséquent, j'aime mes matières.
6) J'aime ce nouveau professeur maintenant.

Page 66 — Words to Compare Things
1) Navid et Pauline sont les plus forts.
2) Ta / Votre grand-mère est plus vieille que mon grand-père.
3) Ce magasin est le moins cher.
4) Julie est aussi active que Thérèse.
5) Ses idées sont les pires.
6) Le français est le meilleur.

Page 67 — Words to Compare Actions
1) Thomas joue du piano **le mieux**.
2) François va à l'étranger **le plus fréquemment**.
3) Lucie court **plus que** Emmanuel.
4) Je regarde la télévision **le moins souvent**.
5) Tu ris **autant que** moi.
6) Je chante **pire que** toi.

Page 68 — Words to Say How Much
1) Elle est **très** vive.
2) Ils ont **un** peu d'eau.
3) Le musicien est **vraiment** doué.
4) C'est **assez** intéressant.
   'Assez' (quite) isn't followed by 'de' here because it's an intensifier.
5) Tu as beaucoup **de** chaussettes.
6) L'homme a trop **de** chocolat.

Page 69 — I, Me, You, We, Them
1) Hélène **lui** donne le livre.
2) **Elle** aime les chiens.
3) Tu peux **les** voir?
4) Avez-vous le livre? Non, elle **l'**a.
5) **Nous** allons au cinéma.
6) Non, **elles** ne sont pas ici.

Page 70 — Something, There, Any
1, 4 and 6 are correct. The others should be:
2) **Tout** le monde sait que c'est vrai.
3) A-t-elle des livres? Oui, elle **en** a.
5) Tu connais le château? J'**y** suis allé(e).

Answers

Page 71 — Position and Order of Object Pronouns
1) Il le lui donne. *He gives it to him / her.*
2) C'est moi qui l'ai écouté. *It's me who listened to him.*
3) Tu l'as écrit toi-même. *You wrote it yourself.*
4) Vous y êtes allés avec nous. *You went there with us.*
5) Elle t'a dit. *She told you.*
6) Je vais lui en parler. *I'm going to talk to him / her about it.*

Page 72 — Relative and Interrogative Pronouns
1) L'homme qui est sportif.
2) La pizza que j'aime manger.
3) J'ai cinq crayons qui sont rouges.
4) Tu cours avec qui? / Avec qui cours-tu?
5) La voiture qu'elle conduit est lente.
6) À quoi penses-tu?

Page 73 — Possessive and Demonstrative Pronouns
1) Le stylo là est **le tien**.
2) Celle-là est **la sienne**.
3) **Cela** n'est pas drôle!
4) Ces chiens sont **les nôtres**.
5) Où as-tu vu **ça / cela**?
6) C'est **le / la vôtre**.

Page 74 — Prepositions
1) Je joue au foot.
2) Elle rend visite à Manu.
3) Il s'agit d'un jeune garçon.
4) un pull en laine
5) Je joue de la clarinette.
6) Ils / Elles habitent en France.
7) Il va à la banque.
8) Tu viens du pays de Galles.

Page 75 — Prepositions
1) Je suis **chez** Paul avec Dima.
2) Le magasin est **sous** le pont.
3) Je vais aller en vacances **pour** deux semaines.
4) Je travaille à la pharmacie **depuis** six mois.

Page 76 — Joining Words
1) d   2) b   3) e   4) a   5) c   6) f

Page 77 — Verbs in the Present Tense
1) je parle
2) il établit
3) nous remplissons
4) tu réponds
5) elles entendent
6) vous commencez
7) vous perdez
8) ils grossissent
9) j'allume
10) on vend

Page 78 — Irregular Verbs in the Present Tense
1) nous **devons**
2) je **veux**
3) vous **êtes**
4) tu **dois**
5) elle **va**
6) ils **font**
7) elles **peuvent**
8) on **sait**
9) ils **ont**
10) nous **faisons**

Page 79 — More About the Present Tense
1) Je commence à comprendre.
2) Je veux manger de la pizza.
3) J'étudie le français depuis deux ans.
4) Je joue au foot depuis 1999.
5) Aimes-tu / Aimez-vous les prunes?
6) Joues-tu / Jouez-vous du piano?

Page 80 — Talking About the Past
1) j'ai parlé
2) il a élargi
3) nous avons fini
4) tu as vendu
5) on a grandi
6) elles ont mangé
7) j'ai répondu
8) vous avez cherché

Page 81 — Talking About the Past
1) elles ont mis
2) nous avons lu
3) tu as dit
4) je suis allé(e)
5) elle est arrivée
6) nous avons dû
7) ils sont retournés
8) je me suis lavé(e)

Page 82 — Talking About the Past
The imperfect verb phrases are:
1) nous venions
3) elle faisait
4) vous veniez
8) tu étais

Page 83 — Talking About the Past
1) J'ai couru. (perfect)
2) Ils / elles ont mangé. (perfect)
3) Tu riais. (imperfect)
4) Il était pénible / embêtant. (imperfect)
5) C'était terrifiant. (imperfect)
6) Elle a pleuré. (perfect)
7) Je jouais au basket. (imperfect)
8) Je rangeais (imperfect) quand elle est arrivée. (perfect)

Page 84 — Talking About the Future
1) il va aller / il ira
2) je vais avoir / j'aurai
3) nous allons finir / nous finirons
4) tu vas regarder / tu regarderas
5) elles vont dire / elles diront
6) vous allez faire / vous ferez
7) tu vas pouvoir / tu pourras
8) elle va venir / elle viendra
9) ils vont être / ils seront
10) on va vendre / on vendra

Page 85 — Reflexive Verbs and Pronouns
1) nous nous couchons
2) vous vous disputez
3) elles se lèvent
4) il s'intéresse à
5) tu t'es amusé(e)
6) je vais me détendre
7) elle s'est sentie
8) nous allons nous plaindre

Page 86 — Negative Forms
1) Je ne mange jamais de viande.
2) Il n'a pas de chien.
3) Tu ne bois que de l'eau.
4) Ils n'aiment personne.
5) Nous ne vivons / habitons plus ensemble.
6) Vous n'y allez jamais.

Page 87 — Would, Could and Should
1) tu améliorerais
2) il élargirait
3) nous rendrions
4) je ferais
5) elles iraient
6) vous viendriez
7) on serait
8) elle aurait
9) ils se laveraient
10) vous chercheriez

Page 88 — Giving Orders
1) Finissez vos devoirs!
2) Organisons une fête!
3) Écoute!
4) Mangeons!
5) Ne va pas!
6) Ne courez pas!
7) Couche-toi!
8) Ne vous disputez pas!

Page 89 — 'Had done' and '-ing'
1) j'avais joué
2) nous nous étions disputé(e)s
3) vous étiez arrivé(e)s
4) elles avaient été
5) en aidant
6) en restant
7) après être parti(e)(s)
8) après avoir détruit

Page 90 — The Passive
The passive sentences are:
1) L'homme est heurté par la voiture.
4) La pomme sera mangée par mon oncle.
6) La tasse a été cassée.

Page 91 — Impersonal Verbs and the Subjunctive
The phrases containing a verb in the subjunctive are:
3) avant que vous alliez
4) bien qu'elles soient
6) pour que nous puissions
8) bien qu'il puisse

Transcripts

Section 1 — General Stuff

Track 1 — p.3

E.g. **F1:** Et maintenant, écoutez le proviseur pendant cinq minutes, lorsqu'il fait des annonces.

1) **M1:** D'abord, nous avons les résultats de notre sondage sur les habitudes de nos élèves. Le sondage nous a montré que la plupart des élèves se lèvent à sept heures moins le quart. Les cours commencent à huit heures et demie. La plupart des élèves pensent qu'ils commencent trop tôt.

Deuxièmement, il y a maintenant des cours de danse le mardi et le jeudi dans le gymnase — inscrivez-vous !

Et pour finir, ce collège a été établi en mille neuf cent quatre-vingt-seize, donc cette année il y aura une fête pour célébrer son vingtième anniversaire.

Track 2 — p.10

1) (i) **F1:** Quelquefois j'aime faire du sport. J'adore jouer au foot car c'est bon pour la forme. Je m'amuse bien avec mon équipe. Mais je n'aime pas faire du sport quand je suis fatiguée. Je n'aime pas lire. Moi, j'adore les films. J'en regarde beaucoup — les films d'action, les films d'horreur… même les films romantiques.

(ii) **M1:** Je ne m'intéresse pas trop au sport, mais la natation me plaît car c'est relaxant. Personnellement, je préfère les livres. En ce moment, je lis un roman formidable. L'histoire est vraiment intéressante. Les comédies m'énervent. Mais regarder un film me plaît si les acteurs sont bons. La semaine dernière, j'ai vu un film d'action. C'était formidable.

Section 2 — About Me

Track 3 — p.13

E.g. **F1:** Alors, Fabien, tu habites toujours à la maison. Parle-moi un peu de ta famille.

1) (i) **M1:** Chez moi, il y a toujours du bruit — ma famille est très vive. J'ai deux sœurs et un frère qui sont tous plus jeunes que moi. Mes sœurs sont jumelles. Elles ont toutes les deux les cheveux roux et les yeux verts. J'ai aussi un demi-frère aîné qui n'habite plus à la maison.

(ii) **M1:** Ma mère est toujours calme et souriante. Elle a les yeux bleus et les cheveux blonds, courts et raides. Mon père est sympa. Il est grand et il a une barbe. Physiquement, je ressemble plus à ma mère qu'à mon père.

Track 4 — p.15

1) **M1:** Chaque semaine, je promène le chien de mon voisin. Duc est un très beau chien, avec des poils tout noirs et de grands yeux adorables. Pourtant il est très jeune, donc il n'aime pas rentrer à la maison quand je l'appelle. J'adore les cochons d'Inde car ils sont mignons et affectueux. Pourtant, j'aime surtout les chats — je les trouve très élégants. J'aimerais avoir des chats, et aussi des chiens, quand je serai adulte. À l'avenir, je voudrais habiter à la campagne où je pourrais avoir beaucoup d'animaux autour de moi. J'en ai marre d'habiter en ville.

Section 3 — Daily Life

Track 5 — p.21

E.g. **F1:** Comme je suis musulmane, je ne peux pas manger de porc parce que ma religion me l'interdit.

1) **M1:** J'adore les légumes, en particulier les petits pois et les champignons. Je mange aussi du chou-fleur de temps en temps. Qu'est-ce que tu aimes, Élodie ?

F2: J'aime beaucoup la nourriture épicée, mais ma petite sœur déteste ça ! Elle mange beaucoup de nourriture sucrée. Ce n'est pas bon pour la santé !

M1: Moi, je suis végétarien. Je ne mange jamais de viande. Ma mère me cuisine des plats avec des légumes. J'aime manger des pommes de terre avec des tomates et des petits pois.

F1: Je préfère les fraises aux framboises, et je déteste l'ananas : c'est trop acide. Je ne peux pas manger les noix car je suis allergique.

Track 6 — p.23

E.g. **F1:** À mon avis, faire des courses en ligne est plus facile que de les faire en magasin.

1) **F1:** Cependant, on ne peut pas demander conseil au vendeur — je n'aime pas ça, parce que parfois c'est utile de demander l'avis d'une autre personne.

M1: J'aime le fait qu'on ne fait pas la queue à la caisse, alors on gagne du temps. J'ai toujours beaucoup de choses à faire donc c'est un avantage important pour moi. Aussi, les supermarchés vous livrent vos courses quand vous le désirez. Par contre, c'est difficile d'acheter des vêtements en ligne parce qu'on ne peut pas les essayer et qu'on n'est pas certain si la taille sera bonne.

Transcripts

Section 4 — Free-Time Activities

Track 7 — p.29

E.g. **M1:** Je m'appelle Youssou. La semaine dernière, j'ai célébré mon seizième anniversaire.

1) **M1:** Mon anniversaire était jeudi. J'ai dû aller au lycée, donc j'ai décidé d'ouvrir mes cadeaux le soir. Je n'ai pas voulu me lever tôt pour le faire le matin ! On m'a offert des baskets, un jeu vidéo et un livre d'histoires mythologiques. J'ai fêté le jour de mon anniversaire avec ma famille. Mon père m'a cuisiné mon plat préféré et ma sœur m'a préparé un gâteau.

Le week-end après mon anniversaire, j'ai retrouvé mes amis pour le célébrer encore. C'était la fête du travail donc il y avait des feux d'artifice. C'était bien de fêter ça avec ma famille et mes amis.

Track 8 — p.31

1) (i) **F1:** Bonjour Joël. Merci d'avoir accepté de répondre à nos questions. Depuis quel âge joues-tu d'un instrument de musique ?

M1: J'ai appris à jouer de la guitare quand j'avais 12 ans, mais mon premier amour, c'est le violon. J'ai commencé à en jouer à cinq ans, et à l'âge de sept ans, je jouais déjà dans un orchestre.

F2: C'était difficile d'apprendre à jouer d'un instrument ?

M1: Oui, au début ce n'était pas facile car je ne m'entendais pas avec mon professeur. Il était trop strict. Heureusement, ma mère m'a trouvé un nouveau professeur.

(ii) **F1:** Et pourquoi l'envie de faire partie d'un groupe plutôt que de faire une carrière solo ?

M1: À l'âge de 15 ans, j'ai assisté à mon premier concert. J'ai trouvé l'ambiance géniale et j'adorais la musique du groupe. Au concert j'ai compris que faire partie d'un groupe était plus amusant que jouer tout seul.

F1: Et qu'est-ce qu'il faut faire pour réussir à devenir un musicien célèbre ?

M1: Naturellement il faut aimer la musique. Mais le plus important, c'est de répéter régulièrement et de toujours essayer de faire de son mieux.

F1: Merci Joël, et bonne continuation.

Section 6 — Travel and Tourism

Track 9 — p.44

1) **M1:** Après l'école, nous nous retrouverons au café de la Belle Époque. Pour y aller, prends l'autobus numéro 15. Descends à la gare routière et change d'autobus. Prends le numéro 23 vers le centre-ville. Descends à la Grand-Place, à côté du marché.

J'espère que tu vas te rappeler de tout ! Attends, malheureusement je n'ai pas fini les instructions, bon alors, puis tourne tout de suite à gauche et continue jusqu'à la bibliothèque.

Traverse la rue aux feux et continue dans le même sens. Après environ cent mètres, tu trouveras la Belle Époque à gauche.

Section 7 — Current and Future Study and Employment

Track 10 — p.46

E.g. **M1:** Je m'appelle Nicolas. Ma matière préférée c'est la chimie parce que c'est vraiment intéressant, et je crois que cette matière me sera utile dans l'avenir.

1) **M1:** Je pense que l'école commence trop tôt — mon premier cours est à huit heures et demie ! En plus, je suis souvent en retard parce que j'y vais avec mon petit frère, et il marche trop lentement. J'étudie neuf matières à l'école. Je n'aime pas le mardi parce que j'ai deux heures de chimie et deux heures de physique et, en tout, ça fait quatre heures de science. Je trouve ça fatigant. Mais heureusement, nous n'avons pas d'école le mercredi.

Track 11 — p.49

E.g. **F1:** L'année dernière, j'ai fait un échange scolaire en France.

1) (i) **F1:** Je suis allée chez mon correspondant, Marc, pendant deux semaines. Avant d'aller en France, j'écrivais à Marc régulièrement. En France, je suis allée à l'école. C'était différent car les cours étaient plus longs que mes cours ici en Angleterre.

(ii) **F1:** Aussi, je ne déjeunais pas à la cantine comme je fais ici : Marc habite près du collège et sa mère nous préparait à manger tous les jours. Après avoir mangé à la maison, nous retournions aux cours. Le soir, après avoir fini nos devoirs, Marc et moi bavardions ou regardions la télé. J'ai adoré mon échange car la famille de Marc m'a très bien accueillie et j'ai pu améliorer mon français.

Index

FER41